CALL to CELEBRATE
SACRAMENTS SOURCE BOOK

W9-DHK-962

Author
Maureen A. Kelly, MA

Program Consultants
Nylda Aldarano

Mary Birmingham

Rita Ferrone

Gael Gensler, OSF

Mary Ann Getty-Sullivan

Rev. Joe Kempf

Tom Kendzia

Rev. Paul Turner

Contributing Writers
Rita Ferrone

Linda Gaupin, CDP, Ph.D.

Carol Gura

David Haas

Larry Livingston

Debi Mahr

C. J. Willie, S.C.

Harcourt Religion Publishers
www.harcourtreligion.com

For permission to reprint copyrighted material, grateful acknowledgment is made to the following sources:

Costello Publishing Company, Inc.: From *Vatican Council II*: *The Basic Sixteen Documents*, edited by Reverend Austin Flannery, O.P. Text copyright © 1996 by Reverend Austin Flannery, O.P.

Division of Christian Education of the National Council of the Churches of Christ in the U.S.A.: Scripture quotations from the *New Revised Standard Version Bible: Catholic Edition*. Text copyright © 1993 and 1989 by the Division of Christian Education of the National Council of the Churches of Christ in the U.S.A.

International Commission on English in the Liturgy: From the English translation of the *General Instruction of the Roman Missal*. Translation © 2002 by International Committee on English in the Liturgy, Inc. From the English translation of the *Rite of Baptism for Children*. Translation © 1969 by International Committee on English in the Liturgy, Inc.

United States Catholic Conference, Washington, D.C.: From the English translation of the *Catechism of the Catholic Church* for the United States of America. Translation copyright © 1994 by United States Catholic Conference, Inc. – Libreria Editrice Vaticana. From the English translation of the *Catechism of the Catholic Church*: *Modifications from the Editio Typica*. Translation copyright © 1997 by United States Catholic Conference, Inc. – Libreria Editrice Vaticana. From *General Directory for Catechesis*. Text copyright © 1998 by United States Conference of Catholic Bishops. From *National Directory for Catechesis*. Text copyright © 2005 by United States Conference of Catholic Bishops.

Printed in the United States of America

ISBN 0-15-901641-X

1 2 3 4 5 6 7 8 9 10 073 11 10 09 08 07 06

Contents

See the Sacraments Source Book CD for English and Spanish handouts as well as background materials and session resources in Spanish.

Dedication

We stand on the shoulders of those who have gone before us and we reap the harvest of what they have planted.

African Proverb

Christiane Brusselmans

Probably no other individual contributed as much to changing the hearts, minds, and paradigms of those involved in parish life in the United States, Canada, Great Britain, and Australia than this vibrant Belgian woman. Christiane came on the scene of American catechetics in the late 1960s with a concept of sacramental preparation of children that was so foreign to the way things were being done that it was difficult at first to see how it would be possible to implement. Programs that involved parents over a period of time and a catechesis that was ritually based were unheard of at that time. Liturgical catechesis as a method of preparation was incomprehensible to many.

However, Christiane's storytelling emphasis on the essential and constitutive nature of the family, religious education, and the worshipping community, and her attention to the scriptural and doctrinal bases for the Sacraments convinced more than a few people to try it. And in the implementation, those initial pioneers witnessed such a flowering of faith and conversion in parents and children that gradually the word got around and what was once considered a new idea became the norm.

It was her own dissertation on Infant Baptism that plunged her into a study of the baptismal catechumenate. She used the resulting model to educate people on the topic even before the Rite of Christian Initiation of Adults was issued in 1972.

Over the years, Christiane's vision and philosophy were shared with students in workshops, institutes, and symposia, as well as in university settings, including the Catholic University of Louvain in Belgium and Fordham University in New York. Through her teaching and her keen interest in her students, she formed another generation of ministers who were seduced by a passion for initiation.

I cannot help but believe that the journey we are on today with lifelong and intergenerational catechesis, a journey that involves the whole parish assembly and family members in liturgical catechesis, owes much to the travels and teachings of this modern-day Saint Paul.

Thank you, Christiane.

> **The sacramental resources for *Call to Celebrate* are lovingly dedicated to Christiane Brusselmans 1931–1991**

CALL to CELEBRATE

Sacraments Source Book

Overview

Vision

"The liturgy is the summit toward which the activity of the church is directed; it is also the source from which all its power flows."

Constitution on the Sacred Liturgy, 10

Call to Celebrate

Call to Celebrate flows from the traditional Church teachings that:

- Liturgy, the public worship of the Church, is the central activity of the People of God.
- The Eucharist is where the faithful come together to offer praise and thanks and to celebrate God's presence and promise.
- In the Sacraments, the People of God are transformed by their immersion in symbols, rituals, prayers, and participation in the Body and Blood of Jesus Christ.
- Participation in the Sacraments urges the faithful to apostolic witness and action for justice in the world.

Call to Celebrate embodies the principles that preparing children for participation in the sacraments is both:

- a process of initiation that is best done in the midst of family, peers, and the whole community
- a process of liturgical catechesis that respects how individuals, both children and adults, come to know the mysteries of faith, through symbol and ritual

Catechetical Process

At its heart, **Call to Celebrate** follows a liturgical-catechetical method in three steps:

Celebrate   Every session begins with a celebration that includes a ritual focus. These celebrations involve children, families, or whole communities in a gradual unfolding of the rites, symbols, and prayers of the Eucharist. The celebration is immediately followed by a reflection on what was experienced.

Remember   In every session, a scripture passage that pertains to the Eucharist is proclaimed and broken open, the doctrines that form the body of teaching about the Eucharist are presented, and a specific part of the Eucharistic ritual, or Mass, is explained.

Live   Every session includes an activity that helps the children integrate the theme into daily living.

Activity Strand   Every session is developed around a developmental activity strand:

- Reflect
- Share
- Respond

which helps participants integrate catechesis into their life experiences.

Sacraments: An Overview

by Rita Ferrone

"The sacraments are efficacious signs of grace, instituted by Christ and entrusted to the Church, by which divine life is dispensed to us…. They bear fruit in those who receive them with the required dispositions."

Catechism of the Catholic Church, 1131

What Is a Sacrament?

The understanding of sacraments defined by the *Catechism of the Catholic Church* comes out of centuries of understanding and Tradition dating back to the writings of the early Church fathers and continuing through the teachings of the Council of Trent in the sixteenth century and most recently the Second Vatican Council in the twentieth century. Roman Catholics believe that the visible signs, symbols, and rituals that constitute a sacrament point to the invisible reality of God's abiding and salvific presence in his Church, the Body of Christ. Through the celebration of sacraments, we become aware of the mystery of the presence and action of the God we cannot see. In fact, early Church fathers used the Greek word *mysterion*, which means "mystery," to describe sacraments. While sacraments do not exhaust God's mystery, they allow us through signs and words to draw near to it and be transformed by it.

Sacraments and Covenant

In Latin the word for sacrament is *sacramentum*, which means "oath." In classical antiquity *sacramentum* referred to symbolic gestures that committed people to future action. A soldier's declaration of allegiance was a *sacramentum*. When two persons made an agreement, the *sacramentum* was a sum of money set aside and forfeited by anyone who failed to keep his or her part of the bargain. The Christian description of sacrament took shape in this cultural context, which helps us to understand that sacraments are inextricably linked with faithfulness and covenant. Sacraments are effective signs of God's fidelity and love, and a pledge of our future inheritance. We call them "the sacraments of the New Covenant" (*CCC*, 1091).

> **❝ Through the celebration of sacraments, we become aware of the mystery of the presence and action of the God we cannot see. ❞**

Christian Sacraments

The most visible sign of God's presence in human history is Jesus Christ. Through the welcoming, healing, and forgiving words and actions of his life, especially his death and Resurrection, we see the institution of Christian sacraments. Through the power of the Holy Spirit, sacraments remember and make present his life in the Body of Christ, the Church. They affirm and complete the natural signs of God's presence in creation and the signs that belonged to God's people in preceding ages. The sacraments sustain the Church and give her life. In modern times, the Second Vatican Council affirmed the great importance of the sacraments in Christian life.

"The purpose of the sacraments is to sanctify people, to build up the body of Christ, and, finally, to worship God. Because they are signs they also [instruct]" (*Constitution on the Sacred Liturgy, 59*). The Council went on to say that sacraments "nourish, strengthen, and express" faith, and lead to a life of charity (59).

Sacraments not only reveal the presence and action of God, they are also an effective means by which grace—the pledge of God's own life—is given to us to be shared with others. In a certain sense, the Church is also a sacrament, because the Church is a sign of God's presence and an instrument of grace in the world (*CCC*, 738, 849).

Seven Sacraments

The Catholic Church teaches that each of the sacraments was instituted by Christ and is rooted in his words and deeds. Naming, enumerating, and defining the sacraments was a gradual process, however. By the thirteenth century the Catholic Church had identified seven sacraments: Baptism, Confirmation, Eucharist, Penance, Anointing of the Sick, Holy Orders, and Marriage. This list remains unchanged.

The *Catechism of the Catholic Church* groups the seven sacraments into three subcategories. Baptism, Confirmation, and Eucharist are called Sacraments of Initiation. Penance and Anointing of the Sick are identified as Sacraments of Reconciliation and Healing. Finally, Marriage and Holy Orders are both considered Sacraments in Service to Communion. Such groupings help to illustrate how all the sacraments work together to build up the Body of Christ.

Catholics believe that the sacraments effect what they symbolize, when those who receive them are open to God's grace. Preparation, catechesis, and the full use of the sacramental symbols help us to achieve that openness and experience the power of the sacraments. Sacraments are the work of God, not simply a human custom or ceremony. Care in preparing for and celebrating the sacraments opens the way for their fruitful reception.

> **" Catholics believe that the sacraments effect what they symbolize, when those who receive them are open to God's grace. Preparation, catechesis, and the full use of the sacramental symbols help us to achieve that openness and experience the power of the sacraments. Sacraments are the work of God, not simply a human custom or ceremony. "**

For Reflection

• What experiences of sacraments have helped you become more aware of God's presence?

Baptism

"Holy Baptism is the basis of the whole Christian life...and the door which gives access to the other sacraments."

Catechism of the Catholic Church, 1213

Introduction

The Sacrament of Baptism confers on us both an identity and a mission. The identity is that of a Christian and member of the Church, and the mission is that of Christ and the Holy Spirit (*CCC*, 738). By water and the Spirit, those who are baptized become children of God, sharing in God's own life. Whether this life begins as an infant or at a later age, Baptism marks us with a dignity and a sacramental character that is permanent and can never be taken away.

Symbolism

The primary symbol for Baptism is water. The original Greek word for baptism, *baptizein*, means to plunge or immerse. Baptism plunges or immerses us into Christ's death and Resurrection. This is most vividly experienced when the sacrament is celebrated by immersion into the waters of baptismal pools or fonts.

In Baptism, we also receive the Light of Christ. The candle lit from the Paschal candle is handed to the newly baptized or, in the case of infants, to the parent or godparent with the exhortation to "walk always as children of the light" (*The Rite of Baptism for Children*, 64). Baptism signifies enlightenment.

The waters of Baptism also signify cleansing and the purification from all sin. Baptism brings about forgiveness of sins and new birth in the Holy Spirit. Saint Paul taught that the baptized share in Christ's Paschal mystery and so are "dead to sin, but alive for God" (*Romans 6:11*). In Jesus' own baptism the Spirit hovered over him (*Matthew 3:16*), foreshadowing the role of the Holy Spirit in Christian Baptism. In the Gospel according to John, the necessity of Baptism is expressed in the words of Jesus: "...no one can enter the kingdom of God without being born of water and the Spirit." (*John 3:5*).

Sacrament of Initiation

Baptism is one of three Sacraments of Initiation. Through it we are baptized into a community of believers and incorporated into the Church. We become children of God and brothers and sisters to one another. Together, we are empowered to spread God's kingdom of justice, love, and peace. Baptism makes us sharers in the common priesthood of the faithful, offering to God our lives.

When adults and older children are baptized, they normally receive the Sacraments of Confirmation and Eucharist in the same celebration. The same is true for infants in Eastern Rite Catholic Churches. Infants who are baptized according to the Roman Rite, however, do not celebrate Confirmation or Eucharist until a later age. Nevertheless, there is a unity to these three sacraments.

Sacrament of Faith

Baptism is a sacrament of faith. For those baptized in infancy, the faith of the Church is passed on by their parents. The parents and godparents make the baptismal promises for the child and take responsibility for raising the child in the faith with the help of the believing community.

Adults and older children, who are capable of accepting the faith for themselves, are led to Baptism by means of a process called the catechumenate. This is a gradual process, described in the *Rite of Christian Initiation of Adults*. The community surrounds those preparing for Baptism, and helps them by prayer and example to embrace the way of life of a Christian. These older catechumens approach Baptism with an enlightened faith and a willing spirit.

The Rite

Immersing a catechumen in water, or the pouring of water over a catechumen's head, is the essential sign of Baptism, along with an invocation of the Trinity. The ordinary minister of the sacrament of Baptism is a priest or a deacon, but in an emergency, anyone can baptize. Additional signs, such as anointing with chrism, clothing with a new garment, and the giving of a lighted candle underscore the transformation brought about by the sacrament.

> 66 We become children of God and brothers and sisters to one another. Together we are empowered to spread God's kingdom of justice, love, and peace. Baptism makes us sharers in the common priesthood of the faithful, offering to God our lives. 99

For Reflection

- Which of the images of Baptism is most meaningful to you?

Confirmation

"For 'by the sacrament of Confirmation, [the baptized] are more perfectly bound to the Church and are enriched with a special strength of the Holy Spirit. Hence they are, as true witnesses of Christ, more strictly obliged to spread and defend the faith by word and deed.'[LG 11; cf. OC, Introduction 2]"

Catechism of the Catholic Church, 1285

Introduction

The Sacrament of Confirmation celebrates an outpouring of the Holy Spirit and increases his gifts in us. These gifts give us the opportunity to be strong in the profession of our faith. Confirmation completes baptismal grace. The Spirit has already been active in the sacrament of Baptism, bringing to birth a "new creature." Confirmation strengthens our bonds with the Church and empowers us to witness. Just as the Apostles went forth fearlessly to proclaim the Good News after Pentecost, so those who receive the Holy Spirit's outpouring in Confirmation become the bearers of glad tidings in word and deed. Pope Paul VI, in his *Apostolic Constitution on the Sacrament of Confirmation,* said that this sacrament "in a certain way perpetuates the grace of Pentecost in the Church." (*The Rites,* p. 474).

66 **Confirmation strengthens our bonds with the Church and empowers us to witness. Just as the Apostles went forth fearlessly to proclaim the Good News after Pentecost, so those who receive the Holy Spirit's outpouring in Confirmation become the bearers of glad tidings in word and deed.** 99

Symbolism and History

The Sacrament of Confirmation was originally a rite that involved the laying on of hands and anointing with fragrant oil, which immediately followed Baptism and "confirmed" it. This anointing was carried out by the bishop. As the young Church grew and communities of Christians became more numerous and far-flung, the bishop was unable to be present at every Baptism. Two responses to this situation developed. In the Roman Rite, the hand-laying and anointing were delayed until a later time when the bishop could carry it out in person. This was the origin of Confirmation as a separate sacramental celebration. In the Eastern Rite Churches, on the other hand, the priest who baptized would anoint the newly baptized immediately. Because the fragrant oil used for this anointing is consecrated by the bishop, the bishop's presence is considered implicit in the rite itself.

In the Roman Rite today, the priest who baptizes adults and older children also confirms them immediately after Baptism. Children who are baptized as infants in the Roman Rite, however, are confirmed at a later date, usually by the bishop. The unity of the three Sacraments of Initiation (Baptism, Confirmation, and Eucharist) is a key element of our Catholic understanding. When Confirmation is celebrated apart from Baptism, therefore, it normally includes both a renewal of baptismal promises and a celebration of the Eucharist.

The essential Rite of Confirmation is the anointing with sacred chrism on the forehead. This gesture is accompanied by the laying on of hands and words that invoke the Holy Spirit. In the Eastern Rite Churches, the oil is called *myron*, and the sacrament is called *Chrismation*.

Anointed for Mission

Like Baptism, the Sacrament of Confirmation configures us to Christ. It therefore leaves an indelible mark upon the soul and can never be repeated. The title *Christ* (*Christos* in Greek) means "the Anointed One." Anyone who is baptized and confirmed becomes "another Christ" anointed, as Jesus was, for his mission. The ancient gesture of anointing with oil calls to mind all of the great figures of Scripture who were anointed for the special work they were given to do. Every Christian stands in the tradition Jesus himself claimed when he read from the book of the prophet Isaiah: "The Spirit of the LORD is upon me, because he has anointed me…" (*Luke 4:18, Isaiah 61:1*).

For Reflection

- In what ways does the phrase "another Christ" help you to understand your Christian call?

Eucharist

"…the Eucharist is the sum and summary of our faith: 'Our way of thinking is attuned to the Eucharist, and the Eucharist in turn confirms our way of thinking.' [St. Irenaeus, *Adv. haeres.* 4, 18, 5: PG 7/s11, 1028.]*"*

Catechism of the Catholic Church, 1327

Introduction

The word "Eucharist" is derived from the Greek word *eucharistein*, which means thanksgiving. In the Eucharistic Prayer, the Church gives thanks to God the Father for all the goodness of creation. It gives thanks, above all, for the gift of God's Son, whose Paschal mystery is the wellspring of our salvation. The Eucharist is the solemn memorial of Christ's death and Resurrection. By keeping this memorial, the Church fulfills the command of Jesus: "Do this in memory of me." (Luke 22:19). In the Eucharist, the sacrifice of Christ is re-presented, and the faithful share in its abundant fruits.

Source and Summit

The Eucharist stands out as the center and high point of the Church's whole sacramental life. The Second Vatican Council taught that "the other sacraments, and indeed all ecclesial ministries and works of the apostolate are bound up with the Eucharist and are directed towards it." (*Decree on the Ministry and Life of Priests,* 5). In the Eucharist, Christian initiation reaches its culmination, and the Eucharist is repeated throughout the Christian life. Indeed, all the way up to the hour of death, when it is offered as viaticum, the Eucharist sustains the faithful on their pilgrim way. It is also a foretaste of the banquet feast of heaven, and so points beyond death to life eternal.

Christ is present in the Eucharist in the gathered assembly as they pray and sing, in the word of Sacred Scripture, in the person of the minister, and above all in the eucharistic elements of bread and wine. Through the words of consecration and the power of the Holy Spirit, the bread and wine offered to the Father in the Eucharist become the Body and Blood of Jesus. Catholics believe in the real and substantial presence of Christ under the forms of bread and wine.

Symbolism and Celebration

The Eucharist is a sacred meal, a paschal banquet. Shared in communion, the sacrament draws the faithful closer to Christ and one another in charity and love. It cleanses and protects them from sin, commits them to the poor whom Christ loved, and gives them spiritual food and drink for the journey of life (*CCC*, 1391–1397).

The liturgical celebration of the Eucharist is composed of two main parts, which together form one act of worship: the Liturgy of the Word and the Liturgy of the Eucharist. In the Liturgy of the Word, the great works of God are proclaimed and preached, and the people respond with renewed conversion of heart. In the Eucharist, "thanks is given to God for the whole work of salvation, and the offerings become the Body and Blood of Christ." (*General Instruction to the Roman Missal*, 72). The ministers and the assembly each have a part to play in the celebration. In the celebration of the Eucharist, the reality of the Church is seen.

Following the Eucharistic celebration, any of the Blessed Sacrament that is not consumed is stored in the tabernacle, so that it may be brought to the sick and homebound, and to the dying. The reserved Host also receives due worship and adoration from the faithful, because of Christ's continuing presence. Eucharistic devotions and prayer before the Blessed Sacrament are traditional forms of Catholic piety encouraged by the Church as part of the Eucharistic mystery in all its fullness (*Holy Communion and Worship of the Eucharist Outside Mass*, 4).

> ❝ Christ is present in the Eucharist in the gathered assembly as they pray and sing, in the word of Sacred Scripture, in the person of the minister, and above all in the Eucharistic elements of bread and wine. ❞

For Reflection

- Which image of the Eucharist is most meaningful for you?

Reconciliation

"During his public life Jesus not only forgave sins, but also made plain the effect of this forgiveness: he reintegrated forgiven sinners into the community of the People of God from which sin had alienated or even excluded them."

Catechism of the Catholic Church, 1443

Introduction

Reconciliation means to reunite or to come together. Today we use this term along with the terms penance or confession to name the Sacrament of Healing in which our sins are forgiven and sinners are reunited to God, the Church, their brothers and sisters, and themselves. In this sacrament through the words and actions of an ordained priest, God restores broken and wounded relationships. The fact that we use several words to describe this sacrament points to the varied practices and emphases of the sacrament over the years.

Jesus and Reconciliation

In the beginning God "looked at everything he had made, and he found it very good." (*Genesis 1:31*) But sin entered the world as a result of the choice of the first humans to disobey God and to follow their own will rather than God's. That choice, which we call original sin, wounded humanity's relationship with God and all of creation. It ruptured the original harmony that existed between God and all of creation. Original Sin describes the personal sin of Adam and Eve as well as the fallen state of humans, which we are all born into. However, the Father did not abandon his creation. He reconciled a sinful world to himself in Jesus Christ, his Son. Jesus began his work on earth by preaching repentance "repent and believe in the good news." (*Mark 1:15*) He went beyond preaching to people about repentance and actually welcomed sinners, he ate and drank with them (*Luke 5:33–34*) and he reconciled them with the Father (*Luke 5:17–26*). His death on the cross was the ultimate act of reconciliation.

The Church and Reconciliation

The Church in apostolic times was confident that Baptism began a new life in which grave sin would have no place. However, it is obvious in the Scriptures of the New Testament that forgiveness and confession of sin were an important element

in the life of the community (*James 5:16*). Eventually some of the early Christians did sin gravely, for example, by giving up their faith under persecution, rather than endure martyrdom. Such public betrayal of Christ was deemed unforgivable by many, as were other grave violations of the moral law, such as murder or adultery. Yet many such sinners repented, and wished to return to the relationship with God and Church that they once had cherished. Clearly, some way had to be found for the community to be faithful to the gospel of mercy, yet to maintain its moral standards. It was out of this need that the Sacrament of Reconciliation developed, as a visible and ecclesial ritual to reconcile or reunite and come back to community and the sharing in the Eucharist. Throughout the history of the Church, the sacrament has taken different forms both public and private and individual and communal. However, the basic theology of the sacrament remained intact, even when different aspects of the sacrament were highlighted in different periods of Church history.*

> 66 The revised Rite of Penance restores the original purpose of the sacrament, which is reconciliation with God and the Church. It emphasizes the importance of conversion and the need to rearrange our lives according to the holiness and love of God. 99

Revision of the Rite of Penance

The Second Vatican Council declared that "the rite and formularies for the Sacrament of Penance are to be revised so that they more clearly express both the nature and the effect of the sacrament."

The revised Rite of Penance restores the original purpose of the sacrament, which is reconciliation with God and the Church. It emphasizes the importance of conversion and the need to rearrange our lives according to the holiness and love of God. By providing three different rites: (1) a rite for Reconciliation that is individual (one penitent and one priest), as well as a new rite offering communal rites for the celebration of the sacrament (2) for individuals with the priest and (3) for communal celebrations with a priest within an assembly, the revision affirms that the celebration of the sacrament is primarily a liturgical action and corporate act of worship which builds up the Body of Christ. It is not a "private function (s), but …celebration(s) belonging to the Church" (*Constitution on the Sacred Liturgy*, 26) and "Whenever rites, according to their specific nature, make provision for communal celebration involving the presence and active participation of the faithful, it is to be stressed that this way of celebrating them is to be preferred, as far as possible, to a celebration that is individual and, so to speak, private" (*Constitution on the Sacred Liturgy*, 27). Interpersonal forgiveness and reconciliation are expectations of this sacrament. As a Church we stress the relation between divine forgiveness and forgiving our brothers and sisters.

*For further information on the history of Reconciliation, see pp. 40–41.

For Reflection

- What is the relationship of using the term reconciliation for this sacrament and the revision of the Rite to include communal celebrations?

Anointing of the Sick

"'Heal the sick!' [Mt 10:8] *The Church has received this charge from the Lord and strives to carry it out by taking care of the sick as well as by accompanying them with her prayer of intercession."*

Catechism of the Catholic Church, 1509

Introduction

The Sacrament of the Anointing of the Sick is rooted in Jesus' compassion and love for those who are sick. During his lifetime on earth, Jesus touched and healed many who were sick, and taught his followers to do the same (*James 5:14–15*). Yet Jesus was more than a wonder-worker. He came to call people into a deeper relationship with God and neighbor, healing their spiritual and moral ills as well as their physical ailments (*CCC, 1503*). He often praised those who turned to him in need, sometimes amid great obstacles. Indeed, illness can be a formidable trial to the human person, but it can also be an occasion for great faith.

> 66 Indeed, illness can be a formidable trial to the human person, but it can also be an occasion for great faith. 99

Symbol and Rite

The Sacrament of Anointing of the Sick draws upon God's power to heal and comfort. It supports the person's faith in the midst of suffering. Finally, it calls the faithful to an awareness of the gift that the sick person brings to the whole community. Christians are called to share in the Passion of the Lord. Those who unite their suffering with his become a living sign of the Paschal mystery (*Romans 8:17*).

The sacrament is celebrated with anyone who is seriously or chronically ill, facing surgery, or infirm because of old age. It is not reserved for those near death, but may be celebrated at any time. Anointing can take place in hospitals, homes, parish churches, or wherever needed. The Christian community takes part, praying for and with those who are sick. The minister of the sacrament is a priest, who anoints the forehead and hands of the sick person with oil blessed by the bishop. When the sacrament is celebrated with the dying, it is usually accompanied by *viaticum* (communion) and prayers for this unique time.

For Reflection

- How has illness and/or healing been an occasion of faithfulness for you?

Matrimony

"The consent by which the spouses mutually give and receive one another is sealed by God himself. [cf. Mk 10:9] *From their covenant arises 'an institution, confirmed by the divine law,…even in the eyes of society.'* [GS 48§1]*"*

Catechism of the Catholic Church, 1639

Introduction

The Sacrament of Matrimony mirrors both the original blessing of God in creation, and the steadfast love of Christ for his Church. When a man and a woman enter into this permanent, lifelong relationship, they vow to be faithful to one another and love one another throughout their lives. Marriage is an "intimate partnership of life and … love" (*Pastoral Constitution on the Church in the Modern World*, 48). It is this community and sacramental union that becomes the heart of the family, which is a source of blessing not only for the family and for the Church, but also for all of society.

Symbols and Rite

The priest or deacon who witnesses the marriage vows of a couple does so on behalf of the Church, but the man and the woman are the ministers of the sacrament. The vows that are exchanged are the essential sign and symbol of the sacrament. Additional symbolic actions may be added, however, such as an exchange of rings. The loving support of the community of faith is expressed through active participation in the wedding liturgy.

The Sacrament of Matrimony is more than an agreement or a legal contract. It is a covenant, and must be entered into freely, without coercion, and with sufficient maturity to make such lasting promises. Marriage requires faithful love, and by its nature also requires openness to procreation and the upbringing of children.

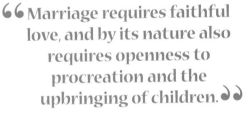

66 Marriage requires faithful love, and by its nature also requires openness to procreation and the upbringing of children. 99

Through the grace of marriage, each of the spouses calls the other to growth in faith and holiness. The action of the Holy Spirit working in and through their union beckons them to a life of self-giving and perfection in following the way of Christ who dwells in them, giving them strength in times of trial and a foretaste of eternity in their joys.

For Reflection

• Name some marriages in which you have seen signs of God's presence.

Holy Orders

"This sacrament configures the recipient to Christ by a special grace of the Holy Spirit, so that he may serve as Christ's instrument for his Church."

Catechism of the Catholic Church, 1581

Sacrament of Service

Holy Orders, along with the Sacrament of Matrimony, is a Sacrament at the Service of Communion. Through this sacrament, bishops, priests, and deacons are empowered by the Holy Spirit for service to the Church. Sustaining the Church's unity with God and the unity of the faithful with one another is their constant calling. Through preaching, teaching, celebrating the sacraments, and governing the community of faith, they exercise this service for which Holy Orders prepares them.

The word communion, *communio* in Latin and *koinonia* in Greek, expresses a New Testament concept of great importance to the Catholic understanding of the Church. Communion is the unity of heart and mind that comes from the Holy Spirit. Communion is experienced first of all in the renewed relationship of love between the human race and God, won by the cross of Christ. It then spills over into a renewed relationship of humans with one another.

> 66 **Through this sacrament, bishops, priests, and deacons are empowered by the Holy Spirit for service to the Church. Sustaining the Church's unity with God and the unity of the faithful with one another is their constant calling.** 99

Bishops, Priests, Deacons

The Sacrament of Orders exists in three degrees. The episcopate (bishops) has the role of teaching, sanctifying, and governing. The presbyterate (priests) works with the bishop to carry out these ministries, and represents the bishop in local assemblies. The deaconate (deacons) shares in Christ's mission by assisting bishops and priests, and through various forms of service.

The essential rite of Holy Orders is the imposition of the bishop's hand on the head of the candidates, with a solemn consecratory prayer to the Holy Spirit. Like Baptism and Confirmation, Holy Orders indelibly marks the candidate, and cannot be repeated or considered temporary. The ministerial priesthood is different from the priesthood of all the baptized, yet all find their inspiration and model in Jesus Christ.

For Reflection

• Why is ordination important for the life of the Church?

Program Components

Child's Book helps children reflect on the mystery of the Eucharist and Reconciliation through celebrations, colorful and appealing visuals, and interactive pages with activities and prayers. Faith at Home features and pages help families support children in their preparation.

Catechist Edition provides everything the catechist needs to be successful—easy-to-use planners, theological, spiritual, and historical background, an easy-to-use three-step lesson process, a wealth of resources and activities, plus activity masters and Scripture pantomimes, dramas, and narrations.

Family Guide features reflections for all adult family members who are involved in preparing children and also offers step-by-step outlines for families preparing children in the home.

Songs of Celebration CD offers the songs used in the celebrations for *Call to Celebrate: Eucharist* and *Call to Celebrate: Reconciliation*. It may be used in the catechetical sessions and by families at home.

My Mass Book and **My Reconciliation Book** are delightfully illustrated guidebooks for children that present and guide them through both sacraments.

Stories of Celebration include two separate videos that present dialogue with children, parents, and noted catechists and liturgists to help parents and catechists reflect and understand their role in preparing children for First Communion and Reconciliation.

Certificates are full-color mementoes that you may personalize for each child once the first Sacrament of the Eucharist or the Rite of Reconciliation has been celebrated. Each certificate provides a space for the pastor to sign and the church seal to be affixed so families have an official record of the celebration to take home and frame if desired.

Sacraments Source Book provides a wealth of information and practical resources, including professional development articles, catechist and parent orientation and training sessions, family centered sessions, and parish assembly sessions.

 **www.harcourtreligion.com**

These sites provide more background and activities for children, parents, and catechists.

- Print Planner with Links
- Music Sample
- Illustrated Glossary
- Timeline of Jesus' Life
- Catechist Edition Activity Masters
- Catechist Edition Gospels

- FAQs
- Extended Saint Stories
- Symbol Chart

People of Faith: Generations Learning Together Celebrating the Sacraments magazines, Vol. 4, issues 2 and 3, engage all ages in a series of faith-filled articles and activities about the Eucharist or Reconciliation.

Scope and Sequence

Scope and Sequence

	Chapter 1 WE BELONG	Restored Order : Use these sessions if also preparing for Confirmation. GIFTS OF THE SPIRIT	WE ARE HOLY	Chapter 2 WE GATHER	Chapter 3 WE ARE FORGIVEN
Ritual Focus	Renewal of Baptismal Promises	Blessing	Extension of Hands in Blessing	Procession and Gloria	Penitential Rite
Scripture	The Vine and the Branches John 15:1–17	Jesus Promises the Holy Spirit John 14:15–26	Jesus Teaches about Holiness Luke 4:16–30	The Early Christians Acts 2:42–47	The Call of Matthew Matthew 9:9–13
Faith Focus	• A sacrament is a holy sign that comes from Jesus and gives us grace. • Baptism, Confirmation, and Eucharist are Sacraments of Initiation. • The Sacraments of Initiation make us full members of the Church.	• The Holy Spirit is the third Person of the Holy Trinity. • The Holy Spirit is our Advocate, our helper. • We receive the seven gifts of the Holy Spirit at Confirmation.	• The gifts of the Holy Spirit help us do God's work. • The Holy Spirit makes us holy. • Being holy means "being close to God and choosing what God wants."	• The Church is the People of God and Body of Christ. • The Eucharist, or Mass, is the Church's most important action of praise and thanks. • The Introductory Rites gather us as a community of faith.	• The Eucharist is a sacrament of unity and forgiveness. • Sin keeps us from being one People of God. • At Mass we ask God's forgiveness during the Penitential Rite.
Catechism of the Catholic Church	1212, 1275–1277, 1285, 1316–1317, 1321–1327	1830–1831	1302–1305	1153, 1156–1158	1393–1395
Liturgical Focus	Sacraments of Initiation	Bishop's Laying on of Hands, Prayer for the Gifts of the Holy Spirit	Anointing, Final Blessing	Introductory Rites, Gloria	Penitential Rite
Signs of Faith	water Paschal candle Holy Trinity	extending hands chrism bishop	fire miter and crozier saint	assembly procession prayer and singing	Lord Have Mercy silence sprinkling with holy water

	Chapter 4 WE LISTEN	Chapter 5 WE PREPARE	Chapter 6 WE REMEMBER & GIVE THANKS	Chapter 7 WE SHARE A MEAL	Chapter 8 WE GO FORTH
Ritual Focus	Signing	Honoring the Cross	Memorial Acclamation	Sharing a Meal	Blessing for Mission
Scripture	The Sower Matthew 13:1–23	The Washing of the Feet John 13:1–16	The Last Supper Matthew 26:26–28; Luke 22:14–20	I Am the Bread of Life John 6:30–58	Pentecost Acts 2:1–41
Faith Focus	• The Bible is God's word written in human words. • We listen to the word of God during the Liturgy of the Word. • When we listen to God's word, we want to share it with others.	• Jesus sacrificed his life for us when he died on the cross. • The Mass is a sacrifice. • At Mass through the power of the Holy Spirit and the words and actions of the priest, Jesus offers again the gift of himself to his Father.	• The Eucharistic Prayer is a prayer of thanksgiving, remembering, and consecration. • Through the power of the Holy Spirit and the words and actions of the priest, the bread and wine become the Body and Blood of Jesus. • At the Great Amen, the assembly says "yes" to all of God's saving actions and promises.	• The Mass is a meal of thanksgiving. • Jesus is the Bread of Life. • In Holy Communion, we are united to Jesus and the Church. We share in the promise of life forever with God.	• The Eucharist changes us. • The Holy Spirit helps us to live out our mission. • At Mass we are sent forth to love and serve others.
Catechism of the Catholic Church	101–104, 136, 141, 1154, 1190, 1349, 1408	1333–1336	1362–1366	1382–1398	1391–1397
Liturgical Focus	Liturgy of the Word	Preparation of the Altar and Gifts	Eucharistic Prayer, Consecration, Memorial Acclamation, Great Amen	Communion Rite	Dismissal
Signs of Faith	Sign of the Cross Bible readings	cross altar bread and wine	kneeling priest Blessed Sacrament	Sign of Peace paten, ciborium, and chalice Lamb of God	blessing witness deacon

Scope and Sequence

Scope and Sequence

	Chapter 1 **WE ARE CALLED**	Chapter 2 **WE ARE WELCOMED**	Chapter 3 **WE REFLECT**
Ritual Focus	Signing with the Cross	Renewal of Baptismal Promises	Reverencing the Word
Scripture	God Gives Everyone Life (Acts 17:16–34)	Zacchaeus (Luke 19:1–10)	The Great Commandment (Luke 10:25–28)
Faith Focus	• In Baptism, God calls us to a life of happiness with him. • A sacrament is a holy sign that comes from Jesus and gives us grace. • Jesus is the greatest sign of God the Father's love.	• At Baptism we are called to walk in the light. • Sin is a choice. • The Sacrament of Reconciliation forgives sins committed after Baptism.	• We prepare for the Sacrament of Reconciliation with an examination of conscience, using the word of God. • The Holy Spirit guides us in examining our conscience. • Conscience is the capacity to know right from wrong.
Catechism of the Catholic Church	1420–1421, 1425–1429	1441–1445	1454
Liturgical Focus	Sacraments of Initiation	Reception of the Penitent	The Role of Scripture
Signs of Faith	baptismal name Baptism Holy Trinity	holy water candles Reconciliation room	bowing Bible Precepts of the Church

	Chapter 4 **WE ARE SORRY**	Chapter 5 **WE ARE FORGIVEN**	Chapter 6 **WE GO FORTH**
Ritual Focus	Examination of Conscience and Act of Contrition	Prayer Over the Children	Sprinkling Rite and Sign of Peace
Scripture	A Woman Who Was Sorry (Luke 7:36–38, 45–48, 50)	The Forgiving Father (Luke 15:11–24)	Jesus Appears to the Disciples (John 20:19–23)
Faith Focus	• The Holy Spirit helps us be sorry for our sins. • Sorrow for sin is the most important part of the Sacrament of Reconciliation. • A penance is a prayer or action that shows we are truly sorry for our sins.	• God is always ready to forgive us. • God wants us to be one with him. *Reconciliation* means "bringing together again, or reuniting." • Through the power of the Holy Spirit and the ministry of the priest, we are reconciled with God and one another.	• The Sacrament of Reconciliation is a sacrament of conversion. • The mission of reconciliation is to bring forgiveness and peace to others. • The Holy Spirit remains with us to help us grow and become more like Jesus.
Catechism of the Catholic Church	1450–1453	1455–1460	1468–1470
Liturgical Focus	Confession of Sins and Penance	Prayer of Absolution	Proclamation of Praise and Dismissal
Signs of Faith	kneeling contrition penitent	laying on of hands Advent/Lent purple stole	sprinkling with holy water Sign of Peace bishops and priests

Pacing Plans

Pacing Plan: Reconciliation, Eucharist

Reconciliation

Sept.	**Week 2**		Catechist and Parent Orientation
	Week 3		Catechist Training
	Week 4	We Are Called	Adult or Liturgical Catechesis Session (1)
Oct.	**Week 1**	We Are Welcomed	Adult or Liturgical Catechesis Session (2)
	Week 2	We Reflect	Adult or Liturgical Catechesis Session (3)
	Week 3	We Are Sorry	Adult or Liturgical Catechesis Session (4)
	Week 4	Children's Retreat	
Nov.	**Week 1**	We Are Forgiven	Adult or Liturgical Catechesis Session (5)
	Week 2	We Go Forth*	Adult or Liturgical Catechesis Session (6)
	Week 3	Family Retreat	
	Week 4	no meeting—Thanksgiving	
Dec.	**Celebration of Reconciliation**		*May also be used as a mystagogical session after the Celebration of Reconciliation/Penance.

Eucharist

Jan.	**Week 2**		Catechist and Parent Orientation
	Week 3		Catechist Training
	Week 4	We Belong	Adult or Liturgical Catechesis Session (1)
Feb.	**Week 1**	We Gather	Adult or Liturgical Catechesis Session (2)
	Week 2	We Are Forgiven	Adult or Liturgical Catechesis Session (3)
	Week 3	We Listen	Adult or Liturgical Catechesis Session (4)
	Week 4	Children's Retreat	
Mar.	**Week 1**	We Prepare	Adult or Liturgical Catechesis Session (5)
	Week 2	We Remember and Give Thanks	Adult or Liturgical Catechesis Session (6)
	Week 3	We Share a Meal	Adult or Liturgical Catechesis Session (7)
	Week 4	We Are Sent*	Adult or Liturgical Catechesis Session (8)
Apr.	**Week 1**	Family Retreat	
	After Easter Celebration of the Sacrament		*May also be used as a mystagogical session after the Celebration of First Communion.

Pacing Plan: Restored Order (Reconciliation, Confirmation, Eucharist)

Reconciliation

Sept.	**Week 2**		Catechist and Parent Orientation
	Week 3		Catechist Training
	Week 4	We Are Called	Adult or Liturgical Catechesis Session (1)
Oct.	**Week 1**	We Are Welcomed	Adult or Liturgical Catechesis Session (2)
	Week 2	We Reflect	Adult or Liturgical Catechesis Session (3)
	Week 3	We Are Sorry	Adult or Liturgical Catechesis Session (4)
	Week 4	Children's Retreat	
Nov.	**Week 1**	We Are Forgiven	Adult or Liturgical Catechesis Session (5)
	Week 2	We Go Forth*	Adult or Liturgical Catechesis Session (6)
	Week 3	Family Retreat	
	Week 4	no meeting—Thanksgiving	
Dec.	**Celebration of Reconciliation**		*May also be used as a mystagogical session after the Celebration of Reconciliation/Penance.

Confirmation / Eucharist

Jan.	**Week 2**		Catechist and Parent Orientation
	Week 3		Catechist Training
	Week 4	We Belong	Adult or Liturgical Catechesis Session (1)
Feb.	**Week 1**	Gifts of the Spirit	Adult or Liturgical Catechesis Session (RO1)
	Week 2	Family Retreat (Confirmation)	
	Week 3	We Are Holy	Adult or Liturgical Catechesis Session (RO2)
	Week 4	Candidates' Retreat	
Mar.	**Week 1**	We Gather	Adult or Liturgical Catechesis Session (2)
	Week 2	We Are Forgiven	Adult or Liturgical Catechesis Session (3)
	Week 3	We Listen	Adult or Liturgical Catechesis Session (4)
	Week 4	We Prepare	Adult or Liturgical Catechesis Session (5)
Apr.	**Week 1**	We Remember and Give Thanks	Adult or Liturgical Catechesis Session (6)
	Week 2	Children's or Family Retreat (Eucharist)	
	Week 3	We Share a Meal	Adult or Liturgical Catechesis Session (7)
	After Easter	We Are Sent*	Adult or Liturgical Catechesis Session (8)
	Celebration of the Sacraments		*May also be used as a mystagogical session after the Celebration of First Communion.

 Visit **www.harcourtreligion.com** for Restored Order resources.

Implementation Models

Introduction

The practices for preparing children for Reconciliation, Eucharist, and the restored order of Confirmation and First Communion are diverse and varied throughout the Catholic Church today.

The common elements of most of these practices are:

- the involvement of children and parents in some type of immediate preparation for the celebration of these sacraments
- a catechetical model that introduces the child and parent gradually and systematically to the meaning of the rites and symbols of the sacrament the child will be celebrating

What has emerged over the past few decades are structures for catechesis that are:

- family centered
- intergenerational

The emphasis of both the *General Directory for Catechesis* and the *National Directory for Catechesis* for models of formation inspired by the baptismal catechumenate, as well as the impetus for lifelong and whole-community catechesis, has added the dimension of involving the liturgical assembly more fully in the initiation of children. This involvement includes the varying degrees of actual participation of members of the worshipping community in the preparation, from praying for the children and families to participating in intergenerational gatherings and forms of liturgical and doctrinal catechesis along side the children and their families.

Call to Celebrate provides a series of resources for Reconciliation, Eucharist, and the restored order of Confirmation and Eucharist, which are flexibly designed to meet all of these models. *Call to Celebrate* also includes resources for the catechesis of older children for Reconciliation and Eucharist and adult catechesis on these sacraments.

Models

Child-Centered Model (Classroom)

- Children are taught in groups by catechists in a parish religious education setting or in a Catholic school. (**Materials:** *Child's Book, Catechist Edition, Songs of Celebration* CD)
- Catechists are oriented and trained by the DRE or Sacramental Coordinator who oversees the program. (**Materials:** *Sacraments Source Book, Stories of Celebration* Video and Guide, *Catechist Edition*)
- Parents and/or family members are provided with a *Family Guide*, and may or may not attend gatherings for orientation and ongoing catechesis. (**Materials:** *Family Guide, Sacraments Source Book*)
- Children and/or families participate in a child or family retreat. (**Materials:** *Sacraments Source Book*)

Child-Centered Model (Neighborhood)

- Neighborhood children meet in a catechist's home or another location other than the school or parish. (**Materials:** *Child's Book, Catechist Edition, Songs of Celebration* CD)
- Catechists are oriented and trained by the DRE or Sacramental Coordinator who oversees the program. (**Materials:** *Sacraments Source Book, Stories of Celebration* Video and Guide, *Catechist Edition*)
- Parents and/or family members are provided with a *Family Guide*, and may or may not attend gatherings for orientation and ongoing catechesis. (**Materials:** *Family Guide, Sacraments Source Book, People of Faith: Generations Learning Together Celebrating the Sacraments* magazine*, *Songs of Celebration* CD*)
- Children and/or families participate in a child or family retreat. (**Materials:** *Sacraments Source Book*)

* optional resource

Parent-Child Home Model

- Parents and/or family members attend orientation and most or all of the parent-family meetings. (**Materials:** *Sacraments Source Book*)
- Parents and/or family members facilitate preparation sessions at home. (**Materials:** *Family Guide, Child's Book, Songs of Celebration* CD, *People of Faith: Generations Learning Together Celebrating the Sacraments* magazine*)
- Children and/or families participate in a child or family retreat. (**Materials:** *Sacraments Source Book*)

Family Cluster Model

- Parents and/or family members attend orientation and most or all of the parent meetings. (**Materials:** *Sacraments Source Book*)
- Families meet in neighborhood clusters, and various parents or family members lead the sessions. (**Materials:** *Sacraments Source Book, Child's Book, Songs of Celebration* CD, and *Family Guide*)
- Parents and/or family members participate in Faith at Home activities. (**Materials:** *Family Guide, Child's Book, Songs of Celebration* CD, *People of Faith: Generations Learning Together Celebrating the Sacraments* magazine*)
- Children and/or families participate in a child or family retreat. (**Materials:** *Sacraments Source Book*)

Intergenerational Model

- Parents and/or family members attend orientation and most or all of the parent meetings. (**Materials:** *Sacraments Source Book*)
- Parents and/or other family members, along with children and other interested adults and families, meet together at the parish for sessions that involve a celebration and an intergenerational catechetical session (**Materials:** *Sacraments Source Book*), or adults and children meet together for the celebration separate from the catechesis. (**Materials:** *Sacraments Source Book, Child's Book, Catechist Edition*)
- Parents and/or family members participate in Faith at Home activities. (**Materials:** *Family Guide, Child's Book, Songs of Celebration* CD*)
- Children and/or families participate in a child or family retreat. (**Materials:** *Sacraments Source Book*)

Confirmation and Eucharist: Restored Order

Call to Celebrate: Eucharist provides eight chapters in the *Child's Book* and two additional chapters in the *Catechist Edition* for those celebrating Confirmation in the restored order. These two chapters may be reproduced for the child (**Materials:** *Catechist Edition*) and may be used with any of the models described above. (**Materials:** *Sacraments Source Book*)

Adult/Parent Catechesis

All sessions of *Call to Celebrate* include the following:

- an assembly celebration or a large group celebration
- a choice of two forms of parent/adult catechetical sessions:
  - a liturgical-catechetical model that is based on the celebration itself
  - a doctrinal model that is based on the theme of the child's session

* *optional resource*

Liturgical Catechesis
by Rita Feronne

Introduction

From ancient times, liturgy has been the heartbeat of the Church. Through it the Christian people gather for worship, their life in Christ is renewed, and they are sent out in mission. Again and again, at Sunday Eucharist, in the sacraments, and in the Liturgy of the Hours, the church is called to share in the mystery of Christ and to go forth to be leaven in the world. In the words of the *Constitution on the Sacred Liturgy*, "the liturgy is the summit toward which the activity of the church is directed; it is also the source from which all its power flows" (10). Catechesis that leads people to a deep and fruitful experience of the liturgy is therefore of utmost importance. The *General Directory for Catechesis* asserts boldly that "Catechesis is intrinsically bound to every liturgical and sacramental action [CT 23]" (30). It calls liturgical catechesis an "eminent kind of catechesis [CT 23]" (71). Indeed, because of the liturgy's central role in the Church's life, the *Catechism of the Catholic Church* calls liturgy "the privileged place for catechizing the People of God" (1074).

> 66 **The faithful must understand the liturgical signs and symbols.** 99

Catechesis and Liturgy

This truth is being discovered today with new vigor. In the era before the Second Vatican Council, not much effort was made to link catechesis with the liturgy. Historical circumstances had led the Church to focus almost exclusively on the self-sufficiency of the sacraments to do what they did *(ex opere operato)*. Little weight was given either to the experience of the liturgy or to catechesis concerning it. Fortunately, the Church is now in a position to reclaim the deeply traditional relationship between catechesis and liturgy, through the practice of a genuinely liturgical catechesis.

What Is Liturgical Catechesis?

Liturgical catechesis is a way of forming people in the Christian life. It is made up of three moments:

Preparation for the liturgy
In order to participate fruitfully in the liturgy, the faithful must understand the liturgical signs and symbols and the experiences of God's people that gave rise to them. They must also come to the liturgy with the proper dispositions of heart.

Liturgical catechesis therefore includes not only instruction about the liturgy, but also everything that fosters conversion, openness to God's will, and the desire for union with Christ and his Church.

Participation in the liturgy

The liturgical celebration itself contains much teaching. The scripture readings, the homily, the prayers, and the sacred texts spoken in the liturgy are rich expressions of Catholic faith. The signs and symbols also teach, without words. By full, active, and conscious participation in the liturgy, the faithful learn on a deep level what it means to be children of God and brothers and sisters to one another in Christ. They are formed in the prayer of the Church, and in the ways of God.

Reflection on the liturgy

The lessons that liturgy teaches, however, can be lost if there is no reflection on them later. The third moment of liturgical catechesis therefore takes place after the celebration. Using the actual experience of worship as the starting point, liturgical catechesis moves "from the visible to the invisible, from the sign to the thing signified, from the 'sacraments' to the 'mysteries'" (*CCC*, 1075). Because liturgical catechesis draws people into the mystery of Christ, it is sometimes called *mystagogy*.

> 66 By full, active, and conscious participation in the liturgy, the faithful learn on a deep level what it means to be children of God. 99

Liturgical Catechesis: An Example

Thus, a preparation for the Sacrament of Penance would include not only catechesis on the signs of the celebration, but also invite interior conversion and cultivate a desire for forgiveness. The celebration itself might open up the meaning of the Scripture, or some aspect of God's invitation to peace and healing. Reflection afterward might call attention to the priest's gesture of extending his hand, or the penitent's feeling of being forgiven, or to the joy of singing a song to celebrate reconciliation. Liturgical catechesis serves an important function in the reception of first sacraments. Baptism, First Penance, First Eucharist, Confirmation, and indeed all the sacraments are key moments in life when faith can deepen, and awareness of God's redemptive work can crystallize. Liturgical catechesis helps individuals and communities to enter into these sacramental events wholeheartedly, and receive from them an abundance of God's grace.

Likewise, the regular celebration of the Eucharist, the Liturgy of the Hours, and Penance also provide many occasions for liturgical catechesis. By preparing to celebrate, active participation in the liturgies themselves, and reflection afterward, the beneficial effects of these celebrations are harvested and integrated into the whole of Christian life.

For Reflection

- Describe a time when a liturgical experience uncovered something for you about God, the Church, or your own spiritual life.
- What are some ways your parish could be more intentional about doing liturgical catechesis?

Sacraments: Celebrations of Unity and Diversity

by C. J. Willie, S.C.

The Catechism of the Catholic Church *states that "the mystery of Christ is so unfathomably rich that it cannot be exhausted by its expression in any single liturgical tradition"* (1201) *and "the celebration of the liturgy, therefore, should correspond to the genius and culture of the different peoples"* [cf. SC 37–40] (1204).

The celebration of the sacraments, the center of the liturgical life of the Church, highlights both the unity and diversity of the Catholic Church. The sacraments are celebrated throughout the Church in every country and across many cultures as signs of God's love and continuing desire to deepen his relationship with his people. They are tangible reminders of the universality of the Church in that all Catholics everywhere have the privilege of participating in its sacramental life.

At the same time, the Church recognizes that it is also a Church of many faces and languages, a Church of many cultures and life experiences, and that the outward expressions of the reception of the sacraments must reflect the strengths and beauty, the ritual and symbolism of each culture. The Good News of Jesus Christ is intended for people of all cultures and, therefore, all catechesis must be grounded in the cultural environment in which it is presented.

This recognition of both the universality of the sacraments and diverse cultural traditions necessitates an understanding of the cultural heritages of those who are preparing for the sacraments. Catechesis is most effective when it touches the lives of the learners in such a way that it leads to personal transformation. This can only take place when both the material and environment reflect and welcome students of all cultures.

"We can say of catechesis, as well as of evangelization in general, that it is called to bring the power of the Gospel into the very heart of culture and cultures. [CT 53] Catechesis… proposes the Gospel 'in a vital way, profoundly, by going to the very roots of culture and the cultures of mankind' [EN 20]" (**General Directory for Catechesis**, 202, 204).

A Model of Diversity

Jesus was a model teacher. He taught in the synagogues, in towns and villages, on the hillsides, and from a boat. He understood the people to whom he was speaking. He knew their cultures and used that understanding to share his message about the Kingdom of God. He taught people wherever he found them with words and examples that touched their life experiences. He asks the same of us—that we, too, will understand the people to whom and with whom we are speaking. He asks that we, too, take the time to know their cultures and use that understanding to share his message. The sacraments represent significant milestones in life and will be truly meaningful and transformational only when they are embedded in and flow from the rich cultural traditions in which those who prepare and celebrate are immersed.

Cultural Pluralism

The United States Bishops in *The National Directory for Catechesis* state: "Just as all races, ethnicities, and cultures in the world are represented in the population of the United States, so too do they find a home within the Catholic Church. Each group brings its own language, history, customs, rituals, and traditions 'for building up the body of Christ' (Eph 4:12). Since persons can only achieve their full humanity by means of culture, the Catholic Church in the United States embraces the rich cultural pluralism of all the faithful, encourages the distinctive identity of each cultural group, and urges mutual enrichment. At the same time, the Catholic Church promotes a unity of faith within the multicultural diversity of the people" (11, C).

Tapping into the cultural heritages of those preparing for the sacraments and incorporating elements that continually expand their understanding of the universality of the Church will provide new threads of multicolored hues and strengths with which to weave a tapestry that reflects the wonder of our relationship with God, with each other, and with all of creation.

> 66 **The Church recognizes that it is also a Church of many faces and languages; a Church of many cultures and life experiences; and that the outward expressions of the reception of the sacraments must reflect the strengths and beauty, the ritual and symbolism of each culture.** 99

For Reflection

- How much diversity do you experience in your parish community?
- In what ways are distinctive cultural groups recognized and respected in your parish?

The Role of the Family

The Family

The family is the most significant community in a child's life. It is through the relationships experienced in a family that a child perceives what is of value. The most basic instincts, intuitions, and feelings about the world around us are established in our earliest years as members of a family. It is within this structure that we develop a way of relating to others, ourselves, and the world in general. This provides the basis for our beliefs and, for people of faith, our ultimate relationship with God.

Within the Church, there has always been a tremendous respect for the place of the family. The early Church began in house churches, which were the heart of the Christian community. It can be assumed that in these house churches, intergenerational groups gathered, and the call to ministry and a sense of mission developed as members of families engaged in meditation on the Scriptures, the breaking of the bread, and serving the needs of the early Church. Through these relationships, ministers were first called to use their personal gifts to serve the needs of the larger community and witness to the Person and message of Jesus. It is still true today that the family is the most intimate experience of Church, the place where love, forgiveness, and trust should first be encountered.

> 66 **The most basic instincts, intuitions, and feelings about the world around us are established in our earliest years as members of a family.** 99

The Domestic Church

The bishops of the Second Vatican Council treated the topic of marriage and family life in the *Pastoral Constitution on the Church in the Modern World*. It is interesting to note that this document was a direct response to Pope John XXIII's original vision for the Council—that the Church update itself and look to "the signs of the times" in carrying out its gospel mission. At that time, the structures of families were beginning to diversify, and the roles of family members were changing significantly. The document opens with the now classic statement: "The joys and hopes, the grief and anguish of the people of our time, especially of those who are poor or afflicted, are the joys and hopes, the grief and anguish of the followers of Christ as well" (1). The Church declared itself in solidarity with the people of the world and resolved to serve their needs, point to God's presence among us, and read "the signs of the times" in the struggle for human dignity. Then the Council turned to the most basic unit of human society, the family, and observed that fostering healthy marriages and families is fundamental to personal and social well-being. Another document from the Council, the *Dogmatic Constitution on the Church*, proclaimed that families were genuinely "Church." It restored the early Church concept of domestic church: "In what might be regarded as the domestic church, the parents are to be the first preachers of the faith for their children by word and example" (11).

Parents and Sacramental Preparation

Parents hold a privileged and unique role in the sacramental preparation of their children. It is both a privilege and an obligation. Before the Christian community, parents present and name their child and ask the Church for Baptism—the gift of faith and life of grace. In doing so, they accept the responsibility of "training them in the practice of the faith…, to bring them up to keep God's commandments … by loving God and our neighbor" (*RBC*, 39).

Only after acknowledging this responsibility do parents sign their infant child with the cross of salvation, claiming the child for Christ (*RBC*, 41). Through this sacrament, parents ritually express their personal faith commitment to God, to the community of faith, and to their child. It is the promise of this living tradition, of God present in the community of faith—as parish and as domestic church—that is the foundation of hope and our ability to transmit faith from generation to generation.

For children to have faith, parents must first have faith. The adage, "faith is caught, not taught," is true especially for the domestic church. Simply put, parents teach most effectively by example. They profoundly affect the faith of their children by attending first to their own faith and religiosity. As they actively seek growth in adult faith and in the Sacrament of Marriage, when they invest themselves in the life of the parish community and work for peace and justice in the world, parents model faith for their children while deepening their own.

Call to Celebrate takes seriously the ongoing faith development of parents and family members through the variety of resources it provides. Whether parents are very involved in the life of the Church or just coming back, the Faith at Home feature in the *Child's Book*, the *Family Guide*, the parent/adult sessions, and the sessions designed for family-centered catechesis and retreats will assist them in their journey.

For Reflection

- When have you experienced your own family as a domestic Church?
- In what ways can your parish support the family as a faith community?

The Role of the Child

"...Truly I tell you, unless you change and become like children, you will never enter the kingdom of heaven."

Matthew 18:3

Bringing a child to sacraments is not just something a parent does for the child. It also something the child does for the parent. It is not only something the parish does for the family; it is also something the family does for the parish. In regard to children, the inter-workings of the relationships in the faith communities of family and parish conversions and commitments begin in the womb. The most important individual who participates in a process of sacramental preparation is the child. All of the efforts to involve families, train catechists, or engage the assembly are sustained for the ongoing faith development of the child.

The children who come for preparation are individuals and their needs will vary, not only because their family situations and the degree of their participation in the life of the Church will vary, but also their own capacity for reflection, prayer, comprehension, and appropriation of concepts will vary. However, what does not vary is that deep within each of them is a desire and capacity for God (*CCC*, 27). In the book *The Spiritual Life of Children*, Robert Coles writes: "Again and again, children have thought long and hard about who God is, about what God might be like, only to find refuge in the stillness of a room, the stillness of their own minds or souls, as they struggled to express, what might well be, for them, the inexpressible" (Robert Coles. *The Spiritual Life of Children*. Houghton Mifflin. Boston 1990, p. 168).

> 66 **Children are ritual makers. They have an innate and unlearned capacity to express themselves in ritual, which they come to know through their own experiences...** 99

Effective Catechesis

Effective catechesis of the child will take this innate and intuitive sense of God into consideration. This sense of God precedes all the components of a process and it is always the seed to be nurtured and developed. Besides the experience of God that is shaped within the relationships of the faith communities of family and parish, there are other fundamental characteristics of children that are important to remember for good sacramental catechesis.

Children have a sense of awe and wonder. They easily move into the knowledge of mysteries of God and Church that are celebrated in sacraments. In fact, often their observations, spoken, written, or created in an art form, can move the adults around them beyond the limited knowledge *about* these mysteries into the realm of *knowing*. It is important that during the catechetical process, the catechist engages them in activities that tap their imaginations and in questioning that does not limit their responses to narrow categories.

Children come to know through their senses. Each child will have preferred ways of learning. Some of them will be artistic, some verbal, some tactile, some visual. It is important to provide a variety of activities that will meet these different learning styles, and also to identify which ways work best for individual children and provide alternatives for them.

Children are ritual makers. They have an innate and unlearned capacity to express themselves in ritual, which they come to know through their own experiences of communication through family gestures from infancy, and of family rituals around meals, getting up, and going to bed. They engage in ritual and symbolic play, such as playing house, going to work, or being a soldier or entertainer. It is how they get to know life better on their terms. Children are equally at home with familial and communal rites as they are to liturgical rites and symbols that make present to us the presence and mystery of God. It is important to keep this in mind as the basis for using the liturgical catechetical model in sacramental catechesis.

Readiness

Questions about a child's readiness to celebrate the sacraments often are posed. Here are some criteria to use in discernment:

Reconciliation

Children show readiness to celebrate the Sacrament of Reconciliation when:
- They know the difference between right and wrong.
- They know the difference between sin and accidents or mistakes.
- They are capable of saying "I am sorry" on their own.
- They are capable of reflecting on their actions when asked about them.
- They understand that God will always forgive them.
- They show a sincere desire to right wrongs.

Eucharist

Children show readiness to celebrate the Sacrament of Eucharist when:
- They have sufficient knowledge and careful preparation so as to understand the mystery of Christ according to their capacity and can receive the Body of the Lord with faith and devotion (*Canon*, 913).
- They and some family members regularly attend Sunday Eucharist.
- Prayer is a part of the their daily life.
- They show a sense of reverence for God.
- They have a relationship with Jesus.
- They know the difference between ordinary bread and wine and the Body and Blood of Jesus.

Confirmation

Children show readiness to celebrate the Sacrament of Confirmation when:
- They have sufficient knowledge and careful preparation for the celebration.
- They regularly attend Sunday Eucharist.
- They are open to the gifts of the Holy Spirit.
- Prayer is a part of their daily life.
- They show a sense of reverence for God.

The Role of the Assembly

"Among the symbols with which liturgy deals, none is more important than this assembly of believers."

Environment and Art in Catholic Worship, 28

What Is the Assembly?

The term "assembly" comes from the Greek word *ekklesia*, which in Scripture is the word that was used to translate the Hebrew word *qahal*, which was used to describe both the divine call to a gathering as well as those who respond and come together in a community event. In the Old Testament, an assembly was the group gathered together by the Lord for life in the presence of the Lord. In the New Testament, it gradually came to be used for the Church. In liturgical use today, it refers to the people assembled for liturgy and it highlights the fact that we believe the Church is most realized when it gathers for worship.

The documents of Vatican II affirm that:

- the liturgy is the primary means where the faithful can express in their lives and show to others the mystery of Christ and the Church. (*SC*, 2)
- the Church is a sacrament and most fully expresses itself in the liturgical assembly. (*LG*, 1, 28)

There is also the traditional principle *lex orandi legem credendidi statuit*, which means "the rule of prayer establishes the rule of faith." The term also expresses the connection between the Church's faith life and the liturgical celebrations of the assembly. In other words, what the assembly does, says, and celebrates is the faith of the Church.

> 66 An assembly's mere attendance at liturgy is profoundly inadequate toward fulfilling the mandate of corporate worship, and participation is not merely an option, but a liturgical expectation. 99

The Assembly at Prayer

The liturgy of any sacrament unifies the gathering of the faithful and places them on an ongoing and focused journey to meet the Risen Christ. Through prayers, gestures, and symbols, those gathered express their presence and their faith convictions and commitments. An assembly's mere attendance at liturgy is profoundly inadequate toward fulfilling the mandate of corporate worship, and participation is not merely an option, but a liturgical expectation. Members of the assembly are not the equivalent of audience members at a drama, but like the actors, they have a specified role to play at each gathering, a role that is primarily shown through gesture, singing, prayers, and responses. The assembly acts as one body praying and giving expression to faith—the Body of Christ.

As for children in the assembly, they are full participants and should be encouraged to engage fully in their role. They naturally learn from the assembly. How the assembly participates in doing its work will always instruct children as to what and how the assembly believes. Participation in the assembly is one of the ways that faith is handed on to the next generation. It goes without saying that what an involved, enthusiastic assembly teaches differs from that which an uninvolved, passive assembly teaches.

The Assembly and Sacramental Preparation

Recent trends in catechesis, including lifelong catechesis and liturgical catechesis, have drawn the assembly into a more participatory role in sacramental catechesis. *Call to Celebrate* provides several ways to enhance and support the role of the assembly:

Sunday Bulletin Inserts, General Intercessions, and Parish Blessings may be found in this book for the sacraments children are preparing for. They are designed to alert the assembly to the events of sacramental preparation and to give them simple ways of joining in their own reflection on the themes of each session (*Confirmation* p. 45, *Eucharist* pp. 82–83, *Reconciliation* pp. 156–157).

Parish Assemblies for each theme presented for Reconciliation, Confirmation, and Eucharist are developed around a celebration and a catechetical session for those members of the assembly who would like to deepen their experience of the sacrament.

Sunday Connection Strategies that include other ways the parish may be involved with children and families are also provided (p. 42).

The Role of the Catechist

Catechist Formation

Catechesis is the name given to all of the ecclesial activities that bring individuals and communities to faith. In this broad context, there are many who do the work of sacramental catechesis in both formal and informal ways. Parents are catechists, the community catechizes, and those involved in the ministries of liturgy and pastoral care also play a catechetical role.

The models of catechesis for sacramental preparation presented in *Call to Celebrate* involve formal catechesis of adults, children, and families. Persons who are selected to fulfill these roles should be faith-filled persons who have a deep regard and love for the sacramental life of the Church. Since the catechist is first and foremost a witness of faith, he or she needs to possess a capacity to communicate with the age level of the group whom they are catechizing.

> ❝ The catechist is first and foremost a witness of faith; he or she needs to possess a capacity to communicate with the age level of the group whom they are catechizing. ❞

Catechists echo the word by what they say and by how they say it—and by who they are. Through their words and the environment they create, catechists enable those who are being instructed to be led to a deeper understanding of the sacraments. *Call to Celebrate* recognizes that formal catechesis may take place in the home, school, or the parish setting, and provides resources unique to all settings.

In *Call to Celebrate*, catechists are called upon to preside, proclaim the word, listen, reflect, and teach. Their ministry is a gift to each child, adult, and family member, because through their service, those being catechized will come to a deeper appreciation of the sacrament as well as the signs, symbols, and rituals associated with it. This will lead them to a fuller experience of Jesus and the Church.

Catechist Formation

Each section of this *Sacraments Source Book* provides a catechist orientation session and a catechist training session for those involved in formal catechesis. The orientation session is designed to familiarize catechists with the vision and scope of the process and to acquaint them with the basic resources available to them. The training session provides a way to assist the catechists to deepen their understanding of the meaning of the sacrament, using content and methods that they will carry into the catechetical session.

In addition to these sessions, articles are provided to assist the catechist in understanding individual sacraments, the roles of family and the assembly, and the aspect of incorporating cultural diversity, which will enrich the catechists as they prepare for and carry out their call. The *Catechist Editions* and F*amily Guides* for **Call to Celebrate** also present step-by-step lesson plans, additional resources, and background information on the theme of each session.

Ongoing Support of Catechists

All catechists need ongoing support, and their needs will vary. It is important that the catechetical leader who oversees the program uses creativity and imagination to adapt these resources to the specific needs of the catechists in any given situation.

- Plan to hold the orientation and training sessions at times convenient for the catechists.
- Plan individual and/or group meetings with catechists to share ideas, answer questions, and provide additional help.
- Create a catechetical center for additional resources, and locate it in an easily accessible place. These resources and supplies for catechists and children should include items that are suggested in the *Catechist Edition*, along with other pertinent articles, books, or audiovisual materials.
- Continue to affirm the catechists on a regular basis.

The Role of the Prayer Leader

Call to Celebrate is based on a process of liturgical catechesis, which is the activity of bringing communal faith to consciousness through participation in and celebration of the rites of the community. It has a solid historical tradition in our Church, since liturgy has long been regarded as the Church's "school of faith," an expression that recognizes the formative value of ritual celebration on participants. The story of Emmaus (*Luke*, 24) shows that it is precisely in the ritual "breaking of the bread" that the disciples come to know and understand the mystery of Jesus. A significant part of your role as catechist is as leader of prayer.

> 66 Liturgy has long been regarded as the Church's 'school of faith,' an expression that recognizes the formative value of ritual celebration. 99

The Celebration

Each of the celebrations is built around a procession, song, a Scripture reading, and a ritual action. Take time to do the procession reverently and slowly. Involve children in song, either by leading it yourself, using the *Songs of Celebration* CD, or by inviting a song leader into your group. You may choose to proclaim the Scripture from the adapted version in the *Child's Book* or from the Bible. Be sure to familiarize yourself with the ritual action ahead of time so that you are able to be fully engaged in it with the children during the celebration. The celebration is in the *Child's Book*, but if you find that having children use the book during the celebration is distracting, you may wish to do the celebration without books and guide the children's responses.

Leading Prayer

During the celebration, you are the leader of prayer. The way you preside is important. Here are some tips:

- Learn the script ahead of time. Be familiar with it so that you are able lead and be present with the children without being distracted by fumbling for "what comes next."
- Use your body to communicate. Stand tall. Use broad and expansive gestures. Be aware of your facial expressions and tone of voice.
- Watch your timing. Let there be silence between parts of the prayer. Take time with each child during the ritual actions. Do not be afraid of pauses or silence. They often lead children to deeper prayer and reflection.

The Prayer Space

It is very important for you to prepare the prayer space ahead of time and to lead the celebration in a way that will call children to prayer, participation in the ritual action, and reflection after the celebration.

The prayer space needs to be a place where the movement of processions and rituals are easily and reverently participated in. Prepare it ahead of time. You may choose to set aside a space in your meeting place, or you may find the church or another room to be more suitable. When you have chosen a space, arrange it in such a way that children can move easily and can see and hear everything that is happening. Decorate the space with plants or flowers. Always have a large, clear bowl with water, a Bible and stand, and a candle available. Check your planning page each week to be sure you have everything you need for the celebration.

Do This in Memory of Me
A Brief History of the Mass

by Linda L. Gaupin, CDP, Ph.D.

Sunday after Sunday we gather to celebrate the Eucharistic Liturgy in response to Jesus' command at the Last Supper to "Do this in memory of me." The word *eucharist* is taken from the Greek, which means "thanksgiving." The English term *liturgy* comes from the Greek word *leitourgia*, which means the public "work of the people."

The early Christian celebration of the Eucharist combined two forms of worship that were central to Jewish worship: the weekly synagogue service, which centered on the Scriptures, and the Passover/Sabbath meal celebrated in the home. The Eucharistic celebration of the early Christians generally occurred in the homes of the people and/or in secret places during time of persecution. It was celebrated in the language of the people. When Christianity became the official religion of the Roman empire, Christians began to build public places for worship. Rather than using 'temples' Christians modeled their spaces for worship on large public buildings commonly known as basilicas.

All participated fully in the celebration of the Eucharist. The prayers were improvised freely by the bishop who was the normal leader of the assembly since there were no liturgical books at that time. The Eucharistic Prayer, the great prayer of Thanksgiving, was proclaimed by the presider while the assembly stood around the altar expressing their assent in song. At every celebration people brought forth their gifts for the poor and those in need because of the relationship between the Eucharist and social justice.

By the beginning of the Middle Ages, the liturgy had developed and expanded and was prayed in Latin, a language that was unintelligible to most. Gradually the role of the laity lessened and the role of priests and deacons was more prominent. The priest celebrated the Mass with his back to the people and the Eucharistic prayer was prayed silently. A bell was rung during the words of consecration to alert the faithful to what was happening at the altar.

A shift in eucharistic piety during this time gradually led to a growing scrupulosity over the reception of the Eucharist. Fewer people received Communion at Mass because they felt unworthy. By the 13th century people stopped receiving Communion from the cup and received the consecrated host on their tongue. In many cases Communion was no longer distributed at Mass.

The decline in lay participation in the liturgy led some bishops at the Council of Trent [1545] to propose that the laity stay at home and allow the priest to say his Mass without a congregation. Although this proposal was rejected, it indicates how far the Mass had changed from the early church. It is no wonder that the Church issued legislation requiring the reception of communion at least once a year!

The Missal of Pope Pius V was issued following the Council of Trent. The Missal regulated every liturgical detail and included medieval additions such as the Prayers at the Foot of the Altar and the "Last Gospel" at the end of Mass. From this time on, very little was changed in the Mass until the Second Vatican Council some 400 years later.

The liturgical reforms of the Second Vatican Council restored the active participation of the people at Mass and directed that the faithful "should not be there as strangers or silent spectators" (*Constitution on the Sacred Liturgy*, 47). The Constitution also called for a revision of the Mass that simplified the rites and discarded those elements during the passage of time that were duplications or were added with little advantage. Finally, it required the restoration of those elements that had "suffered injury through accident of history" to "be restored to the vigor they had in the traditions of the Fathers" (*CSL*, 50).

To Walk in the Newness of Life

A Brief History of Reconciliation

by Linda L. Gaupin, CDP, Ph.D.

From the earliest times in the Church until today, the Sacrament of Reconciliation has gone through numerous changes. In the early Church, reconciliation was intimately linked with conversion. One was fully initiated into the Body of Christ through Baptism, Confirmation, and Eucharist. Baptism washed away all sin and the Eucharist was seen as a Sacrament of Reconciliation, which mediated the mercy and love of God.

Soon the Church had to face the reality of how to reconcile those who had ruptured their relationship with Christ and the Church especially through such grievous actions as murder, adultery, or denying the faith. Thus began the public order of penitents. The penitents confessed their sins to the Bishop. They wore sackcloth and ashes. Each Sunday they were dismissed to a place separate from the assembly and were excluded from receiving the Eucharist. The community was encouraged to pray and support them in their conversion. On Holy Thursday, the bishop laid hands on them and reconciled them back into the Body of Christ.

This form of penance did not last. It could only be received once in a lifetime. Some penances were severe, lasting for many years or even a lifetime. Many began to wait to confess their sins on their deathbed. Finally, changes in the sacramental practice emerged when Christianity became a privileged religion and spread throughout the Roman empire.

With the rise of monasteries, the practice of seeking spiritual advice in private developed. In the sixth century, the Irish monks took their monastic practice of frequent private confession to the churches in Europe. People began to confess their faults and sins privately to the priest. A private penance was given to them. Lists of sins with corresponding penances were written down in books called Penitentials for use with the uneducated clergy. The sacrament could now be received many times throughout one's life.

In 1215 the Fourth Lateran Council made yearly confession mandatory for all Christians. People were especially encouraged to confess sins during Lent. A uniform rite of private confession was developed. In the 1500s the Council of Trent decreed that the confessing of sins to a priest was mandatory for absolution.

Following the Council of Trent and until the Second Vatican Council, the understanding and practice of the sacrament became somewhat legalistic. Emphasis was placed on an accurate listing of sins and the number of times they were committed. Due to the influence of the heresy of Jansenism, many refrained from receiving Communion unless they went to confession even though they were not in the state of mortal sin. To combat this thinking, Pope Pius X mandated that weekly confession was not required for Holy Communion.

At the Second Vatican Council, it was determined that the sacrament needed reform. The Council required that "the rite and formularies for the sacrament of penance are to be revised so that they more clearly express both the nature and the effect of the sacrament."

The revised Rite of Penance restores the original purpose of the sacrament, that is, reconciliation with God and the Church. It emphasizes the importance of conversion and the need to rearrange our lives according to the holiness and love of God. Lastly, it restores the communal nature of the sacrament with the premise that the celebration of the sacrament is primarily a liturgical action.

Sunday Connection Strategies

Every time a sacrament is celebrated by an individual or a group, it deepens and celebrates the faith of the whole community. The celebration of the sacraments by children is the activity of the whole parish, not just the family, the school, or the religious education program. The following strategies will help to involve more parishioners in these special events:

- Communicate with and seek out the help of the liturgy committee, the musicians, and the art and environment committees to assist with large group celebrations as well as the celebrations in the children's sessions.
- Explain to the Social Concerns or Justice committees the vision of the *Live* and *Faith at Home* activities, which involve apostolic action, and ask them to discern areas and avenues where they might provide support or ideas for children and families to implement these activities.
- Present all the children who are preparing for sacraments at the Sunday Eucharist.

- Arrange for pictures of the children to be displayed in the church.
- Invite parishioners or the hospitality committee to arrange a reception for the families after a Sunday Eucharist, either at the beginning of the process or at the conclusion.
- Involve sewing groups in making banners or some other pieces of artwork for the celebration or as remembrances of the celebration.
- Invite parishioners to become prayer partners for individual children or families. Provide them with the names of children or families, and ask them to pray for them on an ongoing basis. Suggest that they find a way through the written or spoken word to be in touch with the child or family occasionally.
- Use the Bulletin Inserts, General Intercessions, and Parish Blessings that are found on pp. 45, 82–83, and 156–157.

CALL to CELEBRATE

Sacraments Source Book

Confirmation/Eucharist (Restored Order)

Confirmation/Eucharist (Restored Order)
Scope and Sequence

Scope and Sequence

	Chapter 1 WE BELONG	Restored Order: Use these sessions if also preparing for Confirmation.		Chapter 2 WE GATHER	Chapter 3 WE ARE FORGIVEN
		GIFTS OF THE SPIRIT	WE ARE HOLY		
Ritual Focus	Renewal of Baptismal Promises	Blessing	Extension of Hands in Blessing	Procession and Gloria	Penitential Rite
Scripture	The Vine and the Branches John 15:1–17	Jesus Promises the Holy Spirit John 14:15–26	Jesus Teaches about Holiness Luke 4:16–30	The Early Christians Acts 2:42–47	The Call of Matthew Matthew 9:9–13
Faith Focus	• A sacrament is a holy sign that comes from Jesus and gives us grace. • Baptism, Confirmation, and Eucharist are Sacraments of Initiation. • The Sacraments of Initiation make us full members of the Church.	• The Holy Spirit is the third Person of the Holy Trinity. • The Holy Spirit is our Advocate, our helper. • We receive the seven gifts of the Holy Spirit at Confirmation.	• The gifts of the Holy Spirit help us do God's work. • The Holy Spirit makes us holy. • Being holy means "being close to God and choosing what God wants."	• The Church is the People of God and Body of Christ. • The Eucharist, or Mass, is the Church's most important action of praise and thanks. • The Introductory Rites gather us as a community of faith.	• The Eucharist is a sacrament of unity and forgiveness. • Sin keeps us from being one People of God. • At Mass we ask God's forgiveness during the Penitential Rite.
Catechism of the Catholic Church	1212, 1275–1277, 1285, 1316–1317, 1321–1327	1830–1831	1302–1305	1153, 1156–1158	1393–1395
Liturgical Focus	Sacraments of Initiation	Bishop's Laying on of Hands, Prayer for the Gifts of the Holy Spirit	Anointing, Final Blessing	Introductory Rites, Gloria	Penitential Rite
Signs of Faith	water Paschal candle Holy Trinity	extending hands chrism bishop	fire miter and crozier saint	assembly procession prayer and singing	Lord Have Mercy silence sprinkling with holy water

	Chapter 4 WE LISTEN	Chapter 5 WE PREPARE	Chapter 6 WE REMEMBER & GIVE THANKS	Chapter 7 WE SHARE A MEAL	Chapter 8 WE GO FORTH
Ritual Focus	Signing	Honoring the Cross	Memorial Acclamation	Sharing a Meal	Blessing for Mission
Scripture	The Sower Matthew 13:1–23	The Washing of the Feet John 13:1–16	The Last Supper Matthew 26:26–28; Luke 22:14–20	I Am the Bread of Life John 6:30–58	Pentecost Acts 2:1–41
Faith Focus	• The Bible is God's word written in human words. • We listen to the word of God during the Liturgy of the Word. • When we listen to God's word, we want to share it with others.	• Jesus sacrificed his life for us when he died on the cross. • The Mass is a sacrifice. • At Mass through the power of the Holy Spirit and the words and actions of the priest, Jesus offers again the gift of himself to his Father.	• The Eucharistic Prayer is a prayer of thanksgiving, remembering, and consecration. • Through the power of the Holy Spirit and the words and actions of the priest, the bread and wine become the Body and Blood of Jesus. • At the Great Amen, the assembly says "yes" to all of God's saving actions and promises.	• The Mass is a meal of thanksgiving. • Jesus is the Bread of Life. • In Holy Communion, we are united to Jesus and the Church. We share in the promise of life forever with God.	• The Eucharist changes us. • The Holy Spirit helps us to live out our mission. • At Mass we are sent forth to love and serve others.
Catechism of the Catholic Church	101–104, 136, 141, 1154, 1190, 1349, 1408	1333–1336	1362–1366	1382–1398	1391–1397
Liturgical Focus	Liturgy of the Word	Preparation of the Altar and Gifts	Eucharistic Prayer, Consecration, Memorial Acclamation, Great Amen	Communion Rite	Dismissal
Signs of Faith	Sign of the Cross Bible readings	cross altar bread and wine	kneeling priest Blessed Sacrament	Sign of Peace paten, ciborium, and chalice Lamb of God	blessing witness deacon

Restored Order Background

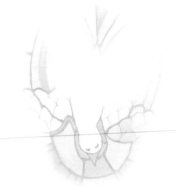

There is a great deal of variation from diocese to diocese for the age of confirmation in the United States. The Sacrament of Confirmation can be celebrated at any time between the age of discretion and sixteen years. It has been determined that a single catechesis cannot be assigned for this sacrament.

See National Directory for Catechesis, 36 A, 2.

In the early Church, Christian Initiation was one event. Adults or children were baptized, anointed, or had hands laid upon them, and then participated in the Eucharist, all at the same celebration. For a variety of reasons this practice gradually became separated into three different events. In 1910, Pius X recommended in his encyclical *Quam Singulari* that the First Communion of children should not be deferred too long after they had reached the age of reason. Previous to his urging, children who had been baptized as infants usually celebrated First Communion in the early teen years, and Confirmation usually was celebrated at an earlier age. However, once children began to participate fully in the Eucharist at an earlier age, the age for Confirmation was varied and not necessarily tied to reception of First Communion.

The Second Vatican Council called for the restoration of the Catechumenate and the revision of all the sacramental rituals. When the Rite of Christian Initiation of Adults, which also includes children of catechetical age, was issued, it restored the order of the Sacraments of Initiation.

> " Once children began to participate fully in the Eucharist at an earlier age, the age for Confirmation was varied and not necessarily tied to reception of First Communion. "

As a result, many dioceses and parishes throughout the United States have adopted the practice of celebrating Confirmation prior to First Communion. This is often referred to as *Restored Order*.

Some of these dioceses celebrate the Sacrament of Confirmation at the same Eucharistic celebration in which children celebrate their First Communion. Other dioceses celebrate at a different time, but before First Communion.

Other dioceses choose to celebrate Confirmation sometime after First Communion. All of these practices are approved by the United States Bishops Conference, which has given approval to the celebration of Confirmation for children baptized as infants anytime between the ages of seven and sixteen.

Call to Celebrate: Eucharist includes two sessions for those parishes that are practicing restored order. These sessions are found on pages CE23–44 of the *Catechist Edition*. If you are preparing children for both sacraments, use these sessions after session one. For *Family Guide* pages for the two additional lessons for Restored Order, visit **www.harcourtreligion.com**.

For Reflection

- What are the positive implications for Restored Order of Confirmation?

Sunday Connection

Bulletin Inserts, General Intercessions, and Parish Blessings

Use these as a way to involve the parish assembly in the preperation for sacraments.

Eucharist 1   We Belong

Bulletin Insert   During the week, our young people who are preparing to receive Holy Communion will be reflecting about Baptism, Confirmation, and the Eucharist. Join them by taking time to think about the effect that belonging to the Church has on your daily life.

Intercession   For young people preparing for Holy Communion, that they may be encouraged by the living faith of this assembly.

Parish Blessing   God, our loving Father, these young people come before you as your children. They belong to you. Send the Holy Spirit upon them as they begin this time of preparation so that they may come to know your presence in all they do. We ask this blessing through Christ our Lord.

Preparing for Confirmation
RO1   Gifts of the Holy Spirit

Bulletin Insert   During the week, our young people who are preparing to celebrate Confirmation and Holy Communion will be reflecting on the Gifts of the Holy Spirit. Join them by taking time to think about how those Gifts are active in your life today.

Intercession   For young people preparing for Confirmation and Holy Communion, that they may be open to receiving the Gifts of the Holy Spirit.

Parish Blessing   God, our loving Father, these young people come before you seeking the Gifts of the Holy Spirit. Open their hearts and minds to his presence and grant them knowledge of his power. We ask this blessing through Christ our Lord.

RO2   We Are Holy

Bulletin Insert   During the week, our young people who are preparing to celebrate Confirmation and Holy Communion will be reflecting on the call to holiness. Join them this week by reflecting on your own witness to the person and message of Jesus.

Intercession   For young people preparing for Confirmation and Holy Communion, that they may see in this community many witnesses to holiness.

Parish Blessing   God, our loving Father, these young people come before you yearning to be like your Son, Jesus. Send them the Holy Spirit that their eyes may be opened and their hearts set on fire with love and knowledge of him. We ask this blessing through Christ our Lord.

Go to pp. 82–83 for the Sunday Connection information for the remainder of the Eucharist sessions.

Catechist Orientation

Goals
• To welcome catechists in a hospitable environment
• To affirm the important role of the catechist
• To reflect on the catechists' experience of Confirmation

• To inform the catechists about **Call to Celebrate: Eucharist** with emphasis on the Confirmation (Restored Order) sessions:
  • the philosophy of the program
  • the content
  • the resources available

Materials	
• Beverages and light refreshments	• A prayer table covered in a white cloth with a candle and a Bible on a stand, a clear glass bowl with water, and a branch or other instrument for sprinkling
• Nametags	
• Copies of **Call to Celebrate: Eucharist** Child's Book	
• Copies of **Call to Celebrate: Eucharist** Catechist Edition	• Matches or lighter
• Songs of Celebration CD	

Welcome and Opening Prayer (30 minutes)

Welcome the catechists and distribute nametags.

Begin the session with welcoming words and introduce yourself.

Have the catechists introduce themselves to one another.

Review the goals and agenda for the gathering.

Gather the group around the prayer setting.

Begin the prayer by singing or listening to "We Are Marching," Songs of Celebration CD, track 2.

Light the candle and lead the catechists in the following reflection. Pause after each question.
• Recall your own Confirmation day.
• Where was it? Who was there?
• Can you recall any significant things that happened that day?
• Do you remember any feelings you may have had during the ceremony?
• How were you prepared for the event?

Invite catechists to share any significant memories they may have of their own Confirmation.

Read John 14:15–26.

Allow silent reflection.

Pause and then discuss the question:
• How do you want the children you will be catechizing to hear the message of this Gospel?

Close with a blessing. Ask the catechists to stand, and extend your hands over them as you say:

Lord God, in your loving kindness strengthen and direct these catechists. Let your Spirit uphold them as they prepare to share their time and talent with your children. We ask this through Christ our Lord. Amen.

Program Overview (15 minutes)

Distribute copies of the Catechist Guide, Child's Book, Songs of Celebration CD, and the Family Guide for **Call to Celebrate: Eucharist**.

Explain what each is for and have catechists page through them.

Discuss any questions the catechists may have about the Restored Order of Confirmation. Refer catechists to p. ix of the Catechist Edition.

Scope and Sequence

Invite catechists to turn to the Table of Contents on p. iii of the Catechist Edition. Point out the articles in the front pages and the Catholic Source Book and Program Resources in the back pages.

Note the two sessions devoted to Confirmation are in the Catechist Edition.

Point out that the Confirmation lessons follow Chapter 1. If you have a different schedule for these sessions, let the catechists know that.

Turn to the Scope and Sequence section on pp. vi–vii. Explain that a scope and sequence gives the overview of the content for each chapter. Note each of the features in the left column and go through one chapter column to explain the format. Go through the Ritual Focus row and show that the flow of the chapters is based on the Order of the Mass.

Note that the Confirmation sessions are based on the Rite of Confirmation.

Lesson Overview (30 minutes)

Child's Book

Use Session 1 of the Confirmation chapter, "Gifts of the Spirit," (pp. CE23–33) to show the three-step process of a session:

Celebrate
- celebration and reflection

Remember
- proclamation and breaking open the Bible reading
- teaching the doctrine
- learning about the ritual action of the sacrament

Live
- making connections to their lives and their families

Point out the Faith at Home boxes in the Remember section and the Signs of Faith feature on the Celebrate and Remember pages.

Catechist Edition

Use Chapter 4 of the *Catechist Edition* as a guide.

Familiarize catechists with the background and resources in the left-hand column on p. 32A.

Encourage them to read and reflect on the essay in the main column as they are planning their lessons. Note the reflection questions and Catechist Prayer.

Review the planner on p. 32B. Note the materials needed for each lesson, and have catechists turn to the pages noted to find the Activity Master CE9 and the Echo Pantomime CE10. Go through the Echo Pantomime with the catechists, and show the variety of Scripture Resources.

Go to pp. 32–41. Alert catechists that the side wrap gives a step-by-step lesson plan for the *Child's Book* pages, and the bottom boxes give them additional background, activities, and tips. Have them page through the lesson, and ask for any questions.

Turn to the Catholic Source Book, pp. 82–105. Have catechists page through it and notice the additional activities provided in the wrap.

Break for refreshments and conversation.

Administrative Details (10 minutes)

Elicit any questions the catechists have about the components and resources.

Allow time for administrative details, such as calendars and class lists.

Remind them of the next session, which will be catechist training on liturgical catechesis. This is the method they will be using throughout the program.

Ask them to read pp. iv–xv before the training session.

Closing Prayer (10 minutes)

Gather the catechists in a circle around the prayer space.

Sing "We Are Marching," *Songs of Celebration* CD, track 2.

Make the Sign of the Cross and say:
Let us call to mind the goodness of God who gives us all good things. I bless you with this water to remind you of the gift of your Baptism and your call to hand on the faith. (Sprinkle the group with water.) Let us join in the prayer that Jesus has taught us.

Pray the Lord's Prayer together.

Thank catechists for their attendance.

Catechist Training

Goals

- To introduce the method of liturgical catechesis
- To present the underlying meaning of the Sacrament of Eucharist
- To show how to design a prayer space and lead prayer
- To explain sacraments as actions of a faith community

Advance Preparation

Familiarize yourself with the ritual action in the opening prayer.

Select three persons to carry the holy water, candle, and Bible in procession.

Rehearse the suggested song, "Yes Lord, I Believe," *Songs of Celebration* CD, track 7.

Materials

- A table covered with a white cloth
- A Bible on a stand
- A large candle
- Candles for each participant
- Matches or a lighter
- A large, clear glass bowl with water
- Plants and flowers, if appropriate
- *Songs of Celebration* CD
- Poster board or chart paper
- *Eucharist Stories of Celebration* video
- Copies of the following articles from the *Sacraments Source Book* CD:
  - "What Is Liturgical Catechesis?"
  - "How to Lead Prayer"
  - "Role of the Prayer Leader"
  - "What Is a Sacrament?"
  - "Eucharist"
  - "Confirmation"

Opening Prayer Service and Reflection (20 minutes)

Sing together, "Yes Lord, I Believe," *Songs of Celebration* CD, track 7.

As you sing, walk forward slowly. Follow the persons carrying the holy water, candle, and Bible.

Lead the opening prayer.

Leader: *Let us begin. God, our loving Father, we are gathered here in your presence. We belong to you. Send us your Holy Spirit to help us live as disciples of your Son, Jesus. We ask this through Jesus Christ our Lord.*

All: *Amen.*

Leader: *On the day of our Baptism, we were claimed for Christ. By water and the Holy Spirit we received the gifts of faith and new life. On that day the faithful remembered their baptismal promises. Today let us once again remember those promises together. Please come forward and gather around the holy water and candle.*

Do you say "no" to sin, so that you can live always as God's children?

All: *We do.*

Leader: *Do you believe in God, the Father almighty?*

All: *We do.*

Leader: *Do you believe in Jesus Christ, his only Son, our Lord?*

All: *We do.*

Leader: *Do you believe in the Holy Spirit?*

All: *We do.*

Leader: *This is our faith. This is the faith of the Church. We are proud to profess it in Christ Jesus.*

All: *Amen.*

Leader: *Let us come to the water and thank God for the gift of our Baptism. Please come to the water and make the Sign of the Cross with the water.*

When everyone has made the Sign of the Cross, light small candles from the large candle and distribute them to each catechist, saying:

[Name], You are the light of Christ.

Have catechists return to their seats.

Leader: *Loving God, we belong to you. We are your children. In Baptism we were united to your Son, Jesus. Open our hearts to the Holy Spirit as we remember our Baptism. We ask this through Jesus Christ our Lord;*

All: *Amen.*

Leader: *The Lord be with you.*

All: *And also with you.*

Leader: *A reading from the holy Gospel of John.*
Read John 15:1–12.
The Gospel of the Lord.

All: *Praise to you, Lord Jesus Christ.*

Leader: *Consider these questions for reflection and discussion: What image or phrase is important for you in this reading? What do Jesus' words "Remain in me as I remain in you" mean for you today?*

When the discussion is finished, continue the prayer.

Let us stand and pray as Jesus taught us.

Pray the Lord's Prayer together.

Let us offer each other the Sign of Peace.

Reflection on Prayer (20 minutes)

If there are a large number of catechists, organize them into smaller groups of 5 to 6 participants.

Invite the catechists to recall the ritual moments of the celebration. Do a guided meditation using the prompts from the celebration. Pause after each prompt.

Pause for a few minutes of silence. Then invite the groups to share their feelings about the celebration in their small group. Encourage them to stay with their feelings. After 5 to 7 minutes, invite sharing with the large group.

Naming (20 minutes)

Ask the participants to name what they learned about God, Jesus, the Church, or their own Christian life from the celebration.

Take each category separately and list their responses on the board or on chart paper. Use phrases from their lists to summarize what they have said about faith, sacrifice, and service. Comment on how much "content" they came up with.

Distribute the article, "What Is Liturgical Catechesis?" Summarize the main parts of the article, and explain that this is the model of catechesis upon which **Call to Celebrate** is based. Encourage catechists to read the article at a later time.

Rotation and Break (5 minutes)

Setting up a Prayer Space and Leading Prayer (30 minutes)

Gather catechists around the prayer space and pass out "How to Lead Prayer." Describe how you set up the space. Give catechists ideas on setting up a prayer space in their meeting place. Note where and how they can obtain materials for the space, and emphasize the importance of a prayer environment.

Distribute the article, "Role of the Prayer Leader," and summarize it with the catechists. Practice leading the procession and prayer gestures with them.

Rotation and Break (5 minutes)

A Theology of Sacrament and Eucharist (30 minutes)

Play Part 3 of the *Eucharist Stories of Celebration* video. After catechists have viewed the video, use the questions in the guide for discussion.

Summarize these important points:
- Sacraments are *actions* of God and a faith community.
- In the Eucharist, we *share in a meal* during which we are fed with the Body and Blood of Jesus.
- The Eucharist is the community's great prayer of thanksgiving.

Distribute the articles, "What Is a Sacrament?" "Eucharist," and "Confirmation." Encourage catechists to read the articles later.

Closing Blessing (5 minutes)

Thank the catechists for attending the session.

Extend your hands over the catechists and pray in these or similar words:

> *God, the Father of mercies, has sent his Son into the world. Through the power of the Holy Spirit, may you continue to be transformed into the Body of Christ and witness his love in the world. Amen.*

Parent Orientation

Goals

- To welcome parents and families in a hospitable environment
- To affirm the importance of parental and family participation in the process
- To inform parents and families about the *Call to Celebrate: Eucharist* program with the Confirmation component for Restored Order
- To inform parents and families about the parish policies and procedures relating to the celebration of Confirmation and First Communion

Environment

- Be sure to clearly identify the meeting place, posting clear directions if necessary.
- Tables and chairs arranged for small groups
- A prayer setting with large candle, Bible on a stand or table, clear bowl filled with water, and a branch or other instrument for sprinkling

> Additional *Family Guide* pages for Restored Order sessions can be found at **www.harcourtreligion.com**.

Materials

- Beverages and light refreshments
- Nametags
- Copies of *Call to Celebrate: Eucharist Family Guide* and *Child's Book*
- Copies of the reproduced Restored Order Confirmation sessions from the *Catechist Edition*, pp. CE25–33 and pp. CE36–44
- Copies of the reproduced catechist pages, pp. CE23–24 and pp. CE34–35 (only for parents doing preparation in the home)
- *Songs of Celebration* CD
- *Eucharist Stories of Celebration* video and guide
- Copies of the following from the *Sacraments Source Book* CD:
  - **Parent Orientation Restored Order Handouts 1 and 2**
  - "Restored Order"
  - "Celebrating Rituals at Home–Letter"
  - **At Home Ritual Preparation Handouts 1–10**

Welcome and Opening Prayer

Welcome parents and other adults and distribute nametags.

Introduce yourself and briefly review the goals and agenda for the gathering.

Gather the group around the prayer setting, or have them pause for a reflective moment.

Begin the prayer by singing or listening to "Yes Lord, I Believe!" from the *Songs of Celebration* CD, track 7.

Light the candle and lead parents in the following reflection. Pause after each question:
- *Recall your own Confirmation day.*
- *Recall any significant things that happened that day or during your preparation.*

Invite parents and family members to share with one or two other persons in the group any significant memories they may have of their own First Communion. Distribute **Parent Orientation Restored Order Handout 1**.

Call the group back together and lead the parents and family members in the Parent's Prayer.

View Video

Show Parts 1 and 2 of the *Eucharist Stories of Celebration* video. Use the questions in the video guide for discussion.

Discuss Restored Order

Use the "Restored Order" article to highlight the important points of celebrating Confirmation before or with the reception of First Holy Communion.

Make the point that there are three Sacraments of Initiation, and full participation in the Eucharist is the fullness of initiation.

Break for refreshments and conversation.

The *Call to Celebrate: Eucharist* Program

Distribute the *Child's Book* and the reproducible child pages from the Catechist Edition, pp. CE25–33 and pp. CE36–44. Lead the parents and family members through the Table of Contents.

Point out that the program:
- introduces the child to an understanding of the Sacrament of Confirmation and the Eucharist.

- is a preparation for a lifetime of celebrating the gifts of the Holy Spirit and the gift of Jesus in the Eucharist.
- introduces children to both the Sacrament of Confirmation and the Sacrament of the Eucharist through rituals and prayers.

Use one chapter of the reproduced pages or the *Child's Book* to show parents and family members the process of a session:

Celebrate
- celebration and reflection

Remember
- proclamation and breaking open the Scripture reading
- teaching the doctrine
- learning about the ritual action of the sacrament

Live
- making connections to their lives and their families

Highlight the three Faith at Home features in the reproduced pages and the *Child's Book*.

Emphasize the importance of doing the activities on the Faith at Home page.

Describe the *Call to Celebrate: Eucharist Family Guide* using one of the two implementation models.

✳ **For programs in which the catechesis is done in a group with a catechist and includes family support**

Distribute the *Call to Celebrate: Eucharist Family Guide*. Point out the differences in the two parts:
- the first part is a reflection tool for parents.
- the second part is a guide for doing home preparation.

Mention the availability of the *Songs of Celebration* CD, which will enhance their time with the child and support the child's learning.

Distribute Restored Order Parent Orientation Handout 2 and go through the frequently asked questions with parents and family members.

Go to Parish Policies and Procedures.

✳ **For programs in which the catechesis is done in the home**

Distribute the *Call to Celebrate: Eucharist Family Guide* and the reproduced *Catechist Edition* pages for the two Confirmation sessions. Point out the difference in the two parts of the guide:
- the first part is a reflection tool for parents.
- the second part is a guide for doing home preparation.

Go through one session of the *Family Guide* and one of the reproduced Confirmation *Catechist Edition* pages, and explain how to use the outline. Point out:
- the parent background essay.
- the easy-to-follow overview.
- the People of Faith story for each session and the importance of telling these stories to children.

Emphasize how essential the ritual prayer is to the session. Go through the prayer as it is written in the session and talk about ways to prepare a prayer space and environment at home.

Distribute Restored Order Parent Orientation Handout 2, "Celebrating Rituals at Home–Letter," and **At Home Ritual Preparation Handouts 1–10**.

Parish Policies and Procedures

Explain the commitment the parish expects of parents and family members for this preparation.

Distribute appropriate schedules or calendars.

Closing Prayer

Gather the parents and family members in a circular grouping around the prayer space.

Begin with the Sign of the Cross, and say these or similar words:

Let us call to mind the goodness of God who gives us all good things. I bless you with this water to remind you of the gift of your Baptism and your call to hand on the faith. (Sprinkle the group with water.)

Sing "Yes Lord, I Believe!" from *Songs of Celebration* CD, track 7.

Pray the Lord's Prayer together.

 Encourage parents and family members to go to **www.harcourtreligion.com** for more ideas and suggestions.

We Belong

Before the Celebration

- Choose a gathering space that will be conducive to prayer and to accommodate the size of the group; the church, a chapel, or a gathering place in the parish hall would each be appropriate. You will want the group to be able to see, hear, and move easily during the ritual.
- Prepare the group for the ritual action of the Renewal of Baptismal Promises and for the reflection on the Scriptures.
- Select a good reader to proclaim the reading.

- Select four people for the entrance procession to carry the Bible, the candle, the bowl of water, and the chrism. Show them where and how to place them in the sanctuary or on the prayer table.
- If not in a church or chapel, place chairs in semicircular rows around the prayer space. Leave enough space for people to move in and out of the rows. If possible, have tables and chairs set up in another space for adult discussion after the celebration.

Materials

- A large, clear bowl with water, or if the celebration is in the church, use the baptismal font or pool
- A large candle or the Paschal candle
- A prayer table for the candle, oil of chrism, a baptismal candle, a Bible, and a stand
- *Songs of Celebration* CD
- Copies of the celebration for the assembly (*Sacraments Source Book* CD)

Gathering Rite

Welcome the gathered assembly.

Rehearse the opening song, and go over the ritual action of the Renewal of Baptismal Promises.

Invite the assembly to stand for the procession.

Opening Song

"Yes Lord, I Believe!," *Songs of Celebration* CD, track 7.

Procession

The presider and persons carrying the bowl with water, candle, and Bible process in while the assembly sings.

> **Leader:** Let us begin with the Sign of the Cross.
> **All:** In the name of the Father, and of the Son, and of the Holy Spirit. Amen.

> **Leader:** May the peace of the Lord be with you.
> **All:** And also with you.

Opening Prayer

> **Leader:** Heavenly Father, at Baptism, we were joined to your Son, Jesus Christ, and welcomed into the family of the Church. Hear our prayer as we remember our Baptism. We ask this through your Son, Jesus, who lives and reigns forever.
> **All:** Amen.

Celebration of the Word

> **Leader:** A reading from the holy Gospel according to John.
> **All:** Glory to you, Lord.
> Read John 15:1–7.
> **Leader:** The Gospel of the Lord.
> **All:** Praise to you, Lord Jesus Christ.
> Sit silently.

Reflection

Invite the assembly to reflect on the Scriptures; use the following question:

- What does the image of the vine and branches suggest to you about your relationship with Jesus?

Ask the assembly to share their responses with one or two people. Be sure to include children in the sharing.

Renewal of Baptismal Promises

Leader: Let us stand and renew our baptismal promises.

Leader: Do you reject sin, so as to live in the freedom of God's children?

All: I do.

Leader: Do you reject the glamour of evil and refuse to be mastered by sin?

All: I do.

Leader: Do you reject Satan, father of sin and prince of darkness?

All: I do.

Leader: Do you believe in Jesus Christ, God's only Son, our Lord?

All: I do.

Leader: Do you believe in the Holy Spirit, the holy catholic Church, the communion of saints, the Resurrection of the body, and life everlasting?

All: I do.

Based on Rite of Chrisian Initiation of Adults, 581

The Lord's Prayer

Leader: Let us join in the words that Jesus has given us.
Say the Lord's Prayer together.

Closing Prayer

Leader: May the Lord bless us, protect us from all evil, and bring us to everlasting life.
All: Amen.
Leader: Our celebration has ended. Let us go forth to love and serve the Lord.
All: Thanks be to God.

Sing the opening song together.

Children go to their group session and adults go to the appointed space for reflection.

- There is a liturgical catechetical session for adults on p. 54.
- There is a parent/adult catechetical session on pp. 55–56.
- There is an intergenerational catechetical session on pp. 57–58.

We Belong

Goals	Materials
• To reflect on the celebration • To review and discuss the effects of Baptism	• Poster board, chart paper, or overhead projector • *Songs of Celebration* CD • Markers • Bible

Reflection (20 minutes)

Invite the adults to gather in groups of five or six.

Begin by recalling the ritual moments of the celebration. Lead a guided meditation using the following prompts. Pause after each prompt.

• Play a few verses of the opening song, "Yes Lord, I Believe," *Songs of Celebration* CD, track 7.
• Ask: "What was it like to renew your baptismal promises?"
• Call to mind the procession to the water and the signing of one another.
• Read a few verses of the Gospel.
• Ask participants to recall their discussion of the Gospel.
• Recall the Lord's Prayer and Dismissal.

Small Group Sharing

Pause for a few minutes of silence. Then invite the participants to share their feelings about the celebration in their small group. Encourage them to stay with their feelings. After 10 to 15 minutes, invite sharing with the large group.

Large Group Sharing

Gather the responses of the small groups on poster board, chart paper, or an overhead projector. Ask for feelings and thoughts about the celebration as a whole, and also for specific parts of the celebration that were meaningful to members of the group.

Naming (30 minutes)

Ask the participants to name what they learned from the celebration about God, Jesus, the Church, Baptism, or their own Christian life.

Take each category separately and list responses on poster board, chart paper, or an overhead projector. When the lists are completed, use them to summarize the theology and meaning of Renewal of Baptismal Promises.

Affirm, add, or enlarge upon the following points:
• Baptism is a sacrament of belonging.
• Baptism is a sacrament of faith and needs a community of believers.
• Baptism makes us members of the Church.
• In Baptism, all sin is forgiven.
• In Baptism, we are made a "new creature."
• In Baptism, we become adopted children of God and temples of the Holy Spirit.

Reflection and Small Group Sharing (20 minutes)

Ask "What will you do this week to nurture your bond with the Holy Spirit?"

Direct participants to reflect in silence for a few minutes, and then share their responses with their group.

Closing Blessing (5 minutes)

Gather and begin with the Sign of the Cross.

> **Leader:** *God, our Father, we praise and thank you for choosing us to be your children.*
> **All:** *Amen.*
> **Leader:** *Jesus our Savior, we praise and thank you for showing us how to live and love.*
> **All:** *Amen.*
> **Leader:** *Holy Spirit, giver of God's gifts, we praise and thank you for guiding us on our way.*
> **All:** *Amen.*

We Belong

Goals	Environment	Materials
• To welcome participants in a hospitable environment • To discuss how one "belongs" to the Church • To help participants come to a deeper understanding of the Sacraments of Initiation	• Be sure to clearly identify the meeting place, posting clear directions if necessary. • Tables and chairs arranged for small groups • A prayer setting with large candle, Bible on a stand or table, clear bowl filled with water, and a branch or other instrument for sprinkling	• Beverages and light refreshments • Copies of *Call to Celebrate: Eucharist* Family Guide • *Songs of Celebration* CD • Copies of **Eucharist Parent/Adult Catechesis Handouts 1:1** and **1:2** (*Sacraments Source Book* CD) • Board or chart paper

Welcome and Opening Prayer (15 minutes)

Begin the session with welcoming words and introduce yourself. Briefly review the goals and agenda for the gathering.

✳ **If this session was preceded by a large group ritual and reflection, go to We Belong. If not, continue with the prayer.**

Gather the group around the prayer setting, if possible; if not, have the group pause for a reflective moment.

Introduce the prayer with the Sign of the Cross.

Sing "Yes Lord, I Believe!" *Songs of Celebration* CD, track 7.

Pray these or similar words:
God, you are the source of life. You have made all things. We live with the breath of your life in us. We give you praise and thanks for these gifts. We belong to you. We are your children and we are never alone because you are present to us in so many ways, especially in the Church. Open our hearts that we may bring your life to those around us. We ask this in the name of your Son, Jesus. Amen.

Read *John 15:1–17*.

Invite the assembly to reflect on the Gospel using the following question:
• What does the image of the vine and branches suggest to you about your relationship with Jesus?

Ask the participants to share their responses with one or two people.

Invite participants to come forward to sign themselves with the holy water as a sign of their belonging to God and the Church.

We Belong (30 minutes)

Write the word *belonging* on the board or on chart paper. Ask the group to give you any word or image that *belonging* brings up for them. Jot down the responses and point out that real belonging involves investment in relationships and causes.

Distribute Eucharist Parent/Adult Catechesis Handout 1:1 and ask participants to complete it. Explain that it will help them see from their own experiences how persons come to belong.

Organize the large group into smaller groups of 5 to 6 people. Ask participants to share their stories of initiation in the small groups.

Direct them to listen for any common characteristics of what happens to people in the process of coming to belong to a group.

Invite participants to share in small groups. Develop a list of characteristics common to everyone's sharing that tells something about how people come to belong. At the end of the sharing, ask volunteers from the small groups to share the lists.

Use ideas from the list and give further input on what it means to belong to the Church. Emphasize that:

- Belonging is a process.
- Usually we are invited in (evangelization) or are really attracted by what we see (Christian witness).
- We make choices about our involvement.
- There are always rituals connected to the process of belonging (sacraments).
- As we become more involved in the group, we change (conversion).
- If it is really important to us, we tell others about it; we invite them in.

Allow some quiet time and ask participants to think about all the things they have just discussed and listened to, and to ask themselves:

- On a scale of 1–10 (10 being the highest), where would you rank yourself as belonging to the Church? Where would you rank yourself as belonging to God?

Break for refreshments and conversation.

What Are the Sacraments of Initiation? (30 minutes)

Use some of the comments from the previous session to move into this segment.

Point out that initiation, or coming to belong, is always a process, and it usually involves symbols, rites, and rituals. It is that way with the Church, too. The Church has three Sacraments of Initiation: Baptism, Confirmation, and Eucharist.

Distribute Eucharist Parent/Adult Catechesis Handout 1:2 and go through it in a conversational style, making comments and explaining as questions arise. You may want to use the questions as a small group resource for sharing.

Allow time for questions, comments, and insights.

Summarize by saying these or similar words:

Baptism, Confirmation, and the Eucharist are the Sacraments of Initiation. These sacraments celebrate our belonging to Jesus Christ and being incorporated into his Body, the Church. Most of us go through a process of understanding what this really means for us. It is important to keep in mind that when we celebrate sacraments without being in relationship with and participating in the community of faith, we miss out on a lot. It is also important to keep in mind that initiation is only a beginning. It is not a graduation.

Parent Moment (10 minutes)

Highlight the three Faith at Home features in the *Child's Book* and show how they will help the parents and family members to participate in the children's preparation.

Emphasize the importance of doing the activities on the Faith at Home page, especially the ritual action.

Closing Prayer (5 minutes)

Gather the participants in a circle around the prayer space. Pray these or similar words:

God, you who call us to yourself, you who long for us to belong to you, we ask for your blessing as we continue our faith journey. May we always be alert to your presence in the sacred signs of our lives and the celebrations of the Church. We ask this in Jesus' name. Amen.

We close by reminding ourselves of our Baptism and our common kinship in God's family. In all that we do, may we reflect the glory of the Father, the Son, and the Holy Spirit. (Sprinkle with water.) Amen.

Thank everyone for their time and participation.

 Encourage parents and family members to go to **www.harcourtreligion.com** for more ideas and suggestions.

We Belong

Objectives

- To guide families to experience a celebration of the word, including Renewal of Baptismal Promises
- To explore the meaning of the ritual action in family groups
- To help family members increase their understanding of the Sacraments of Initiation
- To help family members express that they are followers of Christ

Materials

- Copies of the celebration for the assembly (*Sacraments Source Book* CD)
- *Songs of Celebration* CD
- Prayer table
- Bible
- Candle and matches
- Bowl filled with water
- Chart or poster paper
- Markers
- Pencils
- *Child's Book*

Welcome and Celebration (10–15 minutes)

Welcome the families in the gathering space.

Distribute copies of the celebration.

Select a family to be in the procession. Have them choose a family member to carry the Bible in procession.
- When families are assembled, walk forward slowly. Follow the child carrying the Bible.
- During the procession, lead families in singing "Yes Lord, I Believe," from the *Songs of Celebration* CD, track 7.
- Place the Bible on the prayer table and have family members return to their seats.
- Light the prayer candle.
- Begin prayer with the Sign of the Cross and invite the group to follow the order of the prayer.
- If the group is too large to gather around the water and candle, have families remain seated.
- For the proclamation of the Gospel, you may use a Bible or the adapted reading in the *Child's Book* on pp. 6–7.
- Conclude with the opening song from the *Songs of Celebration* CD, track 7.

New Life individual family unit experience (10 minutes)

Guide family members to reflect on the celebration by asking the following questions:
- What did you see? What did you hear? What did you do?

Ask volunteers to share their responses.

Allow time for children and family members to complete the activity on p. 4 of the *Child's Book*.

The Body of Christ whole-group learning experience (5 minutes)

Select members of several families to share stories or details they know about their own Baptisms.

Direct attention to the bowl of water and the candle on the prayer table. Ask participants how these symbols are related to Baptism.

Explain the Signs of Faith: Water and Paschal Candle by summarizing the text on pp. 4–5 of the *Child's Book*.

Ask for a volunteer to read aloud The Body of Christ section in the *Child's Book*.

We Belong to God family cluster sharing experience (10 minutes)

Organize the large group into small clusters and invite them to reflect on the following question:
- What does Jesus tell us about belonging to God?

Ask volunteers to share their responses.

Ask each family cluster to select a leader to read aloud the first paragraph on p. 6 of the *Child's Book*.

Scripture whole-group learning experience (10 minutes)

Read aloud the Scripture story on pp. 6–7 of the *Child's Book*.

Invite the large group to reflect on the following:
- What was Jesus telling his friends in this story?
- Ask volunteers to share their responses.

Allow silent time for individuals to reflect on how Jesus is their friend. At the end of the reflection, have family members share their responses with one another.

Direct the families to help children complete the Share activity on p. 7 of the *Child's Book*.

Emphasize that Jesus wants us to know we belong to him, and he wants us to love one another.

The Sacraments of Initiation family cluster sharing experience (15 minutes)

Organize the large group into the same family cluster groups as earlier. Be sure each group has selected a leader. Provide one sheet of poster paper for each family cluster and invite them to reflect on the question: Which sacraments are signs of belonging?

Ask each group leader to write down his or her group's responses on the poster paper.

Ask each group leader to select a member of his or her group to read aloud the first paragraph on p. 8 of the *Child's Book*.

Guide family cluster groups to look at the sacraments that they have listed on their chart paper, and have the leaders circle the Sacraments of Initiation.

Explain that Baptism, Confirmation, and Eucharist are the Sacraments of Initiation. These sacraments make us full members of the Church. These sacraments are signs that we belong to God.

Baptism individual family unit experience (5 minutes)

Point out the word "Baptism" in the *Child's Book*.
- Invite family members to group together and have the adults share memories of their Baptisms or that of their child or children.

- Select a child to read aloud about Baptism on p. 8 of the *Child's Book*.

Confirmation and Eucharist whole-group learning experience (10 minutes)

Point out the word "Confirmation" in the *Child's Book*:
- Explain to the large group that the Sacrament of Confirmation strengthens baptized persons with the gifts of the Holy Spirit.
- Read the prayers on p. 9 of the *Child's Book*.
- Ask the families which Person of the Trinity we receive in a special way during Confirmation.
- Select a volunteer to read Signs of Faith: The Trinity.

Point out the word "Eucharist" in the *Child's Book*:
- Select a family member to read aloud from the book about Eucharist.

Clarify that Eucharist is a name used for the whole action of the Mass and that Holy Communion is the receiving of the Body and Blood of Jesus during the Eucharist.

Children of Light individual family unit experience (5 minutes)

Guide families in sharing how they live as followers of Christ using the activity on p. 10 of the *Child's Book*. At the end of the reflection, ask volunteers to share their family's responses.

Closing Blessing (5 minutes)

Invite each family to form a family circle.

Begin with the Sign of the Cross.

Pray the prayer on p. 10 of the *Child's Book*.

Conclude by leading families in singing *Songs of Celebration* CD, track 7, "Yes Lord, I Believe."

Faith at Home

Direct families' attention to the Faith at Home page and encourage them to the activities at home.

Gifts of the Holy Spirit

Before the Celebration		Materials

<table>
<tr><td>

- Choose a gathering space that will be conducive to prayer and that will accommodate the size of the group; the church, a chapel, or a gathering place in the parish hall would each be appropriate. You will want the group to be able to see, hear, and move easily during the ritual.

- Prepare the group for the ritual action of the Blessing and for the reflection on the sacred Scriptures.

- Select a good reader to proclaim the reading.

</td><td>

- Select four people for the entrance procession: to carry the Bible, the candle, the bowl of water, and the chrism. Show them where and how to place them in the sanctuary or on the prayer table.

- If not in a church or chapel, place chairs in semicircular rows around the prayer space. Leave enough space for people to move in and out of the rows. If possible, have tables and chairs set up in another space for adult discussion after the celebration.

</td><td>

- A large, clear bowl with water, or if the celebration is in the church, use the baptismal font or pool

- A branch or aspergellum for sprinkling

- A large candle or the Paschal candle

- A prayer table for the candle, oil of chrism, a baptismal candle, a Bible, and a stand

- *Songs of Celebration* CD

- Copies of the celebration for the assembly (*Sacraments Source Book* CD)

</td></tr>
</table>

Gathering Rite

Welcome the gathered assembly.

Rehearse the opening song with gestures, and go over the ritual action of the Blessing.

Invite the assembly to stand for the procession.

Opening Song

"We Are Called," *Songs of Celebration* CD, track 1.

Procession

The presider and persons carrying the bowl with water, a candle, and Bible process in while the assembly sings.

> *Leader: Let us pray.*
> *Make the Sign of the Cross together.*

Opening Prayer

> ***Leader:*** *God, our Father, we belong to you. We are your children. Open our hearts to the gift of the Holy Spirit. We ask this through Jesus Christ our Lord.*
> ***All:*** *Amen.*

Celebration of the Word

> ***Leader:*** *Jesus is the Light of the World. A reading from the holy Gospel according to John.*
> ***All:*** *Glory to you, Lord.*
> *Read John 14:15–26.*
> ***Leader:*** *The Gospel of the Lord.*
> ***All:*** *Praise to you, Lord Jesus Christ.*
> *Sit silently.*

Reflection

Invite the assembly to reflect on the Gospel. Use the following question:

- When do you feel the presence of the Holy Spirit's help?

Ask the assembly to share their responses with one or two people. Be sure to include children in the sharing.

Blessing

Invite the Confirmation candidates forward with their family members. Invite the family members to extend their hands over the children as you do.

Leader: *In Baptism, you were given the gift of the Holy Spirit. By water and the Holy Spirit, you received the gifts of faith and new life. Let us remember that the Holy Spirit is with us always.*
Extend your hands over the head of each child and pray:

Leader: *[Name], remember that the Holy Spirit is with you always.*

Child: *Amen.*

Closing Prayer

Leader: *Loving Father, we thank you for the gift of your Spirit. Send us forth to bring your love to others. We ask this through Jesus Christ, our Lord.*

All: *Amen.*

Children go to their group session and adults go to the appointed space for reflection.

- There is a liturgical catechetical session for adults on p. 61.
- There is a parent/adult catechetical session on pp. 62–63.
- There is an intergenerational catechetical session on pp. 64–65.

Gifts of the Holy Spirit

Goals

- To reflect on the celebration
- To explore the meaning of Blessing and Gifts of the Holy Spirit
- To review the ritual action of Extension of Hands in the Confirmation Rite

Materials

- Poster board, chart paper, or overhead projector
- Markers
- *Songs of Celebration* CD

Reflection (20 minutes)

Invite the adults to gather in groups of five or six.

Begin by recalling the ritual moments of the celebration. Lead a guided meditation using the following prompts. Pause after each prompt.

- Play a few verses of the opening song "We Are Called," *Songs of Celebration*, track 1.
- Read some verses of the Gospel.
- Ask participants to recall their discussion of the Gospel.
- Call to mind the ritual of blessing the candidates.
- Ask: "What was it like for you observe the candidates being blessed?"

Small Group Sharing

Pause for a few minutes of silence. Then invite the participants to share their feelings about the celebration in their small group. Encourage them to stay with their feelings. After 10 to 15 minutes, invite sharing with the large group.

Large Group Sharing

Gather the responses of the small groups on poster-board, chart paper, or an overhead projector. Ask for feelings and thoughts about the celebration as a whole, and also for comments on specific parts of the celebration that were especially meaningful to members of the group.

Naming (30 minutes)

Ask the participants to name what they learned from the celebration about Blessing, the Holy Spirit, the Church, and their own Christian life.

Take each category separately and list responses on poster board, chart paper, or an overhead projector. When the lists are completed, use them to summarize the theology and meaning of Blessings, Extension of Hands, and Gifts of the Holy Spirit.

Affirm, add, or enlarge upon the following points:

- Blessings call down God's favor on those being blessed. We can bless one another.
- One of the signs the Church uses to call upon the power of the Holy Spirit is the extending of hands.
- During the Sacrament of Confirmation, the bishop and the priests who are with him extend their hands over the candidates and pray that the Holy Spirit will give them the gifts of wisdom, understanding, right judgment, courage, knowledge, reverence, and wonder and awe.
- The Holy Spirit is given to us at Baptism to be our helper and advocate.
- Confirmation increases the gifts of the Holy Spirit in us. The gifts are given for the sake of building up the Church.

Reflection and Small Group Sharing (20 minutes)

Ask "Which of the seven Gifts of the Holy Spirit will you pray for this week? Why?"

Direct participants to reflect in silence for a few minutes and then share their responses with their group.

Closing Blessing (5 minutes)

Gather and begin with the Sign of the Cross.

Instruct participants to face a partner and extend hands over them in blessing, saying:

May the Gifts of the Holy Spirit be active and effective in your life this week.

Gifts of the Spirit

Goals	Environment	Materials
• To welcome participants in a hospitable environment • To teach the meaning of the Holy Spirit • To encourage participants to express their desire for the Gifts of the Holy Spirit	• Be sure to clearly identify the meeting place, posting clear directions if necessary. • Tables and chairs arranged for small groups • A prayer setting with large candle, Bible on a stand or table, clear bowl filled with water, and a branch or other instrument for sprinkling	• Beverages and light refreshments • Nametags • *Songs of Celebration* CD • Copies of **Confirmation Parent/ Adult Catechesis Handouts 1:1** and **1:2** (*Sacraments Source Book* CD) • Poster board or chart paper • Large sheets of newsprint paper and markers

Welcome and Opening Prayer (15 minutes)

Welcome parents and other adults and distribute nametags.

Introduce yourself and briefly review the goals and agenda for the gathering.

✳ **If this session was preceded by a large group ritual and reflection, go to Gifts of the Holy Spirit. If not, continue with the prayer.**

Gather the group around the prayer setting, if possible, or have the group pause for a reflective moment.

Introduce the prayer with the Sign of the Cross.

Sing or listen to "We Are Called," *Songs of Celebration* CD, track 1.

Pray these or similar words:

Lord God, send us the Holy Sprit to help and guide us. May he fill our hearts with life, may he lead us to truth and right living, and give us the courage to preach the Gospel at all times. Open our hearts to his presence that we may bring your life to those around us, we ask this in Jesus' name. Amen.

Read *John 14:15–26*.

Invite the assembly to reflect on the Gospel using the following question:
• When do you feel the presence of the Holy Spirit's help?

Ask the participants to share their responses with one or two people.

Invite participants to stand and face a partner.

Say: In Baptism, you were given the gift of the Holy Spirit. By water and the Holy Spirit, you received the gifts of faith and new life. Let us remember that the Holy Spirit is with us always.

Ask pairs to extend their hands over the heads of their partners and say:

Remember that the Holy Spirit is with you always.

Conclude the prayer by praying in these or similar words:
May the gifts of the Holy Spirit be poured out on us in abundance. We ask this in the name of Jesus, believing in his promise. Amen.

Gifts of the Holy Spirit (30 minutes)

Distribute Confirmation Parent/Adult Catechesis Handout 1:1.

Invite a volunteer to read the prayer from the rite.

Point out that this is a prayer prayed by the bishop during the Confirmation celebration.

Briefly explain each of the gifts.

Allow time for the participants to complete the activity on the handout.

Organize the large group into smaller groups of 5 to 6 people.

Ask participants to choose one of the gifts they feel they use frequently and one they want to practice. Have them share their choices with their small groups. At the conclusion of the sharing, ask participants to stand in their small groups, and offer this short prayer:

Come, Holy Spirit, we thank you for your gifts (Ask participants to name aloud in their small groups the gifts they feel they have and use frequently.), *and we pray that you will increase in us.* (Ask participants to name aloud the gifts they want increased.) *We ask this in the name of Jesus. Amen.*

Break for refreshments and conversation.

Who Is the Holy Spirit? (30 minutes)

Invite participants back and ask them to return to their small groups. Have large sheets of newsprint and markers available for each group.

Tell the groups to create word and picture collages that best describe their image of the Holy Spirit. When the collages are complete, display them around the meeting space and have a representative from each group explain the work. During the explanation, jot down points you want to refer back to during the input.

Summarize the group's input.

Distribute Confirmation Parent/Adult Catechesis Handout 1:2. In a conversational style, use the symbols of the Holy Spirit to describe who the Holy Spirit is.

Conclude with the following points:
- The Holy Spirit is the third Person of the Trinity.
- The Holy Spirit comes to us at Baptism and his gifts are strengthened in us at Confirmation.
- The Holy Spirit enlightens us and guides us.

Parent Moment (10 minutes)

Highlight the three Faith at Home features in the *Child's Book* and show how they will help the parents and family members to participate in children's preparation.

Emphasize the importance of doing the activities on the Faith at Home page, especially the ritual action.

Closing Prayer (5 minutes)

Gather participants in a circular grouping around the prayer space and pray together:

Come, Holy Spirit, fill the hearts of your faithful and kindle in them the fire of your love. Send forth your Spirit and they shall be created. And you shall renew the face of the earth.

We close by reminding ourselves of our Baptism and our common kinship in God's family. In all that we do, may we reflect the glory of the Father, the Son, and the Holy Spirit. (Sprinkle with water.) Amen.

Thank everyone for their time and participation.

 Encourage parents and family members to go to **www.harcourtreligion.com** for more ideas and suggestions.

Gifts of the Holy Spirit

Objectives	Materials
• To guide families to experience a celebration of the word, including a Blessing • To explore the meaning of the ritual action in family groups • To proclaim Jesus' words about the Holy Spirit • To teach the meaning of the Holy Spirit • To describe part of the Rite of Confirmation • To encourage family members to express their desire for the gifts of the Holy Spirit	• Copies of the celebration for the assembly (*Sacraments Source Book* CD) • *Songs of Celebration* CD • Prayer table • Bible • Cross or crucifix • Candle and matches • Bowl filled with water • Chart or poster paper • Markers • Pencils

Welcome and Celebration (10–15 minutes)

Welcome the families in the gathering space.

Distribute copies of the celebration.

Select a family to be in the procession. Have them choose a family member to carry the Bible in procession.
• When families are assembled, walk forward slowly. Follow the child carrying the Bible.
• During the procession, lead families in singing "We Are Called," from the *Songs of Celebration* CD, track 1.
• Place the Bible on the prayer table and have the family members return to their seats.
• Light the prayer candle.
• Begin prayer with the Sign of the Cross and invite the group to follow the order of the prayer.
• For the proclamation of the Gospel, you may use a Bible or the adapted reading in the *Catechist Edition* on p. CE28.
• Invite families to come forward one by one.
• Extend your hands over each family and say, "Remember that the Holy Spirit is with you always."

• Pray the closing prayer.
• Conclude with the opening song from the *Songs of Celebration* CD, track 1, or another appropriate song from your parish repertoire.

The Holy Spirit individual family unit experience (10 minutes)

Guide family members to reflect on the celebration by asking the following questions:
• What did you see? What did you hear? What did you do?
Ask volunteers to share their responses.

Guide families to reflect further on being called by name, using the activity on p. CE26 of the *Catechist Edition*. Allow time for family members to share their responses to the activity.

The Gift of the Holy Spirit whole-group learning experience (10 minutes)

Invite families to name some of the many gifts that God gives us.

Write responses on a sheet of chart paper in front of the large group.

Summarize the first paragraph on p. CE27 of the *Catechist Edition*.

Select family members to read the next two paragraphs aloud.

Jesus Promises the Holy Spirit whole-group learning experience (10 minutes)

Invite the large group to reflect on the following:
• What does Jesus tell us about the Holy Spirit?

List all responses on the next sheet of chart paper.

Read aloud the first paragraph from p. CE28 of the *Catechist Edition*.

Scripture whole-group learning experience (10 minutes)

Select a family member to read aloud the Gospel story from p. CE28 of the *Catechist Edition*.

Invite family members to turn toward one another and discuss the following questions:
• Why did the disciples need a helper?
• How can the Holy Spirit help you?

Have family members discuss times and circumstances when they might pray to the Holy Spirit.

Allow time for families to pray together the Prayer to the Holy Spirit from p. CE30 of the *Catechist Edition*.

The Gifts of the Holy Spirit whole-group learning experience (10 minutes)

Gather families in small clusters and provide each group with a sheet of poster paper.

Ask each family cluster to select a leader.

Direct group leaders to read aloud from p. CE29 of the *Catechist Edition*, and to write the seven gifts of the Holy Spirit on the poster paper provided. For each gift, have group members discuss ways in which that gift can be used.

Ask group leaders to share responses with the large group.

Confirmation whole-group learning experience (10 minutes)

Summarize the first three paragraphs from p. CE30 of the *Catechist Edition*.

Read aloud the prayers of the Rite on p. CE30 and have families repeat the prayers after you.

Invite family members to silently reflect on which gift of the Holy Spirit they need the most.

The Holy Spirit Is with Us individual family unit experience (5 minutes)

Have families work together to complete the activity on p. CE31 of the *Catechist Edition*.

Allow time for family members to discuss how the Holy Spirit will help them show God's love to one another.

Closing Blessing (5 minutes)

Invite each family to form a family circle.

Begin with the Sign of the Cross.

Pray the prayer on p. CE31 of the *Catechist Edition*.

Conclude by leading families in singing *Songs of Celebration* CD, track 1 "We Are Called," or another appropriate song from your parish music repertoire.

Faith at Home

Direct families' attention to the Faith at Home page and encourage them to do the activities at home.

We Are Holy

Before the Celebration		Materials

Before the Celebration

- Choose a gathering space that will be conducive to prayer and that will accommodate the size of the group; the church, a chapel, or a gathering place in the parish hall would each be appropriate. You will want the group to be able to see, hear, and move easily during the ritual.
- Prepare the group for the ritual action of the Extension of Hands in Blessing and for the reflection on the sacred Scriptures.
- Select a good reader to proclaim the reading.

- Select four people for the entrance procession: to carry the Bible, the candle, the bowl of water, and the chrism. Show them where and how to place them in the sanctuary or on the prayer table.
- If not in a church or chapel, place chairs in semicircular rows around the prayer space. Leave enough space for people to move in and out of the rows. If possible, have tables and chairs set up in another space for adult discussion after the celebration.

Materials

- A large, clear bowl with water, or if the celebration is in the church, use the baptismal font or pool
- A large candle or the Paschal candle
- A prayer table for the candle, oil of chrism, a baptismal candle, a Bible, and a stand
- *Songs of Celebration* CD
- Copies of the celebration for the assembly (*Sacraments Source Book* CD)

Gathering Rite

Welcome the gathered assembly.

Rehearse the opening song and go over the ritual action of the Extension of Hands in Blessing.

Invite the assembly to stand for the procession.

Opening Song

"We Are Marching," *Songs of Celebration* CD, track 2.

Procession

The presider and persons carrying the bowl with water, candle, and Bible process in while the assembly sings.

> *Leader:* Let us pray.
> Make the Sign of the Cross together.

Opening Prayer

> *Leader:* God our Father, send your Holy Spirit upon us to open our hearts and fill us with the flame of your love. We ask this through Christ our Lord.
> *All:* Amen.

Celebration of the Word

> *Leader:* A reading from the holy Gospel according to Luke.
> Read Luke 4:16–30.
> *Leader:* The Gospel of the Lord.
> *All:* Praise to you, Lord Jesus Christ.
> Sit silently.

Reflection

Invite the assembly to reflect on the Gospel. Use the following question:

- What does the Gospel reading say about being holy?

Ask the assembly to share their responses with one or two people. Be sure to include children in the sharing.

Extension of Hands in Blessing

Invite the Confirmation candidates forward with their families. Have them face the assembly.

Leader: *We are called by the Holy Spirit to do the things that Jesus did. We are called to bring the good news and the light of Christ to others. Let us remember that the Holy Spirit keeps the light of Christ alive in us always.*

Invite the assembly and family members to extend hands with you as you pray:

Leader: *May the Holy Spirit dwell in you and help you bring the light of Christ to others.*

Child: *Amen.*

Closing Prayer

Leader: *Loving God, we thank you for the gifts of the Holy Spirit. Send us forth to bring your love to others. We ask this through Jesus Christ our Lord.*

All: *Amen.*

Children go to their group session and adults go to the appointed space for reflection.

- There is a liturgical catechetical session for adults on p. 68.
- There is a parent/adult catechetical session on pp. 69–70.
- There is an intergenerational catechetical session on pp. 71–72.

We Are Holy

<table>
<tr><th>Goals</th></tr>
<tr><td>

- To reflect on the celebration
- To explore the meaning of holiness and its connection to anointing

</td></tr>
</table>

<table>
<tr><th>Materials</th></tr>
<tr><td>

- Poster board, chart paper, or overhead projector
- Markers
- *Songs of Celebration* CD

</td></tr>
</table>

Reflection (20 minutes)

Invite the adults to gather in groups of five or six.

Begin by recalling the ritual moments of the celebration. Lead a guided meditation using the following prompts: Pause after each prompt.
- Play a few verses of the opening song, "We Are Marching," *Songs of Celebration* CD, track 2.
- Read some verses of the Gospel.
- Ask participants to recall their discussion of the Gospel.
- Call to mind the ritual of blessing the candidates.
- Ask: "What was it like for you to extend your hands in blessing over the candidates?"

Small Group Sharing

Pause for a few minutes of silence. Then invite the participants to share their feelings about the celebration in their small group. After 10 to 15 minutes, invite sharing with the large group.

Large Group Sharing

Gather the responses of the small groups on poster board, chart paper, or an overhead projector. Ask for feelings and thoughts about the celebration as a whole, and also for specific parts of the celebration that were meaningful to members of the group.

Naming (30 minutes)

Ask the participants to name what they learned from the celebration about God, Jesus, the Church, Scripture, or their own Christian life.

Take each category separately and list responses on poster board, chart paper, or an overhead projector. When the lists are completed, use them to summarize the theology and meaning of the call to holiness in the Rite of Confirmation.

Affirm, add, or enlarge upon the following points:
- Blessings call down God's favor on those being blessed. We can bless one another.
- The Holy Spirit is given to us at Baptism to be our helper and advocate.
- In Baptism, we are called to walk as children of the light to bring the light of Christ to others.
- The anointing or sealing with the Holy Spirit is the symbol of our being set apart or holy.
- Our holiness is manifested when we proclaim the values of God's kingdom in our words and deeds, judgment, courage, knowledge, reverence, and wonder and awe.

Reflection and Small Group Sharing (20 minutes)

Ask "What will you do this week to nurture your bond with the Holy Spirit?"

Direct participants to reflect in silence for a few a minutes and then share their responses with their group.

Closing Blessing (5 minutes)

Gather and begin with the Sign of the Cross.

Instruct participants to face a partner and extend hands over them in blessing, saying:

> **Leader:** *Come Holy Spirit, form us into a holy people.*
> **All:** *Come Holy Spirit, come.*
>
> **Leader:** *Come Holy Spirit, fill us with the fire of your love.*
> **All:** *Come Holy Spirit, come.*
>
> **Leader:** *Come Holy Spirit, guide us to be witnesses of the Gospel.*
> **All:** *Come Holy Spirit, come.*

Sing the opening song from the celebration.

We Are Holy

Goals	Environment	Materials
• To welcome participants in a hospitable environment • To discuss the characteristics of holy people • To help participants come to a deeper understanding of the nature of holiness	• Be sure to clearly identify the meeting place, posting clear directions if necessary. • Tables and chairs arranged for small groups • A prayer setting with large candle, Bible on a stand or table, clear bowl filled with water, a branch or other instrument for sprinkling, and small candles for participants	• Beverages and light refreshments • Nametags • Copy of the *Rite of Confirmation* • *Songs of Celebration* CD, track 2 • Copies of **Confirmation Parent/Adult Catechesis Handouts 2:1** and **2:2** (*Sacraments Source Book* CD) • Poster board or chart paper • Large sheets of newsprint paper and markers

Welcome and Opening Prayer (15 minutes)

Welcome parents and other adults and distribute nametags.

Introduce yourself and briefly review the goals and agenda for the gathering.

✳ **If this session was preceded by a large group ritual and reflection, go to We Are Holy. If not, continue with the prayer.**

Gather the group around the prayer setting, if possible, or have the group pause for a reflective moment.

Introduce the prayer with the Sign of the Cross.

Sing "We Are Marching," *Songs of Celebration* CD, track 2.

Pray these or similar words:

God of all faithfulness, you alone are holy. You are the source of our holiness. Send the Holy Spirit to make us holy that we may be a sign of your goodness to all those we meet. May he fill our hearts with love and justice and lead us to live as your children. We ask this in the name of your Son, Jesus, who lives and reigns forever. Amen.

Read *Luke 4:16–30.*

Invite the assembly to reflect on the Gospel using the following questions:
• What does Jesus teach about holiness?

Ask participants to share their responses with one or two people.

We Are Holy (30 minutes)

Ask the large group:
• How would you respond if someone met you in a social situation and said, "You are really a holy person?"

Invite volunteers to respond.

Distribute Confirmation Parent/Adult Catechesis Handout 2:1. Light the candles and follow the order of prayer.

Read slowly and comment on the Homily or Instruction, *Rite of Confirmation*, 39.

Organize the large group into smaller groups of 5 to 6 people. Introduce the activity by saying that sometimes it is easier to understand holiness by observing it in others.

Ask participants to identify one or two people whom they know that they consider "holy" and think about what characteristics of those people make them seem holy.

Have them share their reflections in the group and create a list of the characteristics of holy people. Each group should collate its list on a large piece of newsprint paper and display it in the meeting place. Have a member of each group present the lists.

Summarize the characteristics in the large group, and compare them to the characteristics of Jesus as we know him from the Gospel.

Remind the group that through the Gifts of the Holy Spirit, we are all called to this holiness.

Ask participants to reflect silently on their own lives, and answer this question for themselves:
- On a holiness scale of 1–10 (10 being the highest), where am I?

Break for refreshments and conversation.

What Is Holiness? (30 minutes)

Invite participants back into the large group.

Distribute Confirmation Parent/Adult Catechesis Handout 2:2. Allow time for the participants to read the quotes on the handout.

Organize the large group into smaller groups of 5 to 6 people. Assign each group a quote. Have them discuss it in the group and develop a response to the question that they can share with the large group. When the groups are ready, have them share their statements with the large group.

Allow time for questions, comments, and insights.

Summarize the comments.

Conclude with the following points:
- *Holiness* means "living a life modeled after the example of Jesus."
- Following the call to holiness requires sacrifice and dying to some of our life patterns and choices.
- The Holy Spirit inspires and strengthens us to be holy.

Parent Moment (10 minutes)

Highlight the three Faith at Home features in the *Child's Book* and show how they will help the parents and family members to participate in the children's preparation.

Emphasize the importance of doing the activities on the Faith at Home page, especially the ritual action.

Closing Prayer (5 minutes)

Gather participants in a circle around the prayer space and pray these or similiar words.

Spirit of the Living God, come to make us holy. Fill our hearts with love and give us the wisdom and courage we need to show the face of God to others that they will come to know the goodness of God.

We close by reminding ourselves of our Baptism and our common kinship in God's family. In all that we do, may we reflect the holiness of the Father, the Son, and the Holy Spirit. (Sprinkle with water.) Amen.

Thank everyone for their time and participation.

 Encourage parents and family members to go to **www.harcourtreligion.com** for more ideas and suggestions.

We Are Holy

Objectives

- To guide families to experience a celebration of the word, including the Extension of Hands in Blessing
- To explore the meaning of the ritual action in family groups
- To explain that we are called to bring the light of Christ to others
- To proclaim Jesus' words about the Holy Spirit being upon him
- To describe parts of the Rite of Confirmation
- To help families understand the connection between holiness and being living witnesses

Materials

- Copies of the celebration for the assembly (*Sacraments Source Book* CD)
- *Songs of Celebration* CD
- Prayer table
- Bible
- Cross or crucifix
- Candle and matches
- Bowl filled with water
- Chart or poster paper
- Markers
- Crayons
- Pencils
- Blank sheets of white paper

Welcome and Celebration (10–15 minutes)

Welcome the families in the gathering space.

Distribute copies of the celebration.

Select a family to be in the procession. Have them choose a family member to carry the Bible in procession.

- When families are assembled, walk forward slowly. Follow the child carrying the Bible.
- During the procession, lead families in singing the suggested song, "We Are Marching," from the *Songs of Celebration* CD, track 2.
- Place the Bible on the prayer table and have family members return to their seats.
- Light the prayer candle.
- Begin prayer with the Sign of the Cross and invite the group to follow the order of the prayer.
- For the proclamation of the Gospel, you may use a Bible or the adapted reading in the *Catechist Edition* on p. CE39.

- Invite families to come forward one by one.
- Extend your hands over each family and say, "May the Holy Spirit dwell in your family and help you bring the light of Christ to others."
- Pray the closing prayer.
- Conclude with the opening song from the *Songs of Celebration* CD, track 2.

The Holy Spirit individual family unit experience (10 minutes)

Guide family members to reflect on the celebration by asking the following questions:
- What did you see? What did you hear? What did you do?

Ask volunteers to share their responses.

Guide families to reflect further on being called by name, using the activity on p. CE37 of the *Catechist Edition*.

Allow time for family members to share their responses to the activity.

The Light of Christ whole-group learning experience (10 minutes)

Invite families to reflect on ways they do God's work at home.

Ask volunteers to share responses.

Select family members to read the last paragraph aloud.

Summarize the first two paragraphs on p. CE38 of the *Catechist Edition*.

Jesus Teaches About Holiness whole-group learning experience (10 minutes)

Invite the large group to reflect on the following:
- What was Jesus telling the people about the Holy Spirit?
- What are some ways that people today can be witnesses of Christ?

Ask volunteers to share responses to the questions.

Direct the families to help children complete the Share activity on p. CE39 of the *Catechist Edition*.

Emphasize that Jesus wants us to know we belong to him, and he wants us to love one another.

Holiness whole-group learning experience (15 minutes)

Gather families in small clusters and provide each group with a sheet of paper.

Assign family clusters to agree upon one person living in the world today that they think is a living witness of Jesus. Have leaders write the person's name on the paper provided.

Invite family cluster leaders to share with the large group the name selected by their group, and to explain how the person is a living witness of Jesus in the world today.

Divide a sheet of poster paper in two columns in front of the large group, and write the word *holy* on one side and *sanctify* on the other.

Discuss the meaning of the words *holy* and *sanctified* from p. CE40 of the *Catechist Edition*.

Select a group leader to read the last paragraph aloud to the large group.

Sealed with the Spirit whole-group learning experience (10 minutes)

Summarize the first two paragraphs from p. CE41 of the *Catechist Edition*.

Discuss the meaning of the bishop's blessing at Confirmation. Select a family member to read aloud the bulleted items.

Invite family members to reflect on how they can be a sign of God's presence in the family.

Ask volunteers to share responses.

Being Holy individual family unit experience (5 minutes)

Have families work together to complete the activity on p. CE42 of the *Catechist Edition*.

Allow time for family members to discuss responses.

Closing Blessing (5 minutes)

Invite each family to form a family circle.

Begin with the Sign of the Cross.

Pray the prayer on p. CE42 of the *Catechist Edition*.

Conclude by leading families in singing *Songs of Celebration* CD, track 2, "We Are Marching."

Faith at Home

Direct families' attention to the Faith at Home page and encourage them to do the activities at home.

Gifts of the Holy Spirit

Outline	Environment	Materials
1. Gathering and Opening Prayer **2.** Activity Centers • Activity 1: Mobiles—*The Fire of the Spirit* • Activity 2: Johnny Appleseed Story—*The Fruits of the Spirit* • Activity 3: Pinwheels—*The Holy Spirit Is Like the Wind* • Activity 4: Bible Search—*Who Is the Holy Spirit?* **3.** Peer Group Time **4.** Family Time **5.** Closing Prayer	• A space large enough to accommodate – four corner activity centers – a center prayer table covered with a red cloth with a Bible on a stand – tables for families (2 or 3 families to a table) to gather and eat lunch • A separate place for children to hear and discuss story • 4 activity center facilitators • Volunteers to distribute/serve lunch	• Lunch, refreshments • Nametags (color coded for activity centers) • 4 large tables for activity centers • Votive candles for each child • Paper and pencils • Large candle on or near Prayer Table • *Songs of Celebration* CD • Bibles (suitable for age group) 1 per family • *Old Turtle* by Douglas Wood* • Apples, 1 per family • Additional materials needed are listed within each activity

Gathering and Opening Prayer (20 minutes)

Welcome the participants and explain the agenda for the gathering. Have facilitators distribute nametags and invite families to enjoy the light refreshments as they find a place to sit in the circle of chairs.

Invite the children who are confirmation candidates to assemble together for a procession. Tell each to each bring an unlit votive candle from their tables. Be sure all candidates have a candle.

Sing "We Are Marching," *Songs of Celebration* CD, track 2.

Have the candidates gather around the prayer table with the large candle. As the singing continues light each child's votive candle, and direct them to return to their table and place the lighted candles on the table.

Direct the group to sit.

Proclaim *Acts 2:1–43.*

Reflection The same Holy Spirit who came to the Apostles on Pentecost is the Spirit given to us in the Sacrament of Confirmation. Direct the families to silently think about why the Holy Spirit is so important. Ask them to share their ideas at their tables.

Close the prayer by asking the participants to stand and pray together with you.

Leader: Open our hearts to receive the gifts and fruits of the Holy Spirit.

All: Come, Holy Spirit.

Leader: Open our hands and feet to serve others.

All: Come, Holy Spirit.

Leader: Be with us today to inspire, guide, and direct us.

All: Come, Holy Spirit.

Leader: Come, Holy Spirit, fill the hearts of your faithful and kindle in us the fire of your love.

All: Come, Holy Spirit, fill our hearts with your love. Amen.

*Old Turtle, Douglas Wood. Scholastic Incorporated, New York, NY, 2001.

Activity Centers

Direct the participants to note the color code on their nametag and ask them to move to the appropriate center.

Tell the group that the lunch break will occur after the families have visited two centers. The remaining two centers can be visited after lunch.

Activity 1: Mobiles–*The Fire of the Spirit*
(30 minutes)

Materials Needed
- Long narrow strips of red fabric (6–7" long, 7 per family)
- Permanent markers
- Wire coat hangers (1 per family)
- Red yarn or string (6–7" long, 7 lengths per family)
- Stapler
- Construction paper (8.5 x 11", white or yellow, 2 per family)

Direct the families to talk about all the things that fire can do. One symbol for the Holy Spirit is fire. What does that tell us about the Holy Spirit? After a short discussion invite the parents to help children write their responses on the seven strips of red fabric provided for each family.

How to Make a Mobile
1. Staple one red fabric strip to each length of yarn.
2. Cover both sides of the wire coat hanger with construction paper.
3. Decorate the paper and write "Holy Spirit" on it with the markers.
4. Staple the yarn to the decorated coat hanger, creating a mobile of the tongues of fire to symbolize the Holy Spirit.

Rotation and Break (5 minutes)

Activity 2: Johnny Appleseed Story–*The Fruits of the Spirit* (30 minutes)

Materials Needed
- Story of Johnny Appleseed*
- **Family Confirmation Retreat Handout 1**
- Pencils

Show participants an apple and ask them to share what they know about Johnny Appleseed.

Tell the story of the man who took it upon himself to travel in the wilderness around the Great Lakes planting apple seeds. This was his gift to the human family. End by saying that we enjoy the fruit of his planting today every time we bite into a crisp apple.

Explain that the work of the Holy Spirit in us is similar to Johnny Appleseed and his apples. In the Sacrament of Confirmation, the Holy Spirit plants the seeds, which are called the gifts of the Spirit. The Holy Spirit also tends these gifts in our hearts like seeds so that our lives will bear fruit. We bear the fruit of the Spirit's presence when we live as holy people.

Introduce **Family Confirmation Retreat Handout 1** with these or similar words:

The Holy Spirit lives in you. He helps us live as God wants us to live. We cannot live like God wants us to without help. So the Holy Spirit helps us. When we use the gifts of the Holy Spirit, people can see it! They see the fruits of God's action in us. The fruits of the Holy Spirit are love, joy, peace, patience, kindness, goodness, faithfulness, gentleness, and self-control. We are confirmed in the Holy Spirit so that we might walk in His ways.

Direct the parents to work on the **Family Confirmation Retreat Handout 1** with their children.

Lunch (45 minutes)

*Johnny Appleseed, Jane Yolen. Harper Collins World, New York, NY, 2006.

Activity 3: Pinwheels–*The Holy Spirit Is Like the Wind* (30 minutes)

Materials Needed
- Squares of paper (4" x 5")
- Permanent markers
- Scissors
- Pushpins
- Small wooden dowels and pencils (1 per family)
- Two large sheets of newsprint taped to the wall
- Children's Bible

Begin by blowing on a pinwheel.

Ask: what is making the paper turn? Do you see the air I am blowing? Can you see the Holy Spirit?

Tell the story of Nicodemus (*John 3:1–8*).

Ask the participants: What does this story tell us about the Holy Spirit?

Invite participants to share all the things that are important about the wind, air, and breath. Write these down on the newsprint.

Direct each family to make a pinwheel as a reminder of the presence of the Holy Spirit.

How to Make a Pinwheel

1. Distribute paper squares. Fold the square corner to corner, and then unfold. Do this with all four corners.
2. Make a pencil line about 1/3 of the way from the center on all four folds. Cut a slit on each fold line up to the pencil line.
3. Write a word or phrase that tells how the Spirit is like the wind on each of the four sections.
4. Bring every other point into the center and stick a push pin through all four points. The head of the pin forms the hub of the pinwheel.
5. Turn your pinwheel over. Make sure the pin pokes through in the exact center. Roll the pin around in little circles to enlarge the hole a little. Then push the pin into a thin dowel, but not too far.
6. Blow and let your Spirit wheel spin.

Rotation and Break (5 minutes)

Activity 4: Bible Search–*Who Is the Holy Spirit?* (30 minutes)

Materials Needed
- Children's Bible for each family
- Cards with Bible citations (do not write the qualities on the card)
- Pencils

Passages: *Romans 8:14–16* (leads); *Romans 8:26* (prays for us); *John 14:26* (teacher); *John 16:13* (guides, shows the truth); *John 15:26* (helper); *Ephesians 1:13–14* (supporter)

Distribute the cards with various Bible passages on them. Ask the families to look up their chosen passages.

Direct them to read the passage and then discuss: What does this passage say about the qualities of the Holy Spirit? Give each family an opportunity to write their response on the back of their card. These can then be shared in the large group.

Peer Group Time (20 minutes)

Adult Session:

Begin by asking the parent(s) to share their experience of Confirmation with others at their table. Invite a few to share in the large group.

Ask: When have you felt the presence and power of the Holy Spirit in your life?

Invite each participant to share his or her response with the person next to him or her.

Make the following points:
- The Holy Spirit is real and personal, not a vague, ethereal shadow, nor an impersonal force.
- The Spirit is God, a Person equal in every way with God the Father and God the Son.
- A primary role of the Holy Spirit is to be the presence of God to the Church for all times.
- The Spirit teaches us all truth, revealing God's will and guiding us in all decisions.

- The Spirit is our Advocate: praying, pleading and presenting us to the household of God and making us a holy people.
- The Holy Spirit is the motivating force behind all our prayers, our good choices, and our loving actions.

Invite the parents to add their ideas about the Holy Spirit.

<u>Children's Session:</u>

Gather the children in a story circle.

Read or tell the story, *Old Turtle*, by Douglas Wood.

Discuss how the Spirit of God has been with us since the beginning of creation and is still with us now.

Closing Prayer (20 minutes)

Gather the families back at the tables.

Ask the families to work together to write a prayer to the Holy Spirit.

Distribute Family Confirmation Retreat Handout 2 to help guide this process.

Invite the participants to gather and process into the worship space singing "We Are Marching," *Songs of Celebration* CD, track 2, as they wave their Spirit wheels.

Read *John 14:16–18.*

Have each family pray aloud its Prayer to the Holy Spirit. The mingling voices will echo the Pentecost scene.

Pray the following prayer:
Come, Holy Spirit, fill the hearts of your faithful and kindle in us the fire of your love.

Invite all to extend a Sign of Peace to one another.

Distribute an apple to each family.

Thank the families for participating in the retreat.

Holiness and the Fruits of the Holy Spirit

Outline

1. Gathering and Opening Prayer
2. Activity Centers
   - Activity 1: Banner of Fire
   - Activity 2: Fruits of the Holy Spirit
   - Activity 3: Spirit Books
3. Closing Prayer

Environment

- 2 catechists
- At least 2 to 4 facilitators depending on the number of candidates
- Prayer table covered with a red cloth, Bible on a stand
- Tables and chairs

Materials

- Children's Bible
- Nametags (numbered for table places)
- Music sheets
- *Songs of Celebration* CD
- Healthy snacks and lunch
- Large candle
- Several unlit votive candles
- Apples (1 for each candidate)
- Additional materials needed are listed within each activity

Gathering and Opening Prayer (20 minutes)

Welcome the candidates and gather them in a circle around the prayer table.

Sing "We Are Marching," *Songs of Celebration* CD, track 2.

Ask catechists and facilitators to light the votive candles while the rest of the group is singing.

Proclaim *Acts 2:1–4.*

Have candidates sit on the floor after the reading.

Help them break open the word by asking the following questions:

- Why were the smaller candles on the altar lighted?
- Does the reading tell us anything about fire?
- What are some important things we know about fire?
- How does fire help us? Hurt us? What does the symbol of fire tell us about the Holy Spirit?

Share the meaning of Pentecost and the importance of the coming of the Holy Spirit. Point out that this same Spirit will be given to us in the Sacrament of Confirmation. Summarize the symbolism of fire by pointing out that the Holy Spirit warms our hearts to love, ignites or sparks us to be good, lights the path to truth, and melts away any anger or fear.

Activity Centers

Direct the candidates to note the number on their nametags and ask them to move to the appropriate table.

Activity 1: Banner of Fire (20 minutes)

Materials Needed

- Large, red fabric shaped like a tongue of fire ironed on to freezer paper (11" x 17", 1 per candidate)
- Permanent markers
- Yarn or string (10–12" per candidate)
- Foam shapes
- Glue
- Staplers
- Dowels (1 per candidate)

Direct the candidates to their tables where the materials (except the dowels and staplers) are located at each place. Be sure to have enough materials for each candidate.

Ask them to think about this phrase: *The Holy Spirit is like fire because….* After a time of reflection, direct them to write those words, filling in the blank with a word or phrase on the red fabric.

(The ironed-on freezer paper keeps the cloth stable and can be peeled off when they have finished.) They can decorate their Spirit banner with bits of yarn, drawn pictures, and foam shapes. As they are finishing, the catechists or facilitators should come to each table and staple the banner onto a thin wooden dowel. Direct the candidates to place their banners under their chairs to be used later.

Rotation and Break (5 minutes)

Activity 2: The Fruits of the Spirit (20 minutes)

Materials needed
- 1 apple per candidate
- Story of Johnny Appleseed*
- Copies of **Candidates' Confirmation Retreat Handout 1**
- Pencils

Gather the candidates back in the center around the prayer table.

Show them an apple and ask them to share what they know about Johnny Appleseed.

Tell the story of the man who took it upon himself to travel in the wilderness around the Great Lakes planting apple seeds. This was his gift to the human family. End by saying that we enjoy the fruit of his planting today every time we bite into a crisp apple. The work of the Holy Spirit in us is similar to Johnny Appleseed and his apples. In the Sacrament of Confirmation, the Holy Spirit plants the seeds, which are called the gifts of the Spirit. The Holy Spirit also tends these seeds in our heart so that our lives will bear fruit. We bear the fruit of the Spirit's presence when we live as holy people.

Introduce Candidates' Confirmation Retreat Handout 1 with these or similar words:

The Holy Spirit lives in you. He helps us live as God wants us to live. We cannot live like God wants us to without help. So the Holy Spirit helps us. He helps us to live our lives in love, joy, peace, patience, kindness, goodness, faithfulness, gentleness, and self-control. We call these the fruits of the Holy Spirit. We are confirmed in the Holy Spirit so that we might walk in His ways.

Lunch (30–45 minutes)

Activity 3: Spirit Books (20 minutes)

Materials needed
- Several sheets of construction paper or card stock, with three holes punched into the left side
- Art supplies
- Three-hole folders
- Copies of **Candidates' Confirmation Retreat Handout 2**
- Pencils
- Appropriate magazine pictures
- Permanent markers
- Glue

Direct the candidates back to their tables, where supplies for making their Spirit book are located.

Instruct them to create a book about the Holy Spirit by making a list of the qualities of the Holy Spirit.

Explain they can use the words, drawings, and pictures. After they have worked for a while, distribute Handout 2, which will help them create a prayer to the Holy Spirit. The catechists and facilitators should assist candidates.

Assemble the books into three-hole folders. Ask the candidates to spend the remaining time decorating their book covers and reviewing the handout.

Closing Prayer (20 minutes)

Invite the candidates to retrieve their Spirit banners and gather them into a procession. As they process, have them sing, "We Are Marching" from the *Songs of Celebration* CD, track 2 as they wave their banners.

Gather candidates in a circle around the altar.

Read *John 14:16–18*.

Invite all the candidates to read aloud their composed Prayer to the Holy Spirit. The mingling voices will echo the Pentecost scene.

Close by inviting all to extend a Sign of Peace to one another.

Distribute an apple to each candidate.

Johnny Appleseed, Jane Yolen. Harper Collins World, New York, NY, 2006.

Restored Order
Songs of Celebration CD

Eucharist, Chapter 1—Track 7
Yes Lord, I Believe!
© 2000 John Burland

RO1—Track 1
We Are Called
David Haas. © GIA Publications

RO2—Track 2
We Are Marching
South African Traditional

Eucharist, Chapter 2—Track 8
Glory to God
Marty Haugen. © GIA Publications

Eucharist, Chapter 3—Track 9
Create in Me
© Tom Kendzia. Published by OCP

Eucharist, Chapter 4—Track 10
Open My Eyes
© Jesse Manibusan. Published by OCP

Eucharist, Chapter 5—Track 11
We Praise You
© Damean. Published by OCP

Eucharist, Chapter 6—Track 12
Te alabaré, Señor/I Will Praise You, Lord
Tony Alonso. © GIA Publications

Eucharist, Chapter 7—Track 13
We Come to the Table
© 2004 John Burland

Eucharist Chapter 8—Track 14
Lead Us to the Water
© Tom Kendzia. Published by OCP

Restored Order
Optional Music Suggestions

Restored Order 1
"Envia tu espíritu," © Bob Hurd. Published by OCP

"Send Down the Fire," Marty Haugen. © GIA Publications

Restored Order 2
"You Have Anointed Me," Mike Balhoff, Gary Daigle, Darryl Ducote. © Damean Music/GIA Publications

"Turn My Heart, O God," Marty Haugen. © GIA Publications

Mystagogy for Confirmation/ Eucharist (Restored Order)

Mystagogical Catechesis

Mystagogical catechesis is the name given to the process of gradually uncovering the meaning of the mysteries of sacraments that have already been celebrated. This type of catechesis was first done by the early Church Fathers in sermons preached to the neophytes after their initiation at the Easter Vigil. We still possess some of those sermons. They are instructions rich in images and symbols that help the newly initiated come to a fuller understanding of the sacraments they have celebrated and are now living out. Mystagogical catechesis is based on the principle that as we live out the commitments of sacraments, we experience a fuller, deeper, more personal and communal meaning of them.

The Rite of Christian Initiation

The Rite of Christian Initiation, which was promulgated after the Second Vatican Council, restored the catechumenate and the full initiation process. It designates the Easter Season as the Period of Mystagogy and sets it aside as a period for both the neophytes and the assembly to grow together "in deepening their grasp of the paschal mystery and in making it part of their lives through meditation on the Gospel, sharing in the eucharist, and doing the works of charity." (*RCIA*, 244)

Here are some practical suggestions to involve children and their families in mystagogical catechesis:

- Shortly after the celebration of Confirmation and First Communion, gather children and/or family members to reflect on their experience of the celebration. Use the process outlined in the *Catechist Edition* for reflecting on each celebration.

- Arrange with the parish liturgy director to involve those who have been confirmed this year in the parish Pentecost celebration.
- Periodically hold gatherings of those who have recently celebrated Confirmation and First Communion to reflect on the Scripture readings that are in the child's lessons. Focus the gatherings on how the children are experiencing themselves as being fully initiated into the Body of Christ.
- Over a period of 18 months, select three short-term (2–3 hours) service projects and invite the children and their family members to participate in them. Situate the service project in an initial "Sending Forth" ritual and a reflection process at the end of the project.
- Plan a family gathering during the Easter season with the families of children who have celebrated Confirmation and First Communion and the families of neophytes to share their experiences of coming to the table and entering more fully into the life of the parish.
- Encourage members of the assembly to seek out and welcome the children who have celebrated Confirmation and First Communion.
- Encourage catechists in all levels of your catechetical program to create prayer spaces that include the primary symbols of water, oil, cross, Bible or lectionary, bread and wine. Encourage them to help children reflect on the symbols often.

CALL to CELEBRATE

Sacraments Source Book

Eucharist

Eucharist
Scope and Sequence

Scope and Sequence

	Chapter 1 WE BELONG	Chapter 2 WE GATHER	Chapter 3 WE ARE FORGIVEN
Ritual Focus	Renewal of Baptismal Promises	Procession and Gloria	Penitential Rite
Scripture	The Vine and the Branches John 15:1–17	The Early Christians Acts 2:42–47	The Call of Matthew Matthew 9:9–13
Faith Focus	• A sacrament is a holy sign that comes from Jesus and gives us grace. • Baptism, Confirmation, and Eucharist are Sacraments of Initiation. • The Sacraments of Initiation make us full members of the Church.	• The Church is the People of God and Body of Christ. • The Eucharist, or Mass, is the Church's most important action of praise and thanks. • The Introductory Rites gather us as a community of faith.	• The Eucharist is a sacrament of unity and forgiveness. • Sin keeps us from being one People of God. • At Mass we ask God's forgiveness during the Penitential Rite.
Catechism of the Catholic Church	1212, 1275–1277, 1285, 1316–1317, 1321–1327	1153, 1156–1158	1393–1395
Liturgical Focus	Sacraments of Initiation	Introductory Rites, Gloria	Penitential Rite
Signs of Faith	water Paschal candle Holy Trinity	assembly procession prayer and singing	Lord Have Mercy silence sprinkling with holy water

	Chapter 4 WE LISTEN	Chapter 5 WE PREPARE	Chapter 6 WE REMEMBER & GIVE THANKS	Chapter 7 WE SHARE A MEAL	Chapter 8 WE GO FORTH
Ritual Focus	Signing	Honoring the Cross	Memorial Acclamation	Sharing a Meal	Blessing for Mission
Scripture	The Sower Matthew 13:1–23	The Washing of the Feet John 13:1–16	The Last Supper Matthew 26:26–28; Luke 22:14–20	I Am the Bread of Life John 6:30–58	Pentecost Acts 2:1–41
Faith Focus	• The Bible is God's word written in human words. • We listen to the word of God during the Liturgy of the Word. • When we listen to God's word, we want to share it with others.	• Jesus sacrificed his life for us when he died on the cross. • The Mass is a sacrifice. • At Mass through the power of the Holy Spirit and the words and actions of the priest, Jesus offers again the gift of himself to his Father.	• The Eucharistic Prayer is a prayer of thanksgiving, remembering, and consecration. • Through the power of the Holy Spirit and the words and actions of the priest, the bread and wine become the Body and Blood of Jesus. • At the Great Amen, the assembly says "yes" to all of God's saving actions and promises.	• The Mass is a meal of thanksgiving. • Jesus is the Bread of Life. • In Holy Communion, we are united to Jesus and the Church. We share in the promise of life forever with God.	• The Eucharist changes us. • The Holy Spirit helps us to live out our mission. • At Mass we are sent forth to love and serve others.
Catechism of the Catholic Church	101–104, 136, 141, 1154, 1190, 1349, 1408	1333–1336	1362–1366	1382–1398	1391–1397
Liturgical Focus	Liturgy of the Word	Preparation of the Altar and Gifts	Eucharistic Prayer, Consecration, Memorial Acclamation, Great Amen	Communion Rite	Dismissal
Signs of Faith	Sign of the Cross Bible readings	cross altar bread and wine	kneeling priest Blessed Sacrament	Sign of Peace paten, ciborium, and chalice Lamb of God	blessing witness deacon

Eucharist
Sunday Connection: Eucharist
Bulletin Inserts, General Intercessions, and Parish Blessings

Use these as a way to involve the parish assembly in the sacramental preparation.

Session 1   We Belong

Bulletin Insert   During the week, our young people who are preparing to receive Holy Communion will be reflecting about Baptism, Confirmation, and the Eucharist. Join them by taking time to think about the effect that belonging to the Church has on your daily life.

Intercession   For young people preparing for Holy Communion, that they may be encouraged by the living faith of this assembly.

Parish Blessing   God, our loving Father, these young people come before you as your children. They belong to you. Send the Holy Spirit upon them as they begin this time of preparation so that they may come to know your presence in all they do. We ask this blessing through Christ our Lord.

Session 2   We Gather

Bulletin Insert   During the week, our young people who are preparing to receive Holy Communion will be reflecting about how we, as the People of God and the Body of Christ, gather on Sundays to give praise and thanks. Join them by reflecting on the words of the *Gloria* and the reasons you have to praise and thank God.

Intercession   For young people preparing for Holy Communion, that they may be aware of God's glory and blessings.

Parish Blessing   God, our loving Father, these young people gather with us, your people, to give you glory. Send the Holy Spirit upon them to help them recognize you in all the ways you show yourself to them and to help them continually give you thanks and praise. We ask this blessing through Christ our Lord.

Session 3   We Are Forgiven

Bulletin Insert   During the week, our young people who are preparing to receive Holy Communion will be reflecting about the Eucharist as a sacrament of unity and forgiveness. Join them by reflecting on the words of the *Confiteor* and how you have experienced God's mercy and forgiveness.

Intercession   For young people preparing for Holy Communion, that they may experience God's mercy and forgiveness.

Parish Blessing   God, our loving Father, these young people come before you seeking the goodness of your mercy and forgiveness. Send the Holy Spirit upon them to help them know you as always kind and merciful. We ask this blessing through Christ our Lord.

Session 4   We Listen

Bulletin Insert   During the week, our young people who are preparing to receive Holy Communion will be reflecting about listening to God's word and reverencing the Scriptures. Join them by reflecting on this week's Sunday readings and asking the question: "What are these readings calling me to do?"

Intercession   For young people preparing for Holy Communion, that they may be open to the presence of God as they listen to the Scriptures.

Parish Blessing   God, our loving Father, these young people come before you to listen and be fed by your word. Send the Holy Spirit upon them so that they may hear your word and be empowered to live by it. We ask this blessing through Christ our Lord.

Session 5 We Prepare

Bulletin Insert   During the week, our young people who are preparing to receive Holy Communion will be reflecting about the gift of Jesus' sacrifice on the Cross and the Mass as a sacrifice. Join them by reflecting on what gifts of sacrifice and service you bring to the altar each Sunday.

Intercession   For young people preparing for Holy Communion, that they may come to know the Cross as a symbol of love, life, and giving.

Parish Blessing   God, our loving Father, these young people come before you knowing the great love you showed by sending your Son who gave his life so that we might live as your children. Send the Holy Spirit upon them to show them how they can give their lives in love and service to others. We ask this blessing through Christ our Lord..

Session 6 We Remember and Give Thanks

Bulletin Insert   During the week, our young people who are preparing to receive Holy Communion will be reflecting about the Eucharistic Prayer being one of remembering and giving thanks. Join them by reflecting on what it means for you to say "Amen" or "yes" to all God's actions and promises.

Intercession   For young people preparing for Holy Communion, that they will continue to re-member God's constant love and give thanks for the greatest gift, Jesus, the Son of God.

Parish Blessing   God, our loving Father, these young people come before you knowing that Jesus is always with us. Send the Holy Spirit upon them so they will come to know Jesus more fully and share his love with others. We ask this blessing through Christ our Lord.

Session 7 We Share a Meal

Bulletin Insert   During the week, our young people who are preparing to receive Holy Communion will be reflecting about the Eucharist as a meal where we are nourished by the Body and Blood of Jesus. Join them by reflecting on your experience of the presence of Jesus in the Eucharist.

Intercession   For young people preparing for Holy Communion, that as they come to the table to be nourished by the presence of Jesus, they will also find him in us as a community.

Parish Blessing   God, our loving Father, these young people come before you ready to come to the table and share the meal of Jesus, the Bread of Life. Send the Holy Spirit upon them that they may be transformed as they partake in the Lord's Supper. We ask this blessing through Christ our Lord.

Session 8 We Go Forth

Bulletin Insert   During the week, our young people who are preparing to receive Holy Communion will be reflecting about how the Eucharist changes us and the Holy Spirit helps us live out our mission. Join them by reflecting on your experience of living out the mission of your Baptism.

Intercession   For young people preparing for Holy Communion, that they may be strengthened to go forth and live as disciples.

Parish Blessing   God, our loving Father, these young people come before you ready to do your will. Send the Holy Spirit upon them that they may be a sign and witness to all they meet of your presence in the world. We ask this blessing through Christ our Lord.

Eucharist
Catechist Orientation

Goals	Materials

Goals

- To welcome catechists in a hospitable environment
- To affirm the important role of the catechist
- To reflect on the catechists' experience of First Communion
- To inform the catechists about *Call to Celebrate: Eucharist*
  - the philosophy of the program
  - the content
  - the resources available

Materials

- Beverages and light refreshments
- Nametags
- Copies of *Call to Celebrate: Eucharist* Child's Book
- Copies of *Call to Celebrate: Eucharist* Catechist Edition
- *Songs of Celebration* CD
- A prayer table covered in a white cloth with a candle and a Bible on a stand, a clear glass bowl with water, and a branch or other instrument for sprinkling
- Matches or lighter

Welcome and Opening Prayer (30 minutes)

Welcome the catechists and distribute nametags.

Begin the session with welcoming words and introduce yourself.

Have the catechists introduce themselves to one another.

Review the goals and agenda for the gathering.

Gather the group around the prayer setting.

Begin the prayer by singing or listening to "Open My Eyes," *Songs of Celebration*, track 10.

Light the candle and lead the catechists in the following reflection. Pause after each question.
- Recall your own First Communion day.
- Where was it? Who was there?
- Can you recall any significant things that happened that day?
- Do you remember any feelings you may have had during the ceremony?
- How were you prepared for the event?
- Was there anything that stood out for you as memorable about your preparation or celebration?

Invite catechists to share any significant memories they may have of their own First Communion.

Read *Luke 2:14–20.*

Allow silent reflection.

Pose and then discuss the question:
- How do you want the children you will be catechizing to hear the message of this Gospel?

Close with a blessing, Ask the catechists to stand, and extend your hands over them as you say:
> *Lord God, in your loving kindness strengthen and direct these catechists. Let your Spirit uphold them as they prepare to share their time and talent with your children. We ask this through Christ our Lord. Amen.*

Program Overview (15 minutes)

Components

Distribute copies of the *Catechist Guide, Child's Book, Songs of Celebration* CD, and *Family Guide* for **Call to Celebrate: Eucharist**.

Explain what each is for and have catechists page through them.

Scope and Sequence

Invite catechists to turn to the Table of Contents on p. iii of the *Catechist Edition*. Go through it quickly, pointing out the articles in the front pages and the Catholic Source Book and Program Resources in the back pages.

Note the number of chapters (8) in the *Child's Book*.

Turn to the Scope and Sequence section on pp. vi–vii. Explain that scope and sequence gives the overview of the content for each chapter. Note each of the features in the left column, and go through one chapter column to familiarize catechists with the format. Go through the Ritual Focus row and point out that the flow of the chapters is based on the Order of the Mass. Review the Order, if necessary.

Tell catechists that each chapter is structured with a three-step process: Celebrate, Remember, and Live, and point out the family-oriented Faith at Home page.

Lesson Overview (30 minutes)

Child's Book

Use Chapter 4 of the *Child's Book* and show the process of a session:

Celebrate
- celebration and reflection

Remember
- proclamation and breaking open the Scripture reading
- teaching the doctrine
- learning about the ritual action of the sacrament

Live
- making connections to their lives and their families

Point out the Faith at Home boxes in the Remember section and the Signs of Faith feature in the Celebrate and Remember pages.

Catechist Edition

Use Chapter 4 of the *Catechist Edition* as a guide.

Familiarize catechists with the background and resources in the left-hand column on p. 32A.

Encourage them to read and reflect on the essay in the main column as they are planning their lessons.

Note the reflection questions and Catechist Prayer.

Review the planner on p. 32B. Note the materials needed for each lesson, and have catechists turn to the pages noted to find the Activity Master CE9 and Echo Pantomime CE10. Go through the Echo Pantomime with catechists, and show the variety of Scripture Resources.

Alert the catechists that the side wrap on pp. 32–41 gives a step-by-step lesson plan for the *Child's Book* pages, and the bottom boxes gives them additional background, activities, and tips. Instruct them to page through the lesson and ask any questions.

Turn to the Catholic Source Book, pp. 82–105. Have catechists page through it and notice the additional activities provided in the wrap.

Break for refreshments and conversation.

Administrative Details (10 minutes)

Elicit any questions the catechists have about the components and resources.

Allow time for administrative details, such as calendars and class lists.

Remind them of the next session, which will be catechist training on liturgical catechesis. This which is the method they will be using throughout the program.

Ask them to read pp. iv–xv before the training session.

Closing Prayer (10 minutes)

Gather the catechists in a circle around the prayer space.

Sing "Open My Eyes," *Songs of Celebration* CD, track 10

Make the Sign of the Cross and say:
Let us call to mind the goodness of God who gives us all good things. I bless you with this water to remind you of the gift of your Baptism and your call to hand on the faith. (Sprinkle the group with water.) Let us join in the prayer that Jesus has taught us.

Pray the Lord's Prayer together.

Thank catechists for their attendance.

Eucharist
Catechist Training

Goals

- To introduce the method of liturgical catechesis
- To present the underlying meaning of the Sacrament of Eucharist.
- To show how to design a prayer space and lead prayer
- To explain sacraments as actions of a faith community

Advance Preparation

Familiarize yourself with the ritual action in the opening prayer.

Select three persons to carry the holy water, candle, and Bible in procession.

Rehearse the suggested song, "Yes Lord, I Believe," *Songs of Celebration* CD, track 7.

Materials

- Table covered with a white cloth
- A Bible on a stand
- A large candle
- Candles for each participant
- Matches or a lighter
- A large, clear glass bowl with water
- Plants and flowers, if appropriate
- *Songs of Celebration* CD
- Poster board or chart paper
- *Eucharist Stories of Celebration* video
- Copies of the following articles from the *Sacraments Source Book* CD:
  - "What Is Liturgical Catechesis?"
  - "How to Lead Prayer"
  - "Role of the Prayer Leader"
  - "What Is a Sacrament?"
  - "Eucharist"
  - "History of Eucharist"

Opening Prayer Service and Reflection (20 minutes)

Sing together, "Yes Lord, I Believe," *Songs of Celebration* CD, track 7.
As you sing, walk forward slowly. Follow the persons carrying the holy water, candle, and Bible.

Lead the opening prayer.

Leader: *Let us begin. God, our loving Father, we are gathered here in your presence. We belong to you. Send us your Holy Spirit to help us live as disciples of your Son, Jesus. We ask this through Jesus Christ our Lord.*

All: *Amen.*

Leader: *On the day of our Baptism, we were claimed for Christ. By water and the Holy Spirit we received the gifts of faith and new life. On that day the faithful remembered their baptismal promises. Today let us once again remember those promises together. Please come forward and gather around the holy water and candle.*

Do you say "no" to sin, so that you can live always as God's children?

All: *We do.*

Leader: *Do you believe in God, the Father almighty?*

All: *We do.*

Leader: *Do you believe in Jesus Christ, his only Son, our Lord?*

All: *We do.*

Leader: *Do you believe in the Holy Spirit?*

All: *We do.*

Leader: *This is our faith. This is the faith of the Church. We are proud to profess it in Christ Jesus.*

All: *Amen.*

Leader: *Let us come to the water and thank God for the gift of our Baptism. Please come to the water and make the Sign of the Cross with the water.*

When everyone has made the Sign of the Cross, light small candles from the large candle and distribute them to each catechist, saying:

[Name], You are the light of Christ.

Have catechists return to their seats and continue:

Leader: *Loving God, we belong to you. We are your children. In Baptism we were united to your Son, Jesus. Open our hearts to the Holy Spirit as we remember our Baptism. We ask this through Jesus Christ our Lord;*

All: *Amen.*

Leader: *The Lord be with you.*

All: *And also with you.*

> *A reading from the holy Gospel of John.*
>
> *Read John 15:1–12.*

Leader: *The Gospel of the Lord.*

All: *Praise to you, Lord Jesus Christ.*

Leader: *Consider these questions for reflection and discussion: What image or phrase is important for you in this reading? What do Jesus' words "Remain in me as I remain in you" mean for you today?*

> *When the discussion is finished, continue the prayer.*

Leader: *Let us stand and pray as Jesus taught us.*

> *Pray the Lord's Prayer together.*

Leader: *Let us offer each other the Sign of Peace.*

Reflection on Prayer (20 minutes)

If there are a large number of catechists, organize them into smaller groups of 5 to 6 participants.

Invite the catechists to recall the ritual moments of the celebration. Do a guided meditation using the prompts from the celebration. Pause after each prompt.

Pause for a few minutes of silence. Then invite the groups to share their feelings about the celebration in their small group. Encourage them to stay with their feelings. After 5 to 7 minutes, invite sharing with the large group.

Naming (20 minutes)

Ask the participants to name what they learned about God, Jesus, the Church, or their own Christian life from the celebration.

Take each category separately and list their responses on the board or on chart paper. Use phrases from their lists to summarize what they have said about faith, sacrifice, and service. Comment on how much "content" they came up with.

Distribute the article, "What Is Liturgical Catechesis?" Summarize the main parts of the article, and explain that this is the model of catechesis upon which **Call to Celebrate** is based. Encourage catechists to read the article at a later time.

Rotation and Break (5 minutes)

Setting up a Prayer Space and Leading Prayer (30 minutes)

Gather catechists around the prayer space and pass out "How to Lead Prayer." Describe how you set up the space. Give catechists ideas on setting up a prayer space in their meeting place. Note where and how they can obtain materials for the space, and emphasize the importance of a prayer environment.

Distribute the article, "Role of the Prayer Leader," and summarize it with the catechists. Practice leading the procession and prayer gestures with them.

Rotation and Break (5 minutes)

A Theology of Sacrament and Eucharist (30 minutes)

Play Part 3 of the *Eucharist Stories of Celebration* video. After catechists have viewed the video, use the questions in the guide for discussion.

Summarize these important points:

- Sacraments are *actions* of God and a faith community.
- In the Eucharist, we *share in a meal* during which we are fed with the Body and Blood of Jesus.
- The Eucharist is the community's great prayer of thanksgiving.

Distribute the articles, "What is a Sacrament?," "Eucharist," and "History of Eucharist." Encourage catechists to read the articles later.

Closing Blessing (5 minutes)

Thank the catechists for attending the session.

Extend your hands over the catechists and pray in these or similar words:

> *God, the Father of mercies, has sent his Son into the world. Through the power of the Holy Spirit, may you continue to be transformed into the Body of Christ and witness his love in the world. Amen.*

Eucharist
Parent Orientation

Goals	Environment	Materials

• To welcome parents and families in a hospitable environment
• To affirm the importance of parental and family participation in the process
• To introduce parents and families to the **Call to Celebrate: Eucharist** program
• To inform parents and families about the parish policies and procedures relating to the celebration of First Communion
	• Be sure to clearly identify the meeting place, posting clear directions if necessary.
	• Tables and chairs arranged for small groups
	• A prayer setting with large candle, Bible on a stand or table, clear bowl filled with water, and a branch or other instrument for sprinkling
		• Beverages and light refreshments
		• Nametags
		• Copies of **Call to Celebrate: Eucharist** Family Guide and Child's Book
		• Songs of Celebration CD
		• Eucharist Stories of Celebration video and guide
		• Copies of the following from the Sacraments Source Book CD:
		  • **Eucharist Parent Orientation Handouts 1** and **2**
		  • "Celebrating Rituals at Home–Letter"
		  • **At Home Ritual Preparation Handouts 1–8**

Welcome and Opening Prayer

Welcome parents and other adults and distribute nametags.

Introduce yourself and briefly review the goals and agenda for the gathering.

Gather the group around the prayer setting or have them pause for a reflective moment.

Begin the prayer by singing or listening to "Yes Lord, I Believe!" from the Songs of Celebration CD, track 7.

Light the candle and lead parents in the following reflection. Pause after each question:
- *Recall your own First Communion day.*
- *Where was it? Who was there?*
- *Can you recall any significant things that happened that day?*
- *Do you remember any feelings you may have had during the ceremony?*
- *How were you prepared for the event?*
- *Was there any thing that stood out for you as memorable about your preparation or celebration?*

Invite parents and family members to share with one or two other persons any significant memories they may have of their own First Communion.

Call the group back together. Ask the parents and family members to stand. Lead the parents and family members in the Parent's Prayer (from **Eucharist Parent Orientation Handout 1**).

View Video

Show Parts 1 and 2 of the Eucharist Stories of Celebration video.

Use the questions in the video guide for discussion.

Break for refreshments and conversation.

The Call to Celebrate: Eucharist Program

Distribute the Child's Book and walk the parents through the Table of Contents.

Point out that the program:
- introduces the child to an understanding of the Eucharist (Mass).
- is a preparation for a lifetime of celebrating God's gifts, especially the gift of his Son, Jesus.
- introduces children to the Sacrament of Eucharist through its rituals and prayers.

Use one chapter of the Child's Book to show parents and family members the process of a session:

Celebrate
- celebration and reflection

Remember
- proclamation and breaking open the Scripture reading
- understanding the doctrine
- learning about the ritual action of the sacrament

Live
- making connections to their lives and their families

Highlight the three Faith at Home features in the *Child's Book*.

Emphasize the importance of doing the activities on the Faith at Home page, especially the ritual action.

Describe the *Call to Celebrate: Eucharist* Family Guide using one of the two implementation models below.

✳ **For programs where the catechesis is done in a group with a catechist and includes family support**

Distribute the *Call to Celebrate: Eucharist* Family Guide. Point out the difference in the two parts of the guide:
- the first part is for parents and family members to use for their own reflections on community of faith, listening to the word, and the Bread of Life.
- the second part is for those who will be doing the child's preparation at home.

Mention the availability of the *Songs of Celebration* CD, which will enhance their time with the child and support the children's learning.

Emphasize that this time of assisting the child and using the *Family Guide* is an opportunity for parents and family members to grow in their own relationship with God and understanding the meaning of the Eucharist.

Distribute Eucharist Parent Orientation Handout 2 and go through the frequently asked questions with parents. Answer any other questions parents or family members may have.

Go to Parish Policies and Procedures.

✳ **For programs where the catechesis is done in the home**

Distribute the *Call to Celebrate: Eucharist* Family Guide. Point out the difference in the two parts of the guide:
- the first part is for parents and family members to use for their own reflections on community of faith, listening to the word, and the Bread of Life.

- the second part is to help these parents and family members to conduct the sessions at home.

Go through one session of the *Family Guide* and show parents and family members how to use the outline. Point out:
- the parent background essay, an important piece to understanding what the session is about.
- the easy to follow overview.
- the People of Faith story for each session and the significance of telling these stories to children so they can hear and visualize how others lived out their baptismal call.

Emphasize how essential the ritual prayer is to the session. Go through the prayer as it is written in the session, and talk about ways to prepare a prayer space and environment at home.

Distribute Eucharist Parent Orientation Handout 2, "Celebrating Rituals at Home–Letter," and **At Home Ritual Preparation Handouts 1–8**.

Parish Policies and Procedures

Explain the commitment the parish expects of parents and family members for this preparation.

Distribute appropriate schedules or calendars.

Closing Prayer

Gather the parents and family members in a circular grouping around the prayer space and pray together.

Begin with the Sign of the Cross.

Let us call to mind the goodness of God who gives us all good things. I bless you with this water to remind you of your baptism and your call to hand on the faith. (Sprinkle the group with water.)

Sing "Yes Lord, I Believe!" from the *Songs of Celebration* CD, track 7.

Let us join in the prayer that Jesus has taught us.

Pray the Lord's Prayer together.

 Encourage parents and family members to go to **www.harcourtreligion.com** for more ideas and suggestions.

Eucharist Session 1—Whole Community Ritual

We Belong

Before the Celebration		Materials

- Choose a gathering space that will be conducive to prayer and that will accommodate the size of the group; the church, a chapel, or a gathering place in the parish hall would each be appropriate. You will want the group to be able to see, hear, and move easily during the ritual.
- Prepare the group for the ritual action of the Renewal of Baptismal Promises and for the reflection on the sacred Scriptures.
- Select a good reader to proclaim the reading.

- Select four people for the entrance procession: to carry the Bible, the candle, the bowl of water, and the chrism. Show them where and how to place them in the sanctuary or on the prayer table.
- If not in a church or chapel, place chairs in semicircular rows around the prayer space. Leave enough space for people to move in and out of the rows. If possible, have tables and chairs set up in another space for adult discussion after the celebration.

- A large, clear bowl with water, or if the celebration is in the church, use the baptismal font or pool
- A large candle or the Paschal candle
- A prayer table for the candle, oil of chrism, a baptismal candle, a Bible, and a stand
- *Songs of Celebration* CD
- Copies of the celebration for the assembly (*Sacraments Source Book* CD)

Gathering Rite

Welcome the gathered assembly.

Rehearse the opening song, and go over the ritual action of the Renewal of the Baptismal Promises.

Invite the assembly to stand for the procession.

Opening Song

"Yes Lord, I Believe!," *Songs of Celebration* CD, track 7.

Procession

The presider and persons carrying the bowl with holy water, candle, and Bible process in while the assembly sings.

> **Leader:** *Let us begin with the Sign of the Cross.*
> **All:** *In the name of the Father, and of the Son, and of the Holy Spirit. Amen.*

> **Leader:** *May the peace of the Lord be with you.*
> **All:** *And also with you.*

Opening Prayer

> **Leader:** *Heavenly Father, at Baptism, we were joined to your Son, Jesus Christ, and welcomed into the family of the Church. Hear our prayer as we remember our Baptism. We ask this through your Son, Jesus, who lives and reigns forever.*
> **All:** *Amen.*

Celebration of the Word

> **Reader:** *A reading from the holy Gospel according to John.*
> **All:** *Glory to you, Lord.*
> *Read John 15:1–7.*
> **Reader:** *The Gospel of the Lord.*
> **All:** *Praise to you, Lord Jesus Christ.*
> *Sit silently.*

Reflection

Invite the assembly to reflect on the Gospel. Use the following question:
- What does the image of the vine and branches suggest to you about your relationship with Jesus?

Ask the assembly to share their responses with one or two people. Be sure to include children in the sharing.

Renewal of Baptismal Promises

Leader: *Let us stand and renew our baptismal promises.*
Do you reject sin, so as to live in the freedom of God's children?

All: *I do.*

Leader: *Do you reject the glamour of evil and refuse to be mastered by sin?*

All: *I do.*

Leader: *Do you reject Satan, father of sin and prince of darkness?*

All: *I do.*

Leader: *Do you believe in God, the Father almighty, creator of heaven and earth?*

All: *I do.*

Leader: *Do you believe in Jesus Christ, God's only Son, our Lord?*

All: *I do.*

Leader: *Do you believe in the Holy Spirit, the holy catholic Church, the communion of saints, the resurrection of the body, and life everlasting?*

All: *I do.*

Based on *Rite of Christian Initiation of Adults*, 581

The Lord's Prayer

Leader: *Let us pray in the words that Jesus has given us.*
Say the Lord's Prayer together.

Closing Prayer

Leader: *May the Lord bless us, protect us from all evil, and bring us to everlasting life.*

All: *Amen.*

Leader: *Our celebration has ended. Let us go forth to love and serve the Lord.*

All: *Thanks be to God.*

Sing the opening song together.

Children go to their group session and adults go to the appointed space for reflection.
- There is a liturgical catechetical session for adults on p. 92.
- There is a parent/adult catechetical session on pp. 93–94.
- There is an intergenerational catechetical session on pp. 95–96.

We Belong

Goals	Materials
• To reflect on the celebration • To review and discuss the effects of Baptism	• Poster board, chart paper, or overhead projector • Markers • *Songs of Celebration* CD • Bible

Reflection (20 minutes)

Invite the adults to gather in groups of five or six.

Begin by recalling the ritual moments of the celebration. Lead a guided meditation using the following prompts. Pause after each prompt.

- Play a few verses of the opening song, "Yes Lord, I Believe," *Songs of Celebration* CD, track 7.
- Ask: "What was it like to renew your baptismal promises?"
- Call to mind the procession to the water and the signing of one another.
- Read a few verses of the Gospel.
- Ask participants to recall their discussion of the Gospel.
- Recall the Lord's Prayer and Dismissal.

Small Group Sharing

Pause for a few minutes of silence. Then invite the participants to share their feelings about the celebration in their small group. Encourage them to stay with their feelings. After 10 to 15 minutes, invite sharing with the large group.

Large Group Sharing

Gather the responses of the small groups on poster board, chart paper, or an overhead projector. Ask for feelings and thoughts about the celebration as a whole, and also for specific parts of the celebration that were meaningful to members of the group.

Naming (30 minutes)

Ask the participants to name what they learned from the celebration about God, Jesus, the Church, Baptism, or their own Christian life.

Take each category separately and list responses on poster board, chart paper, or an overhead projector. When the lists are completed, use them to summarize the theology and meaning of the Renewal of Baptismal Promises.

Affirm, add, or enlarge upon the following points:

- Baptism is a sacrament of belonging.
- Baptism is a sacrament of faith and needs a community of believers.
- Baptism makes us members of the Church.
- In Baptism, all sin is forgiven.
- In Baptism, we are made a "new creature."
- In Baptism, we become adopted children of God and temples of the Holy Spirit.

Reflection and Small Group Sharing (20 minutes)

Ask "What will you do this week to nurture your bond with the Holy Spirit?"

Direct participants to reflect in silence for a few minutes, and then share their responses with their group.

Closing Blessing (5 minutes)

Gather and begin with the Sign of the Cross.

> **Leader:** *God, our Father, we praise and thank you for choosing us to be your children.*
> **All:** *Amen.*
> **Leader:** *Jesus our Savior, we praise and thank you for showing us how to live and love.*
> **All:** *Amen.*
> **Leader:** *Holy Spirit, giver of Godís gifts, we praise and thank you for guiding us on our way.*
> **All:** *Amen.*

We Belong

Goals	Environment	Materials
• To welcome participants in a hospitable environment • To discuss how one "belongs" to the Church • To help participants come to a deeper understanding of the Sacraments of Initiation	• Be sure to clearly identify the meeting place, posting clear directions if necessary. • Tables and chairs arranged for small groups • A prayer setting with large candle, Bible on a stand or table, clear bowl filled with water, and a branch or other instrument for sprinkling	• Beverages and light refreshments • Nametags • Copies of *Call to Celebrate: Eucharist* Family Guide • *Songs of Celebration* CD • Copies of **Eucharist Parent/Adult Catechesis Handouts 1:1** and **1:2** (*Sacraments Source Book* CD) • Board or chart paper

Welcome and Opening Prayer (15 minutes)

Welcome parents and other adults and distribute nametags.

Introduce yourself and briefly review the goals and agenda for the gathering.

✳ **If this session was preceded by a large group ritual and reflection, go to We Belong. If not, continue with the prayer.**

Gather the group around the prayer setting, if possible; if not, have the group pause for a reflective moment.

Introduce the prayer with the Sign of the Cross.

Sing "Yes Lord, I Believe!" *Songs of Celebration* CD, track 7.

Pray these or similar words:
God, you are the source of life. You have made all things. We live with the breath of your life in us. We give you praise and thanks for these gifts. We belong to you. We are your children and we are never alone because you are present to us in so many ways, especially in the Church. Open our hearts that we may bring your life to those around us. We ask this in the name of your Son, Jesus. Amen.

Read *John 15:1–17*.

Invite the assembly to reflect on the Gospel using the following question:
• What does the image of the vine and branches suggest to you about your relationship with Jesus?

Ask the participants to share their responses with one or two people.

Invite participants to come forward to sign themselves with the holy water as a sign of their belonging to God and the Church.

We Belong (30 minutes)

Write the word *belonging* on the board or on chart paper. Ask the group to give you any word or image that belonging brings up for them. Jot down the responses and point out that real belonging involves investment in relationships and causes.

Distribute Eucharist Parent/Adult Catechesis Handout 1:1 and ask participants to complete it. Explain that it will help them see from their own experiences how persons come to belong.

Organize the large group into smaller groups of 5 to 6 people. Ask participants to share their stories of initiation in the small groups.

Direct them to listen for any common characteristics of what happens to people in the process of coming to belong to a group.

Invite participants to share in small groups. Develop a list of characteristics common to everyone's sharing that tells something about how people come to belong. At the end of the sharing, ask volunteers from the small groups to share the lists.

Use ideas from the list and give further input on what it means to belong to the Church. Emphasize that:

- Belonging is a process.
- Usually we are invited in (evangelization) or are really attracted by what we see (Christian witness).
- We make choices about our involvement.
- There are always rituals connected to the process of belonging (sacraments).
- As we become more involved in the group, we change (conversion).
- If it is really important to us, we tell others about it; we invite them in.

Allow some quiet time and ask participants to think about all the things they have just discussed and listened to, and to ask themselves:

- On a scale of 1–10 (10 being the highest), where would you rank yourself as belonging to the Church? Where would you rank yourself as belonging to God?

Break for refreshments and conversation.

What Are the Sacraments of Initiation? (30 minutes)

Use some of the comments from the previous session to move into this segment.

Point out that initiation, or coming to belong, is always a process, and it usually involves symbols, rites, and rituals. It is that way with the Church, too. The Church has three Sacraments of Initiation: Baptism, Confirmation, and Eucharist.

Distribute Eucharist Parent/Adult Catechesis Handout 1:2 and go through it in a conversational style, making comments, and explaining as questions arise. You may want to use the questions as a small group resource for sharing.

Allow time for questions, comments, and insights.

Summarize by saying these or similar words:

> *Baptism, Confirmation, and the Eucharist are the Sacraments of Initiation. These sacraments celebrate our belonging to Jesus Christ and being incorporated into his Body, the Church. Most of us go through a process of understanding what this really means for us. It is important to keep in mind that when we celebrate sacraments without being in relationship with and participating in the community of faith, we miss out on a lot. It is also important to keep in mind that initiation is only a beginning. It is not a graduation.*

Parent Moment (10 minutes)

Highlight the three Faith at Home features in the *Child's Book* and show how they will help the parents and family members to participate in the children's preparation.

Emphasize the importance of doing the activities on the Faith at Home page, especially the ritual action.

Closing Prayer (5 minutes)

Gather the participants in a circle around the prayer space. Pray these or similar words:

> *God, you who call us to yourself, you who long for us to belong to you, we ask for your blessing as we continue our faith journey. May we always be alert to your presence in the sacred signs of our lives and the celebrations of the Church. We ask this in Jesus' name. Amen.*

> *We close by reminding ourselves of our Baptism and our common kinship in God's family. In all that we do, may we reflect the glory of the Father, the Son, and the Holy Spirit. (Sprinkle with water.) Amen.*

Thank everyone for their time and participation.

 Encourage parents and family members to go to **www.harcourtreligion.com** for more ideas and suggestions.

We Belong

Objectives

- To guide families to experience a celebration of the word, including Renewal of Baptismal Promises
- To explore the meaning of the ritual action in family groups
- To help family members increase their understanding of the Sacraments of Initiation
- To help family members express that they are followers of Christ

Materials

- Copies of the celebration for the assembly (*Sacraments Source Book* CD)
- *Songs of Celebration* CD
- Prayer table
- Bible
- Candle and matches
- Bowl filled with water
- Chart or poster paper
- Markers
- Pencils
- *Child's Book*

Welcome and Celebration (10–15 minutes)

Welcome the families in the gathering space.

Distribute copies of the celebration.

Select a family to be in the procession. Have them choose a family member to carry the Bible in procession.
- When families are assembled, walk forward slowly. Follow the child carrying the Bible.
- During the procession, lead families in singing "Yes Lord, I Believe," from the *Songs of Celebration* CD, track 7.
- Place the Bible on the prayer table and have family members return to their seats.
- Light the prayer candle.
- Begin prayer with the Sign of the Cross and invite the group to follow the order of the prayer.
- If the group is too large to gather around the water and candle, have families remain seated.
- For the proclamation of the Gospel, you may use a Bible or the adapted reading in the *Child's Book* on pp. 6–7.
- Conclude with the opening song from the *Songs of Celebration* CD, track 7.

New Life individual family unit experience (10 minutes)

Guide family members to reflect on the celebration by asking the following questions:
- What did you see? What did you hear? What did you do?

Ask volunteers to share their responses.

Allow time for children and family members to complete the activity on p. 4 of the *Child's Book*.

The Body of Christ whole-group learning experience (5 minutes)

Select members of several families to share stories or details they know about their own Baptisms.

Direct attention to the bowl of water and the candle on the prayer table. Ask participants how these symbols are related to Baptism.

Explain the Signs of Faith: Water and Paschal Candle by summarizing the text on pp. 4–5 of the *Child's Book*.

Ask for a volunteer to read aloud The Body of Christ section in the *Child's Book*.

We Belong to God family cluster sharing experience (10 minutes)

Organize the large group into small clusters and invite them to reflect on the following question:
- What does Jesus tell us about belonging to God?

Ask volunteers to share their responses.

Ask each family cluster to select a leader to read aloud the first paragraph on p. 6 of the *Child's Book*.

Scripture whole-group learning experience (10 minutes)

Read aloud the Scripture story on pp. 6–7 of the *Child's Book*.

Invite the large group to reflect on the following:
• What was Jesus telling his friends in this story?

Ask volunteers to share their responses.

Allow silent time for individuals to reflect on how Jesus is their friend. At the end of the reflection, have family members share their responses with one another.

Direct the families to help children complete the Share activity on p. 7 of the *Child's Book*.

Emphasize that Jesus wants us to know we belong to him, and he wants us to love one another.

The Sacraments of Initiation family cluster sharing experience (15 minutes)

Organize the large group into the same family cluster groups as earlier. Be sure each group has selected a leader. Provide one sheet of poster paper for each family cluster and invite them to reflect on the question: Which sacraments are signs of belonging?

Ask each group leader to write down his or her group's responses on the poster paper.

Ask each group leader to select a member of his or her group to read aloud the first paragraph on p. 8 of the *Child's Book*.

Guide family cluster groups to look at the sacraments that they have listed on their chart paper, and have the leaders circle the Sacraments of Initiation.

Explain that Baptism, Confirmation, and Eucharist are the Sacraments of Initiation. These sacraments make us full members of the Church. These sacraments are signs that we belong to God.

Baptism individual family unit experience (5 minutes)

Point out the word "Baptism" in the *Child's Book*.
• Invite family members to group together and have the adults share memories of their Baptisms or that of their child or children.
• Select a child to read aloud about Baptism on p. 8 of the *Child's Book*.

Confirmation and Eucharist whole-group learning experience (10 minutes)

Point out the word "Confirmation" in the *Child's Book*:
• Explain to the large group that the Sacrament of Confirmation strengthens baptized persons with the gifts of the Holy Spirit.
• Read the prayers on p. 9 of the *Child's Book*.
• Ask the families which Person of the Trinity we receive in a special way during Confirmation.
• Select a volunteer to read Signs of Faith: The Trinity.

Point out the word "Eucharist" in the *Child's Book*:
• Select a family member to read aloud from the book about Eucharist.

Clarify that Eucharist is a name used for the whole action of the Mass and that Holy Communion is the receiving of the Body and Blood of Jesus during the Eucharist.

Children of Light individual family unit experience (5 minutes)

Guide families in sharing how they live as followers of Christ using the activity on p. 10 of the *Child's Book*. At the end of the reflection, ask volunteers to share their family's responses.

Closing Blessing (5 minutes)

Invite each family to form a family circle.

Begin with the Sign of the Cross.

Pray the prayer on p. 10 of the *Child's Book*.

Conclude by leading families in singing *Songs of Celebration* CD, track 7, "Yes Lord, I Believe."

Faith at Home

Direct families' attention to the Faith at Home page and encourage them to the activities at home.

We Gather

Before the Celebration		Materials

Before the Celebration

- Choose a gathering space that will be conducive to prayer and that will accommodate the size of the group; the church, a chapel, or a gathering place in the parish hall would each be appropriate. You will want the group to be able to see, hear, and move easily during the ritual.
- Prepare the group for the ritual action of the Procession and Gloria and for the reflection on the sacred Scriptures.
- Select a good reader to proclaim the reading.

- Select four people for the entrance procession: to carry the Bible, the candle, the bowl of water, and the chrism. Show them where and how to place them in the sanctuary or on the prayer table.
- If not in a church or chapel, place chairs in semicircular rows around the prayer space. Leave enough space for people to move in and out of the rows. If possible, have tables and chairs set up in another space for adult discussion after the celebration.

Materials

- A large clear bowl with water, or if the celebration is in the church, use the baptismal font or pool
- A large candle or the Paschal candle
- A prayer table or setting for the bowl with holy water, candle, a Bible, and a stand
- *Songs of Celebration* CD
- Copies of the celebration for the assembly (*Sacraments Source Book* CD)

Gathering Rite

Welcome the gathered assembly.

Rehearse the opening song, and go over the ritual action of the Procession and Gloria.

Invite the assembly to stand for the procession.

Opening Song

"Glory to God," *Songs of Celebration CD*, track 8.

Procession and Gloria

Have the gathered assembly walk forward slowly singing the opening song and following the persons carrying the candle, bowl of water, and Bible.

Leader: Let us pray.
Make the Sign of the Cross together.

Opening Prayer

Leader: God, our Father, you alone are holy. You give us life and all good things. Help us be grateful children who always remember your glory. We ask this through Jesus Christ our Lord.
All: Amen.

Gloria

Leader: God, our loving Father, we are gathered here in your presence as one. We praise you for your goodness and thank you for the gift of your Son, Jesus. Send us your Holy Spirit to help us live as your children. We ask this through Jesus Christ our Lord.
All: Amen.
Leader: Every Sunday, we come together as God's people to praise him and to give him thanks for all the wonderful things he has done. Today we do the same, offering prayers of praise and thanksgiving.

If the space is conducive, invite the assembly to come forward and gather around the water and candle.

Leader: Lord Jesus, you came to gather all people into the peace of your Father's kingdom.
All: (Sing) Glory to God in the highest.
Leader: Lord Jesus, you came to bring us new life.
All: (Sing) Glory to God in the highest.
Leader: Lord Jesus, you came to save us.
All: (Sing) Glory to God in the highest.
Leader: Let us give praise and thanks to God.
All: (Sing) Glory to God in the highest.

Celebration of the Word

Leader: *A reading from the Acts of the Apostles.*
Read Luke 19:1–10.

Leader: *The word of the Lord*

All: *Thanks be to God.*
Sit silently.

Reflection

Invite the assembly to reflect on the reading. Use the following question:

- What most impresses you about the early Christian community?

Ask the assembly to share their responses with one or two people. Be sure to include children in the sharing.

Closing Prayer

Leader: *Loving God, we praise and thank you for the gifts of your Spirit. Help us to act in ways that show your gifts to others. We ask this through Jesus Christ our Lord.*

All: *Amen.*

Children go to their group session and adults go to the appointed space for reflection.

- There is a liturgical catechetical session for adults on p. 99.
- There is a parent/adult catechetical session on pp. 100–101.
- There is an intergenerational catechetical session on pp. 102–103.

We Gather

Goals	Materials

Goals
- To reflect on the celebration
- To understand the qualities of a community of faith
- To describe the Introductory Rites

Materials
- Poster board, chart paper, or overhead projector
- Markers
- *Songs of Celebration* CD
- Bible

Reflection (20 minutes)

Invite the adults to gather in groups of five or six.

Begin by recalling the ritual moments of the celebration. Lead a guided meditation using the following prompts. Pause after each prompt:
- Play a few verses of the opening song "Glory to God," *Songs of Celebration* CD, track 8.
- Read some verses of the Gospel.
- Ask participants to recall their discussion of the Gospel
- Ask: "What was it like to be in procession, and to sing Glory to God? What was it like to be gathered together?"
- Call to mind the Scripture sharing. Ask: "What did you hear?"

Small Group Sharing

Pause for a few minutes of silence. Then invite the participants to share their feelings about the celebration in their small group. Encourage them to stay with their feelings. After 10 to 15 minutes, invite sharing with the large group.

Large Group Sharing

Gather the responses of the small groups on poster board, chart paper, or an overhead projector. Ask for feelings and thoughts about the celebration as a whole, and also for specific parts of the celebration that were meaningful to members of the group.

Naming (30 minutes)

Ask the participants to name what they learned from the celebration about God, Jesus, the Church, or their own Christian life.

Take each category separately and list responses on poster board, chart paper, or an overhead projector. When the lists are completed, use them to summarize the theology of gathering as a community.

Affirm, add, or enlarge upon the following points:
- We gather as an assembly to give glory to God.
- The Entrance Procession and Introductory Rites of the Mass gather us as a community of faith.
- Other terms for the community of faith are Church, People of God, and Body of Christ.
- Sunday is an important day for Christians because it recalls the Resurrection of Jesus.

Reflection and Small Group Sharing (20 minutes)

Ask "What is one thing you will do this week to strengthen your participation in the parish community?"

Direct participants to reflect for a few minutes and then share their responses with their group.

Closing Blessing (5 minutes)

Gather and begin with the Sign of the Cross.

Leader: *God, our Father, we praise and thank you for gathering us together.*
All: *Amen.*

Leader: *Jesus, our Savior, we praise and thank you for the gift of your Person and message.*
All: *Amen.*

Leader: *Holy Spirit, giver of God's gifts, continue to guide us in the way of faith and form us together into one people.*
All: *Amen.*

We Gather

Goals	Environment	Materials
• To welcome participants in a hospitable environment • To communicate the importance of gathering as a Eucharistic community • To help participants come to a deeper understanding of Catholic liturgy, especially the Introductory Rites	• Be sure to clearly identify the meeting place, posting clear directions if necessary. • Tables and chairs arranged for small groups • A prayer setting with large candle, Bible on a stand or table, clear bowl filled with water, and a branch or other instrument for sprinkling	• Beverages and light refreshments • Nametags • Copies of *Call to Celebrate: Eucharist* Family Guide • *Songs of Celebration* CD • Copies of **Eucharist Parent/Adult Catechesis Handout 2:1** (*Sacraments Source Book* CD) • Pens or pencils • Posterboard or chart paper

Welcome and Opening Prayer (15 minutes)

✳ **Before the session, ask two active members of the parish who are members of the group to prepare a short (two to three minutes in length) presentation of how and why the parish is an important faith community for them. Invite them to make their presentation during the third part of the session.**

Welcome parents and other adults and distribute nametags.

Introduce yourself and briefly review the goals and agenda for the gathering.

Gather the group around the prayer setting. If that is not possible, have the group pause for a reflective moment.

Introduce the prayer with the Sign of the Cross.

Sing "Glory to God," *Songs of Celebration* CD, track 8.

✳ **If this session was preceded by a large group ritual and reflection, go to We Gather. If not, continue with the prayer.**

Pray these or similiar words:
God, our loving Father, we are gathered here in your presence as one. We praise you for your goodness and thank you for the gift of your Son, Jesus. Send us your Holy Spirit to help us grow in faith and understanding. We ask this through Jesus Christ our Lord. Amen.

Read *Acts 2:42-47.*

Allow a few moments of silence.

Invite the participants to share the Sign of Peace with one another.

We Gather (30 minutes)

Distribute Eucharist Parent/Adult Catechesis Handout 2:1.

Allow 5 to 7 minutes for individuals to complete the handout.

Organize the participants into small groups of 5 to 6 people, and have them share their reflections in the small group.

Distribute two large sheets of chart paper or poster board to each group.

Guide the discussion by asking them to share both their responses and insights from the reflection. Then ask them to appoint a recorder and collate two top 10 lists: the first, the top 10 reasons people want to gather; the second, the top 10 reasons that make a gathering "sacred."

Ask each group to display their lists around the gathering space, and invite participants to walk around and read the lists during the break.

Break for refreshments and conversation.

What Is a Community of Faith? (30 minutes)

Invite participants to open to pp. 4–5 of the *Call to Celebrate: Eucharist Family Guide*.

Call on three participants to each read one of the stories on p. 4.

Ask volunteers to respond to the question.

Highlight key characteristics of a faith community:
- believes in Jesus
- is a group of people we share faith with, we imitate, we pray with
- shares a mission

Ask participants to reflect on whom they would include as part of their faith community today.

Invite the parishioners you asked in advance to share their presentation about their relationship to the parish.

Offer input on the importance of gathering to celebrate Eucharist, using this outline as a basis for your remarks.

Refer to the top 10 lists to draw parallels when appropriate.

Make the following points:

- **Christianity is a community-oriented faith.**
  - We believe in a God who is a Triune community of love.
  - In the Incarnation, God entered into intimate community with the human family.
  - We believe that when we gather in community, we become the Body of Christ.

- **In the Eucharistic assembly, we strengthen and support one another.**
  - We bring all that we are, the good and the bad, and present it to God and to one another. We also forgive and pray for one another.
  - We are fed as individuals and as a community and given strength to continue our individual journeys.
  - The community remains with us in spirit as we live our daily lives, strive to make good moral choices, and serve others in Christ's name.

- **The parish is the place where we can be strengthened to live as disciples.**
  - Mention activities such as prayer groups, social activities, and organizations that support parishioners on the journey of discipleship.
  - Describe how the parish reaches out to the sick, the poor, and the larger world.

Invite all to reflect on their involvement in the parish, and encourage them to continue or start being involved. Emphasize the importance of that involvement to the faith life of children.

Parent Moment (10 minutes)

Highlight the three Faith at Home features in the *Child's Book* and show how they will help the parents and family members to participate in the children's preparation.

Emphasize the importance of doing the activities on the Faith at Home page, especially the ritual action.

Closing Prayer (5 minutes)

Gather the parents and family members in a circle around the prayer space and pray these or similiar words.

God of joy, God of life, we praise you. In your goodness, you have given us the gift of Christian community. Help us to better appreciate the support of our brothers and sisters in the bad times, and the blessings that come with sharing our joy with them in the good times. May you, the source of all that is good, bless our parish community, especially our young ones as they prepare to join us at your table. We ask this in Jesus' name. Amen.

As always, we close by reminding ourselves of our Baptism and our common kinship in God's family. In all that we do, may we reflect the glory of the Father, the Son, and the Holy Spirit. (Sprinkle with water.) Amen.

Thank everyone for their time and participation.

 Encourage parents and family members to go to **www.harcourtreligion.com** for more ideas and suggestions.

We Gather

Objectives

- To guide families to experience a celebration of the word, including the singing of the Gloria
- To explore the meaning of the ritual action in family groups
- To help families increase their understanding of the qualities of a community of faith
- To describe the Introductory Rites
- To model ways of praising God

Materials

- Copies of the celebration for the assembly (*Sacraments Source Book* CD)
- *Songs of Celebration* CD
- Prayer table
- Bible
- Candle and matches
- Bowl filled with water
- Copies of Scripture Drama 2, pp. CE4–5
- Props for dramatizing the Gospel story
- Chart or poster paper
- Markers
- *Child's Book*

Welcome and Celebration (10–15 minutes)

Welcome the families in the gathering space.

Distribute copies of the celebration.

Select a family to be in the procession. Have them choose a family member to carry the Bible in procession.

- When families are assembled, walk forward slowly. Follow the child carrying the Bible.
- During the procession, lead families in singing "Glory to God," from the *Songs of Celebration* CD, track 8.
- Place the Bible on the prayer table and have the famiy members return to their seats.
- Light the prayer candle.
- Begin the prayer with the Sign of the Cross and invite the group to follow the order of the prayer.
- If the group is too large to gather around the water and candle, have families stand in place.
- For the proclamation of the Gospel, you may use a Bible or the adapted reading in the *Child's Book* on pp. 16–17.
- Conclude with the opening song from the *Songs of Celebration* CD, track 8.

Gathered Together individual family unit experience
(10 minutes)

Guide family members to reflect on the celebration by asking the following questions:

- What did you see? What did you hear? What did you do?

Ask volunteers to share their responses.

Read aloud page 14 of the *Child's Book*. Allow time for children and family members to complete the activity and share their responses.

We Come Together whole-group learning experience
(5 minutes)

Invite families to reflect on the meaning of prayer. Write the word "prayer" on a sheet of poster paper in the front of the gathering space.

Ask:
- What is prayer?
- When do you pray together as a family?

Invite volunteers to share their responses.

Select a family member to read aloud the We Come Together section in the *Child's Book*.

Point out the Signs of Faith: Assembly and Procession, and ask volunteers to describe them in their own words.

We Gather as God's People family cluster sharing experience
(10 minutes)

Organize the large group into small clusters and invite them to reflect on the following question:
- What is a community of faith?

Ask volunteers to share their responses.

Ask each family cluster to select a leader to read aloud p. 16 of the *Child's Book*.

Scripture whole-group learning experience (10 minutes)

Arrange the space for the Scripture dramatization from pp. CE4–5 of the *Catechist Edition*. Select members of several families to role-play the scripture reading.

Dramatize the reading.

Invite the large group to reflect on the following questions:
- How did others feel when they saw how happy the Christians were?
- What are some ways your family and parish take care of the needs of other Christians?

Ask for volunteers to share their responses.

The People Gather family cluster sharing experience (15 minutes)

Divide the large group into same family cluster groups as before, and be sure each group has selected a leader.

Provide one sheet of poster paper and a marker for each family cluster.

Guide each group to discuss the following question:
- What happens when we gather as a community of faith?

Ask group leaders to write down their group's responses on the poster paper at the end of the reflection.

Invite each leader to share his or her group's responses with the large group.

Ask each group leader to select a member of his or her group to read aloud from p. 18 of the *Child's Book*.

Introductory Rites whole-group learning experience
(10 minutes)

Write the words "Introductory Rites" on poster paper.

Point out that during the Introductory Rites, we greet one another and begin our worship by praising God with songs, prayer, and actions.

Invite families to look at the photographs on p. 18 of the *Child's Book*.

Read aloud the section of the *Child's Book* about Introductory Rites.

Discuss the question. We greet one another, stand together, and pray and sing together.

Give Praise and Thanks individual family unit experience
(5 minutes)

Invite each family to form a family circle.

Ask each person to share with his or her family one thing that he or she is thankful for.

Guide families in sharing how they give God thanks and praise using the activity on p. 20 of the *Child's Book*.

Allow time for families to complete the activity. At the end, ask for volunteers to share their responses.

Closing Blessing (5 minutes)

Invite each family to form a family circle.

Begin with the Sign of the Cross.

Pray the prayer on p. 20 of the *Child's Book*.

Conclude by leading families in singing *Songs of Celebration* CD, track 8, "Glory to God," or another appropriate song from your parish music repertoire.

Faith at Home

Direct families' attention to the Faith at Home page and encourage them to do the activities at home.

We Are Forgiven

Before the Celebration		Materials
• Choose a gathering space that will be conducive to prayer and that will accommodate the size of the group; the church, a chapel, or a gathering place in the parish hall would each be appropriate. You will want the group to be able to see, hear, and move easily during the ritual. • Prepare the group for the ritual action of the Penitential Rite and for the reflection on the sacred Scriptures. • Select a good reader to proclaim the reading.	• If not in a church or chapel, place chairs in semicircular rows around the prayer space. Leave enough space for people to move in and out of the rows. If possible, have tables and chairs set up in another space for adult discussion after the celebration.	• A large clear bowl with water, or if the celebration is in the church, use the baptismal font or pool • A large candle or the Paschal candle • A prayer table for the candle, oil of chrism, a baptismal candle, a Bible, and a stand • *Songs of Celebration* CD • Copies of the celebration for the assembly (*Sacraments Source Book* CD)

Gathering Rite

Note: Because this is a Penitential Rite, there is no entrance procession.

Welcome the gathered assembly.

Rehearse the opening song, and go over the ritual action of the Penitential Rite.

Opening Song

"Create in Me," *Songs of Celebration* CD, track 9.

Opening Prayer

Leader: God our loving Father, you call us to forgiveness and peace. You want us to be united in you. We ask you to help us forgive others as you forgive us. We ask this through Jesus Christ, our Lord.

All: Amen.

Penitential Rite

Leader: Let us pray.
Make the Sign of the Cross together.
May the peace of the Lord be with you.

All: And also with you.

Confiteor

Leader: Every week, we come together as a community of faith. God wants us to be united with him and with one another as one family. Let us be quiet now and think about the times we have not been united to God or others.
Sit silently.
Let us pray for God's forgiveness and mercy.

All: I confess to almighty God, and to you, my brothers and sisters, that I have sinned through my own fault in my thoughts and in my words, in what I have done, and in what I have failed to do; and I ask blessed Mary, ever virgin, all the angels and saints, and you, my brothers and sisters, to pray for me to the Lord our God.

Leader: May God forgive us our sins and unite us in his love.

Celebration of the Word

Leader: *A reading from the holy Gospel according to Matthew.*

All: *Glory to you, Lord.*
Read Matthew 9:9–13.

Leader: *The Gospel of the Lord.*

All: *Praise to you, Lord Jesus Christ.*
Sit silently.

Reflection

Invite the assembly to reflect on the Gospel. Use the following question:

- For you, what was the most important phrase in the Gospel as you heard it?

Ask the assembly to share their responses with one or two people. Be sure to include children in the sharing.

Closing Prayer

Leader: *Let us offer each other the Sign of Peace. Go forth united in God's love.*

All: *Amen.*

Children go to their group session and adults go to the appointed space for reflection.:

- There is a liturgical catechetical session for adults on p. 106.
- There is a parent/adult catechetical session on pp. 107–108.
- There is an intergenerational catechetical session on pp. 109–110.

We Are Forgiven

Goals	Materials
• To reflect on the celebration • To explore the relationship between forgiveness and unity • To reflect on why we pray for forgiveness at Mass	• Poster board, chart paper, or overhead projector • Markers • *Songs of Celebration* CD • Bible

Reflection (20 minutes)

Invite the adults to gather in groups of five or six.

Begin by recalling the ritual moments of the celebration. Lead a guided meditation using the following prompts. Pause after each prompt.
- Play a few verses of the opening song, "Create in Me," *Songs of Celebration* CD, track 9.
- Read a few verses of the Gospel.
- Ask participants to recall their discussion of the Gospel.
- Ask: "What was it like to think about the times we have not been united to God and others?"

Small Group Sharing

Pause for a few minutes of silence. Then invite the participants to share their feelings about the celebration in their small group. Encourage them to stay with their feelings. After 10 to 15 minutes, invite sharing with the large group.

Large Group Sharing

Gather the responses of the small groups on poster board, chart paper, or an overhead projector. Ask for feelings and thoughts about the celebration as a whole, and also for specific parts of the celebration that were meaningful to members of the group.

Naming (30 minutes)

Ask the participants to name what they learned from the celebration about God, Jesus, the Church, or their own Christian life.

Take each category separately and list their responses on poster board, chart paper, or an overhead projector. When the lists are completed, use them to summarize the theology and meaning of the Penitential Rite.

Affirm, add, or enlarge upon the following points:
- The Eucharist is a sacrament of unity and forgiveness.
- The confession of the sins during the Confiteor does not take the place of the Sacrament of Reconciliation.
- The confession of sin during the Confiteor unites us to God and one another.
- The Penitential Rite reminds us that God is merciful and forgiving.
- There are several ways to celebrate the Penitential Rite.
- A Sprinkling Rite, or *Asperges*, sometimes replaces the Penitential Rite.

Reflection and Small Group Sharing (20 minutes)

Ask "What is one thing you will do this week to witness God's forgiveness and mercy?"

Direct participants to reflect for a few minutes and then share their responses with their group.

Closing Blessing (5 minutes)

Gather and begin with the Sign of the Cross.

Leader: God, our Father, we praise and thank you for being a God who forgives.
All: Amen.
Leader: Jesus, our Savior, we praise and thank you for welcoming sinners and showing us how to live and love.
All: Amen.
Leader: Holy Spirit, giver of God's gifts, guide and strengthen us to be a forgiving, united people.
All: Amen.

We Are Forgiven

Goals	Environment	Materials
• To welcome participants in a hospitable environment • To continue to affirm the importance of parent and family participation in the process • To communicate God's forgiveness and the importance of reconciliation with the Christian community • To help participants come to a deeper understanding of Catholic liturgy, especially the Penitential Rite	• Be sure to clearly identify the meeting place, posting clear directions if necessary. • Tables and chairs arranged for small groups • A prayer setting with large candle, Bible on a stand or table, clear bowl filled with water, and a branch or other instrument for sprinkling	• Beverages and light refreshments • Nametags • Copies of *Growing Faith* pamphlet, #26* • Copies of *Call to Celebrate: Eucharist* Family Guide • *Songs of Celebration* CD • Copies of **Eucharist Parent/Adult Catechesis Handouts 3:1** and **3:2** (*Sacraments Source Book* CD) • Board or chart paper

Welcome and Opening Prayer (15 minutes)

Welcome parents and other adults and distribute nametags.

Introduce yourself and briefly review the goals and agenda for the gathering.

✳ **If this session was preceded by a large group ritual and reflection, go to We Are Forgiven. If not, continue with the prayer.**

Gather the group around the prayer setting, if possible, or have the group pause for a reflective moment.

Introduce the prayer with the Sign of the Cross.

Sing "Create in Me," *Songs of Celebration* CD, track 9.

Pray these or similar words:

Lord God, we come before you a sinful people. We don't always do what we should do and we often do what we should not. We ask your forgiveness and the grace of a changed heart. We ask this in the name of your Son Jesus who lives and reigns with you forever. Amen.

Read *Matthew 9:9–13*.

Invite the assembly to reflect on the Gospel, using the following question:
• Why did Jesus eat with sinners?

Ask participants to share their responses with one or two people.

Invite participants to reflect on forgiveness.

We Are Forgiven (30 minutes)

Distribute Eucharist Parent/Adult Catechesis Handout 3:1.

Allow 5 to 7 minutes for individuals to complete the handouts.

Organize the participants into small groups of 5 to 6 people and invite them to share in their small groups, using the following questions:
• Reflect on a time when your relationship with another person was damaged through a disagreement or failure to fulfill a promise. If reconciliation did not take place, what kept it from happening?
• If reconciliation did take place, what steps were taken that allowed it to happen? How did the relationship change after reconciliation?

Distribute the pamphlet, "How Does God Offer Unending Forgiveness?" (*Growing Faith* pamphlet, #26).*

> ***Growing Faith*** project pamphlets can be purchased online by going to **www.harcourtreligion.com.**

Highlight key concepts that address the importance of forgiveness and reconciliation within the Eucharistic community.

Break for refreshments and conversation.

How Is the Eucharist a Sacrament of Forgiveness? (30 minutes)

Offer input on the importance of reconciliation to the celebration of Eucharist. Use this outline as a basis for your remarks:

- **Sin is part of the human experience.**
  - Sin can be understood as an act (or failure to act) that damages a person's relationship with either God or another person or group. Every sin is a violation of the dignity of another person or oneself.
  - Even sins that we consider private harm the community by diminishing our ability to serve others generously and selflessly.
  - Because we live in a broken world, we are all inclined to sin.

- **When we celebrate Eucharist, we forgive one another for our failings and offer mutual support.**
  - In Eucharist, we set aside the conflicts of our daily lives to offer worship to God and to be strengthened by the prayers of the community.
  - We ask forgiveness of God and one another in preparation to come to the Eucharistic table.
  - In the Rite of Peace, we extend good will to others and accept it from them as well as a sign of our unity in Christ.
  - In our common proclamation of the Lord's Prayer, we recognize that we must forgive others just as we desire to be forgiven.

Invite all to participate in the following discussion in their small groups:

- Why is it important to reconcile with the community before we receive Communion?
- What does our common reception of Jesus' Body and Blood say about our unity as a people?
- How do you experience that unity in your day-to-day life?

Distribute Eucharist Parent/Adult Catechesis Handout 3:2 as a personal reflection piece for participants to use during the week.

Parent Moment (10 minutes)

Highlight the three Faith at Home features in the *Child's Book* and show how they will help the parents and family members to participate in the children's preparation.

Emphasize the importance of doing the activities on the Faith at Home page, especially the ritual action.

Closing Prayer (5 minutes)

Gather participants in a circle around the prayer space and pray these or similar words:

Lord of the journey, you celebrate with us when we succeed and you strengthen us when we fail. May we always rely on your forgiveness and the supportive companionship of the Christian community. We especially ask that we may be role models of reconciliation for our young ones as they prepare to come to the Eucharistic table. We ask this through Christ, our Lord. Amen.

As always, we close by reminding ourselves of our Baptism and our common kinship in God's family. In all that we do, may we reflect the glory of the Father, the Son, and the Holy Spirit. (Sprinkle with water.) Amen.

Thank everyone for their time and participation.

 Encourage parents and family members to go to **www.harcourtreligion.com** for more ideas and suggestions.

We Are Forgiven

Objectives

- To guide families to experience a celebration of the word, including praying the Confiteor and extending the Sign of Peace
- To explore the meaning of the ritual action in family groups
- To help families increase their understanding of Jesus as a friend of sinners
- To explain why we pray for forgiveness at Mass
- To review with families signs and prayers of forgiveness

Materials

- Copies of the celebration for the assembly (*Sacraments Source Book* CD)
- *Songs of Celebration* CD
- Prayer table
- Bible
- Candle and matches
- Bowl filled with water
- Copies of Scripture Drama 3, pp. CE7–8
- Props for dramatizing the Gospel story
- Activity Master 3, p. CE6
- Pencils
- *Child's Book*

Welcome and Celebration (10–15 minutes)

Familiarize yourself with the ritual focus for the Penitential Rite.

Set up the prayer table ahead of time. There is no procession in this celebration.

Welcome the families in the gathering space.

Distribute copies of the celebration.
- When families are assembled, have them sit quietly. You may want to play reflective music to center the group.
- Lead families in singing the suggested song, "Create in Me," from the *Songs of Celebration* CD, track 9.
- Light the prayer candle.
- Begin prayer with the Sign of the Cross and invite the group to follow the order of the prayer.
- If the group is too large to gather around the water and candle, have the families stand in place.
- For the proclamation of the Gospel, you may use a Bible or the adapted reading in the *Child's Book* on pp. 26–27.
- Conclude with the opening song from the *Songs of Celebration* CD, track 9.

God's Forgiveness individual family unit experience (10 minutes)

Guide family members to reflect on the celebration by asking the following questions:
- What did you see? What did you hear? What did you do?

Invite family members to turn toward one another and share their responses to the questions.

Guide families to think about a time when they told a family member that they were sorry and the other person forgave them. Use the activity on p. 24 of the *Child's Book*.

Allow time for family members to share with one another and for the children to complete the activity.

Point out that relationships grow and are strengthened when people ask for and receive forgiveness.

Ask a family member to read aloud the text for Signs of Faith: Lord Have Mercy.

We Are One whole-group learning experience (5 minutes)

Invite families to reflect on the following question:
- What does it mean to be united as a family?

Ask for volunteers to share their responses.

Select a family member to read aloud the We Are One section in the *Child's Book*.

Read aloud the text for the Sign of Faith: Silence, and emphasize the importance of reflecting during the Mass.

Jesus Calls Sinners family cluster sharing experience (10 minutes)

Organize the large group into small clusters and invite them to reflect on the following question:
• Why did Jesus eat with sinners?

Allow time for family clusters to share their responses.

Invite volunteers to share their group's responses with the large group.

Ask each family cluster to select a leader to read aloud p. 26 of the *Child's Book*.

Scripture whole-group learning experience (10 minutes)

Select members of several families to dramatize the Scripture reading. Use the Scripture dramatization found on pp. CE7–8 of the *Catechist Edition*.

Invite the large group to reflect on the following questions:
• How do you think Matthew felt when Jesus asked him to become a follower?
• What are some ways that your family can welcome others?

Ask for volunteers to share their responses.

Distribute copies of the Activity Master. Families may complete it during the session or take it home to complete.

Penitential Rite family cluster sharing experience (15 minutes)

Explain to the large group that at the beginning of every Eucharist, we reflect on sin and its consequences, and we pray for God's mercy.

Organize the large group into the same family cluster groups as earlier. Be sure each group has selected a leader. Guide each group to discuss the following question:
• What happens during the Penitential Rite?

Ask each group leader to select a member of his or her group to read aloud p. 28 of the *Child's Book*.

We Are Sorry whole-group learning experience (10 minutes)

Read aloud the first few lines of the Confiteor to the whole group.

Recall that this prayer was part of the opening celebration and that they often hear it at Mass.

Explain that we begin our time as an assembly confessing our sin and asking for God's mercy and forgiveness.

Point out the prayer the priest says at the end of the Penitential Rite on p. 29 of the *Child's Book*.

Discuss the following question.
• Why do you think the Penitential Rite is important?

We Forgive individual family unit experience (5 minutes)

Invite family members to turn to one another and talk about ways they forgive at home.

Direct them to complete the activity on p. 30 of the *Child's Book*.

Select a family or families to come forward and share their bulletin board ideas before the large group and demonstrate ways family members can show forgiveness at home.

Closing Blessing (5 minutes)

Invite each family to form a family circle.

Begin with the Sign of the Cross.

Pray the prayer on p. 30 of the *Child's Book*.

Conclude by leading families in singing *Songs of Celebration* CD, track 9, "Create in Me."

Faith at Home individual family unit experience (5 minutes)

Direct families' attention to the Faith at Home page and encourage them to do the activities at home.

We Listen

Before the Celebration

- Choose a gathering space that will be conducive to prayer and that will accommodate the size of the group; the church, a chapel, or a gathering place in the parish hall would each be appropriate. You will want the group to be able to see, hear, and move easily during the ritual.

- Prepare the group for the ritual action of Signing and for the reflection on the sacred Scriptures.

- Select a good reader to proclaim the reading.

- Select four people for the entrance procession: to carry the Bible, the candle, the bowl of water, and the chrism. Show them where and how to place them in the sanctuary or on the prayer table.

- If not in a church or chapel, place chairs in semicircular rows around the prayer space. Leave enough space for people to move in and out of the rows. If possible, have tables and chairs set up in another space for adult discussion after the celebration.

Materials

- A large, clear bowl with water, or if the celebration is in the church, use the baptismal font or pool

- A large candle or the Paschal candle

- A prayer table for the candle, oil of chrism, a baptismal candle, a Bible, and a stand

- *Songs of Celebration* CD

- Copies of the celebration for the assembly (*Sacraments Source Book* CD)

Gathering Rite

Welcome the gathered assembly.

Rehearse the opening song, and go over the ritual action of Signing.

Invite the assembly to stand for the procession.

Opening Song

"Open My Eyes," *Songs of Celebration* CD, track 10.

Procession

The presider and persons carrying the bowl with water, candle, and Bible process in while the assembly sings.

Leader: Let us pray.
> Make the Sign of the Cross together.

Opening Prayer

Leader: Father, send the Holy Spirit to open our ears and hearts that we may hear and live your word. We ask this in Jesus' name.
All: Amen.

Celebration of the Word

Leader: A reading from the holy Gospel according to Matthew.
All: Glory to you, Lord.

Signing

Invite the assembly to turn to one another and sign each other with the following words. Do the signing in a slow and deliberate gesture.

Leader: Loving Father, we want to live by your word.
> Trace the Sign of the Cross on your partner's forehead.
> May your words be in our minds.

> Trace the Sign of the Cross on your partner's lips.
> May your words be in our mouths.

> Trace the Sign of the Cross on your partner's heart.
> May your words be in our heart.

> We ask this through Jesus Christ our Lord.
All: Amen.
> Read Matthew 13:1–23.

Leader: *The Gospel of the Lord.*
All: *Praise to you, Lord Jesus Christ.*
Sit silently.

Reflection

Invite the assembly to reflect on the Gospel. Use the following question:

- How do you prepare yourself to hear the word of God?

Ask the assembly to share their responses with one or two people. Be sure to include children in the sharing.

Closing Prayer

Leader: *Loving God, we thank you for your word. Help us remember and share it. We ask this through Jesus Christ our Lord.*
All: *Amen.*

Children go to their group session and adults go to the appointed space for reflection.

- There is a liturgical catechetical session for adults on p. 113.
- There is a parent/adult catechetical session on pp. 114–115.
- There is an intergenerational catechetical session on pp. 116–117.

We Listen

Goals	Materials
• To reflect on the celebration • To explain that God is present in the word • To describe the parts of the Liturgy of the Word	• Poster board, chart paper, or overhead projector • *Songs of Celebration* CD • Markers • Bible

Reflection (20 minutes)

Invite the adults to gather in groups of five or six.

Begin by recalling the ritual moments of the celebration. Lead a guided meditation using the following prompts. Pause after each prompt.
- Play a few verses of the opening song, "Open My Eyes," *Songs of Celebration* CD, track 10.
- Call to mind the procession and the signing by praying the words again.
- Ask: "What was it like to have someone else trace the cross on your forehead, lips, and heart?"
- Call to mind the experience of being gathered together.
- Read some verses of the Gospel.
- Ask participants to recall their discussion of the Gospel.

Small Group Sharing

Pause for a few minutes of silence. Then invite the participants to share their feelings about the celebration in their small group. After 10 to 15 minutes, invite sharing with the large group.

Large Group Sharing

Gather the responses of the small groups on poster board, chart paper, or an overhead projector. Ask for feelings and thoughts about the celebration as a whole, and also for specific parts of the celebration that were meaningful to members of the group.

Naming (30 minutes)

Ask the participants to name what they learned from the celebration about God, Jesus, Scripture, or their own Christian life.

Take each category separately and list responses on poster board, chart paper, or an overhead projector. When the lists are completed, use them to summarize the theology and meaning of the Liturgy of the Word.

Affirm, add, or enlarge upon the following points:
- God is present in the sacred Scriptures.
- The word of God is a guide for us.
- We show our reverence for God's word during the liturgy by our gestures.
- The Liturgy of the Word is the first of two principal parts of the Mass.
- There are four readings from Scripture during the Liturgy of the Word, but usually the Psalm is sung or recited.
- The Liturgy of the Word also includes the Creed and the General Intercessions or Prayers of the Faithful, which are a response to the readings.

Reflection and Small Group Sharing (20 minutes)

Ask "What is one thing you will do this week to listen more closely to God's word in the Scriptures?"

Direct participants to reflect in silence for a few minutes and then share their responses.

Closing Blessing (5 minutes)

Gather and begin with the Sign of the Cross.

Leader: *God, our Father, we praise and thank you for all the ways you reveal yourself to us.*
All: *Amen.*

Leader: *Jesus, Word of the Father, we praise and thank you for speaking to us in your words and actions.*
All: *Amen.*

Leader: *Holy Spirit, giver of God's gifts, open our hearts and minds to listen and be guided by God's word.*
All: *Amen.*

Eucharist Session 4–Parent/Adult Catechesis

We Listen

Goals	Environment	Materials
• To welcome participants in a hospitable environment • To continue to affirm the importance of parent and family participation in the process • To communicate the presence of Jesus in the Liturgy of the Word • To help participants come to a deeper understanding of Catholic liturgy, especially the Liturgy of the Word	• Be sure to clearly identify the meeting place, posting clear directions if necessary. • Tables and chairs arranged for small groups • A prayer setting with large candle, Bible on a stand or table, clear bowl filled with water, and a branch or other instrument for sprinkling	• Beverages and light refreshments • Nametags • Copies of **Call to Celebrate: Eucharist** Family Guide • Songs of Celebration CD • Copies of **Eucharist Parent/Adult Catechesis Handouts 4:1** and **4:2** (Sacraments Source Book CD)

Welcome and Opening Prayer (15 minutes)

Welcome parents and other adults and distribute nametags.

Introduce yourself and briefly review the goals and agenda for the gathering.

✳ **If this session was preceded by a large group ritual and reflection, go to We Listen. If not, continue with the prayer. Use Eucharist Parent/Adult Catechesis Handout 4:1 as a prayer aid.**

Gather the group around the prayer setting, if possible, or have the group pause for a reflective moment.

Introduce the prayer with the Sign of the Cross.

Sing "Open My Eyes," Songs of Celebration, track 10.

Pray these or similar words:

Lord God, open our ears and hearts to your word that we may hear you and follow where you lead us. We ask this in the name of your Son Jesus. Amen.

Read Matthew 13:1–23.

Invite the assembly to reflect on the Gospel using the following question:
• Why do we listen to God's word?

Ask participants to share their responses with one or two people.

Invite participants to reflect on the power of listening.

We Listen (30 minutes)

Distribute Eucharist Parent/Adult Catechesis Handout 4:1.

Allow 5 to 7 minutes for inividuals to complete the handout.

Organize participants into small groups of 5 to 6 people, and invite them to share in their small groups.

Introduce the group sharing with a short reflection, using these or similar words:
• Whenever families get together, stories are told. Some are new, others have been told many times before, and some are embellished as time goes by. Recall one of your family stories.
• Think about what it says about what you value as a family.
• How has your listening to the family story over and over again shaped or affected your life?

Direct each group member to share his or her response to the last question without comment or question from anyone else in the group.

Tell group members to think about the effect of listening to stories has on people or communities. At the end of the sharing, invite volunteers to say what they heard about the power of hearing and listening to stories.

Open the Call to Celebrate: Eucharist Family Guide.

Ask a volunteer to read the story on p. 6.

Summarize this section by noting that the Gospel

is the family story of the Church. Listening to it week after week should shape and form us.

Break for refreshments and conversation.

What Is the Liturgy of the Word? (30 minutes)

Offer input on the importance of Liturgy of the Word, using this outline as a basis for your remarks.

- **Storytelling is important for a community.**
  - All people want to know who they are as individuals and in relationship to one another, where they came from, and what their purpose in life is. Sharing traditional stories is a community's way of trying to answer these fundamental human questions.
  - We listen to the same stories over and over again. They connect us with the past, illuminate our lives today, and offer us wisdom for the future.
- **When we share the Word of God in the Liturgy, we share Jesus.**
  - Jesus Christ is the true Word of God (*John 1:1*). All of Scripture reflects Jesus.
  - In the Liturgy of the Word, Jesus is fully present. It is one of the four ways we recognize the presence of Christ in the liturgy (The others are the presiding priest, the sacred assembly, and under the appearance of bread and wine.)
  - We are nourished by God's word just as we are nourished by Jesus in Holy Communion. Together they offer us strength, wisdom, and guidance for acting as Christ in the world.

Distribute Eucharist Parent/Adult Catechesis Handout 4:2, and invite the participants to use it as a reflection during the week.

Parent Moment (10 minutes)

Highlight the three Faith at Home features in the *Child's Book* and show how they will help the parents and family members to participate in the children's preparation.

Emphasize the importance of doing the activities on the Faith at Home page, especially the ritual action.

Closing Prayer (5 minutes)

Gather the participants in a circle around the prayer space and pray these or similiar words:

God of our history, Lord of our sacred story, we ask for your blessing as we prepare to continue our individual journeys. May we always have open ears to hear your word, open minds to receive your wisdom, and open hearts to help bring your saving love to others. Just as you have nourished us with your holy word, nourish our young ones as they prepare to receive you in the Sacrament of Eucharist. We ask this with faith and a spirit of wonder. Amen.

As always, we close by reminding ourselves of our Baptism and our common kinship in God's family. In all that we do, may we reflect the glory of the Father, the Son, and the Holy Spirit. (Sprinkle with water.) Amen.

Thank everyone for their time and participation.

 Encourage parents and family members to go to **www.harcourtreligion.com** for more ideas and suggestions.

We Listen

Objectives

- To guide families to experience a celebration of the word, including Signing before the proclamation of the Gospel
- To explore the meaning of the ritual action in family groups
- To explain that God is present in the word
- To describe the parts of the Liturgy of the Word
- To encourage families to express how they will listen to and share God's word

Materials

- Copies of the celebration for the assembly (*Sacraments Source Book* CD)
- *Songs of Celebration* CD
- Prayer table
- Bible
- Candle and matches
- Bowl filled with water
- Lectionary and/or Book of the Gospels
- Copies of the Echo Pantomime 4, p. CE10
- Pencils
- Chart or poster paper
- Markers

Welcome and Celebration (10–15 minutes)

Welcome the families in the gathering space.

Distribute copies of the celebration.

Select a family to be in the procession. Have them choose a family member to carry the Bible in procession.

- When families are assembled, walk forward slowly. Follow the child carrying the Bible.
- During the procession, lead families in singing "Open My Eyes," from the *Songs of Celebration* CD, track 10.
- Place the Bible on the prayer table and have family members return to their seats.
- Light the prayer candle.
- Begin prayer with the Sign of the Cross and invite the group to follow the order of the prayer.
- Do the signing very reverently and slowly.
- For the proclamation of the Gospel, you may use a Bible or the adapted reading in the *Child's Book* on pp. 36–37.
- Conclude with the opening song from the *Songs of Celebration* CD, track 10.

God's Word individual family unit experience (10 minutes)

Guide family members to reflect on the celebration by asking the following questions:
- What did you see? What did you hear? What did you do?

Invite family members to turn toward one another and share their responses to the questions.

Guide families to review the celebration using the activity on p. 34 of the *Child's Book*. Allow time for family members to share with one another their responses.

Ask participants to silently read the text for Signs of Faith: The Sign of the Cross.

Discuss the importance and meaning of the gesture.

The Bible whole-group learning experience (10 minutes)

Display a Bible so all can see it. Quickly review the differences between the Old and New Testaments.

Ask if any family member can tell the group what is meant by "God's word."

Affirm correct responses.

Select a family member to read aloud The Bible section on p. 35 of the *Child's Book*.

Hear God's Word family cluster sharing experience (10 minutes)

Organize the large group into small clusters and invite them to reflect on the following question:
- Why do we listen to God's word?

Allow time for family clusters to share responses.

Invite volunteers to share their group's responses with the large group.

Ask each family cluster to select a leader to read aloud the first two paragraphs on p. 36 of the *Child's Book*.

Scripture whole-group learning experience (15 minutes)

Tell the Gospel story using Echo Pantomime 3 on p. CE10 of the *Catechist Edition*.

Review the images described in the parable.

Invite the large group to reflect on the following questions:
- What lesson did Jesus teach the people in his story?
- How does your family listen to and follow God's word?

Ask for volunteers to share responses. Remind families that the word *Gospel* means "good news." We are called to listen to God's word and follow it.

The Liturgy of the Word family cluster sharing experience (10 minutes)

Present the lectionary or Book of the Gospels.

Explain that during the Liturgy of the Word at Mass, we listen to God's word.

Emphasize that the Liturgy of the Word is one of the two main parts of the Mass, and Jesus is present in God's word.

Guide each family cluster to discuss the following question:
- What happens during the Liturgy of the Word?

Ask each group leader to select a member of his or her group to read aloud p. 38 of the *Child's Book*.

Our Response whole-group learning experience (10 minutes)

Explain that during the Liturgy of the Word, we not only listen, but also respond to God's word.

Write the terms *homily, Creed,* and *General Intercessions* or *Prayers of the Faithful* on chart paper.

Invite volunteers to read the sentence from the text that describes each term.

Share God's Word individual family unit experience (5 minutes)

Invite family members to turn toward one another and talk about how they will share God's word at home.

Give children time to complete their drawing.

Ask volunteers to share their responses with the large group.

Closing Blessing (5 minutes)

Invite each family to form a family circle.

Begin with the Sign of the Cross.

Pray the prayer on p. 40 of the *Child's Book*.

Conclude by leading families in singing *Songs of Celebration* CD, track 10, "Open My Eyes."

Faith at Home individual family unit experience (5 minutes)

Direct families' attention to the Faith at Home page and encourage them to do the activities at home.

We Prepare

- Choose a gathering space that will be conducive to prayer and that will accommodate the size of the group; the church, a chapel, or a gathering place in the parish hall would each be appropriate. You will want the group to be able to see, hear, and move easily during the ritual.

- Prepare the group for the ritual action of Honoring the Cross and for the reflection on the sacred Scriptures.

- Select a good reader to proclaim the reading.

- Select four people for the entrance procession: to carry the Bible, the candle, the bowl of water, and the chrism. Show them where and how to place them in the sanctuary or on the prayer table.

- If not in a church or chapel, place chairs in semicircular rows around the prayer space. Leave enough space for people to move in and out of the rows. If possible, have tables and chairs set up in another space for adult discussion after the celebration.

Materials

- A large, clear bowl with water, or if the celebration is in the church, use the baptismal font or pool

- A large cross or crucifix; if the group is large, have several crosses or crucifixes ready for the ritual

- A large candle or the Paschal candle

- A prayer table for the candle, oil of chrism, a baptismal candle, a Bible, and a stand

- *Songs of Celebration* CD

- Copies of the celebration for the assembly (*Sacraments Source Book* CD)

Gathering Rite

Welcome the gathered assembly.

Rehearse the opening song, and go over the ritual action of Honoring the Cross.

Invite the assembly to stand for the procession.

Opening Song

"We Praise You," *Songs of Celebration* CD, track 11.

Procession

The presider and persons carrying the bowl with water, candle, and Bible process in while the assembly sings.

> **Leader:** *Let us pray.*
>   *Make the Sign of the Cross together.*

Opening Prayer

> **Leader:** *Gracious God, open our hearts to hear your word. Send us the Holy Spirit to help us do what you want. We ask this through Jesus Christ our Lord.*
> **All:** *Amen.*

Celebration of the Word

> **Reader:** *A reading from the holy Gospel according to John.*
> **All:** *Glory to you, Lord.*
>   *Read John John 13:1–16.*
> **Leader:** *The Gospel of the Lord.*
> **All:** *Praise to you, Lord Jesus Christ.*
>   *Sit silently.*

Reflection

Invite the assembly to reflect on the Gospel. Use the following question:

- If you could only use one word to title this Gospel, what would it be?

Ask the assembly to share their responses with one or two people. Be sure to include children in the sharing.

Honoring the Cross

Leader: *God gives us many gifts. He gives us sun and rain. He gives us family and friends. He gives us our life. The most important gift God gives us is his Son, Jesus. Jesus shows us how to live. When Jesus died on the cross, he gave his life for all people. Let us think about what a wonderful gift Jesus gave us.*
Sit silently.

Direct the children preparing for First Communion to come forward with a family member to honor the cross by placing their hands on it or bowing before it. Invite the family members to place their hands on the child's shoulders as he or she honors the cross. Other family members follow. Then invite the rest of the assembly forward to honor the cross.

Leader: *Lord God, send us the Holy Spirit to show us how to live our lives for others. We ask this in the name of Jesus, your Son.*
All: *Amen.*
Leader: *Let us pray as Jesus taught us.*
Pray the Lord's Prayer together.
Leader: *Let us offer each other the Sign of Peace.*

Closing Prayer

Leader: *Loving God, we thank you for all the gifts you have given us. Send us out to share our lives with others. We ask this through Jesus Christ our Lord.*
All: *Amen.*

Children go to their group session and adults go to the appointed space for reflection.

- There is a liturgical catechetical session for adults on p. 120.
- There is a parent/adult catechetical session on pp. 121–122.
- There is an intergenerational catechetical session on pp. 123–124.

We Prepare

<table>
<tr><th>Goals</th><th>Materials</th></tr>
<tr><td>
<ul>
<li>To reflect on the celebration</li>
<li>To explore the meaning of honoring the Cross</li>
<li>To explain the meaning of the Preparation of the Gifts</li>
</ul>
</td><td>
<ul>
<li>Poster board, chart paper, or overhead projector</li>
<li>Markers</li>
<li>Songs of Celebration CD</li>
<li>Bible</li>
</ul>
</td></tr>
</table>

Reflection (20 minutes)

Invite the adults to gather in groups of five or six.

Begin by recalling the ritual moments of the celebration. Lead a guided meditation using the following prompts. Pause after each prompt.
- Play a few verses of the opening song, "We Praise You," *Songs of Celebration* CD, track 11.
- Call to mind the ritual of honoring the cross.
- Ask: "What was it like for you to honor the cross?"
- Read some verses of the Gospel.
- Ask participants to recall their discussion of the Gospel.

Small Group Sharing

Pause for a few minutes of silence. Then invite the participants to share their feelings about the celebration in their small group. Encourage them to stay with their feelings. After 10 to 15 minutes, invite sharing with the large group.

Large Group Sharing

Gather the responses of the small groups on poster board, chart paper, or an overhead projector. Ask for feelings and thoughts about the celebration as a whole, and also for specific parts of the celebration that were meaningful to members of the group.

Naming (30 minutes)

Ask the participants to name what they learned from the celebration about God, Jesus, the Church, or their own Christian life.

Take each category separately and list responses on poster board, chart paper, or an overhead projector. When the lists are completed, use them to summarize the theology and meaning of the Mass as a sacrifice.

Affirm, add, or enlarge upon the following points:
- The cross is a primary Christian symbol and represents the fact that Jesus died for our sins.
- Through the cross we are offered salvation and forgiveness.
- *Sacrifice* means "to give up something out of love for someone else."
- Jesus modeled sacrifice and service in the washing of the feet.
- We prepare to participate in the sacrifice of the Eucharist by bringing gifts of bread and wine, money, and, most importantly, the gift of our lives.
- The Eucharist is a "re-presentation" of Jesus' sacrifice on the cross.
- The Preparation of the Gifts and the Altar begins the Eucharistic Prayer.

Reflection and Small Group Sharing (20 minutes)

Ask "What is one thing you will do this week to prepare your *self* to celebrate the Eucharist?"

Direct participants to reflect in silence for a few minutes and then share their responses with their group.

Closing Blessing (5 minutes)

Gather and begin with the Sign of the Cross.

Leader: God, our Father, we praise and thank you for the gift of your Son, Jesus.

All: *Amen.*

Leader: Jesus, our Savior, we praise and thank you for giving up your life for us.

All: *Amen.*

Leader: Holy Spirit, we praise and thank you for always being with us.

All: *Amen.*

We Prepare

Goals	Environment	Materials
• To welcome participants in a hospitable environment • To explain the dimensions of personal sacrifice as related to the Eucharist • To help participants come to a deeper understanding of Catholic liturgy, especially the Preparation of the Gifts	• Be sure to clearly identify the meeting place, posting clear directions if necessary. • Tables and chairs arranged for small groups • A prayer setting with large candle, Bible on a stand or table, clear bowl filled with water, a branch or other instrument for sprinkling, a cross or crucifix, and incense	• Beverages and light refreshments • Nametags • *Songs of Celebration* CD • Copies of **Call to Celebrate: Eucharist** Family Guide • Copies of **Eucharist Parent/Adult Catechesis Handouts 5:1** and **5:2** (*Sacraments Source Book* CD) • Board or chart paper

Welcome and Opening Prayer (15 minutes)

Welcome parents and other adults and distribute nametags.

Introduce yourself and briefly review the goals and agenda for the gathering.

✳ **If this session was preceded by a large group ritual and reflection, go to We Prepare. If not, continue with the prayer.**

Gather the group around the prayer setting, if possible, or have the group pause for a reflective moment.

Light the incense, and introduce the prayer with the Sign of the Cross.

Sing "We Praise You," *Songs of Celebration* CD, track 11.

Pray these or similar words:

Lord God, we continue to give you praise and thanks for all the gifts you have given us: the gift of creation, the gift of our lives and those around us. Most especially, we give you thanks for the gift of your Son, Jesus, who through the sacrifice of his life has opened up to us eternal life. Amen.

Read *John 13:1–16*, then pause for silent reflection.

Invite the assembly to reflect on the Gospel using the following question:

- What does Jesus tell us about serving others?

Ask participants to share their responses with one or two people.

Close by praying the Lord's Prayer.

We Prepare (30 minutes)

Introduce this segment by talking about the importance of preparation in daily life.

Distribute Eucharist Parent/Adult Catechesis Handout 5:1.

Allow 5 to 7 minutes for individuals to complete the handout.

Organize the large group into smaller groups of 5 to 6 people. Invite the participants to read Handout 5:1 and respond individually to the reflection. Then, have them share their responses in small groups. At the conclusion of the sharing, ask volunteers to name what they learned about preparing and planning.

Offer input on the importance of the Preparation of the Gifts. Use the outline below as a basis for your remarks:

- **We prepare for things that are important to us.**
  - Preparation implies an investment of thought and energy on the part of everybody present. At Mass, we do not merely watch as the table is set and the gifts are brought forth; we participate in these actions as a community.

- Preparing is a sign of respect. Just as you would not invite somebody to your home without tidying up or putting out refreshments, so, too, would it be inappropriate to enter into the sacred mystery of the Eucharist without preparing our hearts and minds.

- **Our gifts represent ourselves.**
  - Our offerings of money are representative of our labor, our trust in God to provide for our needs, and our recognition that everything we have is a gift from God to be used for God's glory and the service of our brothers and sisters.
  - In the prayer for the preparation of the gifts the priest says, *"Blessed are you, Lord, God of all creation. Through your goodness we have this bread to offer, which earth has given and human hands have made."* He also says, *"Through your goodness we have this wine to offer, fruit of the vine and work of human hands."* The common elements of wheat and grapes symbolize all of creation, given to us as stewards by a loving God, now changed into bread and wine through our labor and given back to God in gratitude.

Break for refreshments and conversation.

What Is Sacrifice? (30 minutes)

Begin this segment by making those points:

- At Mass, when the priest offers the bread and wine, we say: "May the Lord accept the sacrifice of your hands for the praise and glory of his name, for our good and the good of all his Church."
- The Mass re-presents the sacrifice of Jesus on the cross, but it is also our sacrifice. We bring gifts to the altar and we give money in the collection, but we also bring to the altar sacrifices of our lives.

Distribute Eucharist Parent/Adult Catechesis Handout 5:2, and invite participants to complete the activity. When participants are ready, ask them to gather in groups of 2 to 3 and share their quotes and experiences of sacrifice. At the end of the sharing, ask volunteers to share any insights about sacrifice. Write them on the board or on chart paper.

Make the following points about sacrifice and the faithful:

- As disciples, we are called to sacrifice.
- The daily sacrifices we make prepare us to participate in the Eucharist.
- They are gifts we bring and they are responses to Jesus' call, "as I have done for you, you should also do" *(John 13:15)*.

Parent Moment (10 minutes)

Highlight the three Faith at Home features in the *Child's Book* and show how they will help the parents and family members to participate in the children's preparation.

Emphasize the importance of doing the activities on the Faith at Home page, especially the ritual action.

Closing Prayer (5 minutes)

Gather the participants in a circle around the prayer space and pray these or similar words:

Good and gracious God, everything we have comes from you. You give us life, you give us dignity, and you give us people to love in our families and communities. May we be appreciative of your grace, may we be faithful in our stewardship, and may we be generous in sacrificing and sharing your abundance. Mostly we thank you for our young ones, your children and ours, who are now preparing to receive your greatest gift in the Sacrament of Eucharist. Bless them as they continue their journey toward intimate communion with you and with your people. Amen.

As always, we close by reminding ourselves of our Baptism and our common kinship in God's family. In all that we do, may we reflect the glory of the Father, the Son, and the Holy Spirit. (Sprinkle with water.) Amen.

Thank everyone for their time and participation.

 Encourage parents and family members to go to **www.harcourtreligion.com** for more ideas and suggestions.

We Prepare

Objectives

- To guide families to experience a celebration of the word, including Honoring the Cross
- To explore the meaning of the ritual action in family groups
- To help families increase their understanding of sacrifice and service
- To explain why we present gifts at Mass
- To encourage families to serve others and praise God

Materials

- Copies of the celebration for the assembly (*Sacraments Source Book* CD)
- *Songs of Celebration* CD
- Prayer table
- Bible
- Candle and matches
- Cross and crucifix
- Bowl filled with water
- Copies of Scripture Narration 5, p. CE12
- Props for dramatizing the Gospel story
- Copies of Activity Master 5, p. CE11
- Chart or poster paper
- Marker
- Pencils
- *Child's Book*

Welcome and Celebration (10–15 minutes)

Welcome the families in the gathering space.

Distribute copies of the celebration.

Prepare the families ahead of time for the ritual. Explain that they may touch the cross or bow before it at the appropriate time in the celebration.

Select a family to be in the procession. Have them choose a family member to carry the Bible and the cross in procession.
- When families are assembled, walk forward slowly. Follow the child carrying the Bible.
- During the procession, lead families in singing "We Praise You," from the *Songs of Celebration* CD, track 11.
- Place the Bible on the prayer table and have the family members return to their seats.
- Light the prayer candle.
- Begin prayer with the Sign of the Cross and invite the group to follow the order of the prayer.
- Have the families sit silently while others come forward to honor the cross. Invite family groups to come forward one family at a time.

- For the proclamation of the Gospel, you may use a Bible or the adapted reading in the *Child's Book* on pp. 46–47.
- Conclude with the opening song from the *Songs of Celebration* CD, track 11.

The Cross individual family unit experience (15 minutes)

Guide family members to reflect on the celebration using the following questions:
- What did you see? What did you hear? What did you do?

Invite family members to turn toward one another and share their responses to the questions.

Guide families to reflect on the celebration by responding to phrases in the activity on p. 44 of the *Child's Book*.

Invite volunteers to share their responses to the questions with the large group.

Summarize the Signs of Faith: The Cross text for the whole group. Use a cross and a crucifix to show the difference between them.

Sacrifice family cluster sharing experience (5 minutes)

Organize the large group into clusters of two or three families together and ask each group to select a leader. Have cluster leaders read aloud the first two paragraphs on p. 45 of the *Child's Book*.

Ask family groups to reflect on these questions:
- When have you made a sacrifice for someone else?
- Why did you make the sacrifice? How did it feel to sacrifice?

Invite groups to share stories. When they have finished sharing, summarize the last paragraph on p. 45. Use Activity Master 5 on p. CE11 of the *Catechist Edition*, or distribute copies of it to be used at home. Have family cluster leaders read aloud The Altar section on p. 45 of the *Child's Book* to their groups.

We Serve Others whole-group learning experience (15 minutes)

Invite families to look at what is happening in the illustration on p. 46 of the *Child's Book*.

Ask: What does Jesus tell us about serving others?

List the responses on chart paper.

Scripture whole-group learning experience (10 minutes)

Arrange the space for the Scripture Narration from p. CE12 of the *Catechist Edition*. Select members of several families to role-play the Scripture reading.

Invite the large group to reflect on the following question after the performance:
- What does Jesus want your family to do for others?

Direct family members to assist children in the story writing activity.

The Sacrifice of the Mass whole-group learning experience (15 minutes)

Guide families to reflect on the Sacrifice of the Mass using the following question:
- What gifts do we bring to the altar?

Write the terms *Liturgy of the Eucharist, Preparation of the Gifts*, and *sacrifice* on a sheet of poster paper. Explain the terms as you lead families through p. 48 of the *Child's Book*.

Point out that every Mass reminds us of Jesus' sacrifice.

Read aloud the Signs of Faith: Bread and Wine and discuss how bread and wine are not just food for our bodies, but food for our souls when it becomes the Body and Blood of Jesus during Mass.

Preparation of the Gifts whole-group learning experience (10 minutes)

Recall with families that members of the assembly often carry up the gifts at Saturday evening and Sunday Masses. Have families who have carried up the gifts share their experiences.

Ask a volunteer to read aloud the first two paragraphs on p. 49 of the *Child's Book*.

Discuss what the parish does with collection offerings.

Finish reading the text aloud. Invite children to repeat the Mass responses after you.

Discuss the following question to help families reflect on their part in the Preparation of the Gifts:
- What gifts do you bring to Mass?

Point out that during the Preparation of the Gifts, we offer ourselves and our gifts to help others.

I Serve Others individual family unit experience (10 minutes)

Invite family members to turn to one another and brainstorm ways that they can serve others during the week.

Ask each family to work together and complete the activity on p. 50 of the *Child's Book*.

Closing Blessing (5 minutes)

Invite each family to form a family circle.

Begin with the Sign of the Cross.

Pray the prayer on p. 50 of the *Child's Book*.

Conclude by leading families in singing from the *Songs of Celebration* CD, track 11, "We Praise You."

Faith at Home individual family unit experience (5 minutes)

Direct families' attention to the Faith at Home page and encourage them to do the activities at home.

We Remember and Give Thanks

Before the Celebration		Materials

Before the Celebration

- Choose a gathering space that will be conducive to prayer and that will accommodate the size of the group; the church, a chapel, or a gathering place in the parish hall would each be appropriate. You will want the group to be able to see, hear, and move easily during the ritual.
- Prepare the group for the ritual action of the Memorial Acclamation and for the reflection on the sacred Scriptures.
- Select a good reader to proclaim the reading.

- Select four people for the entrance procession: to carry the Bible, the candle, the bowl of water, and the chrism. Show them where and how to place them in the sanctuary or on the prayer table.
- If not in a church or chapel, place chairs in semicircular rows around the prayer space. Leave enough space for people to move in and out of the rows. If possible, have tables and chairs set up in another space for adult discussion after the celebration.

Materials

- A large, clear bowl with water, or if the celebration is in the church, use the baptismal font or pool
- A large candle or the Paschal candle
- A prayer table for the candle, oil of chrism, a baptismal candle, a Bible, and a stand
- *Songs of Celebration* CD
- Copies of the celebration for the assembly (*Sacraments Source Book* CD)

Gathering Rite

Welcome the gathered assembly.

Rehearse the opening song with gestures, and go over the ritual action of the Memorial Acclamation. Invite the assembly to stand for the procession.

Opening Song

"Te albaré, Señor," *Songs of Celebration* CD, track 12.

Procession

The presider and persons carrying the bowl with water, candle, and Bible process in while the assembly sings.

> *Leader:* Let us pray.
> *Make the Sign of the Cross together.*

Opening Prayer

> *Leader:* Loving Father, we come together in your presence to remember and give thanks for what your Son Jesus did for us. Open our hearts to the Holy Spirit that we will understand your word. We ask this through Jesus Christ, our Lord.
> *All:* Amen.

Celebration of the Word

> *Leader:* A reading from the holy Gospel according to Luke.
> *All:* Glory to you, Lord.
> *Read Luke 22:14–20.*
> *Leader:* The Gospel of the Lord.
> *All:* Praise to you, Lord Jesus Christ.
> *Sit silently.*

Reflection

Invite the assembly to reflect on the Gospel. Use the following question:

- What do you like best about the story of the Last Supper?

Ask the assembly to share their responses with one or two people. Be sure to include children in the sharing.

Memorial Acclamation

Leader: *Every time we gather together at the Eucharist, the priest prays the words Jesus said at the Last Supper. We know Jesus comes again to be with us. We are happy. We give God the Father thanks and praise for the mystery of Jesus' presence.*

Invite the assembly to kneel.

Leader: *Let us proclaim the mystery of faith:*
All: *Christ has died. Christ is risen. Christ will come again.*
Stand.
Leader: *Let us pray as Jesus taught us: Pray the Lord's Prayer together. Let us offer each other the Sign of Peace.*

Closing Prayer

Leader: *Loving God, we thank you for the gift of your Son, Jesus. We praise you for all the ways he makes himself known to us. Send us forth to bring his presence to one another. Help us to remember him. We ask this through Jesus Christ our Lord.*
All: *Amen.*

Children go to their group session and adults go to the appointed space for reflection.
- There is a liturgical catechetical session for adults on p. 127.
- There is a parent/adult catechetical session on pp. 128–129.
- There is an intergenerational catechetical session on pp. 130–131.

We Remember and Give Thanks

Goals	Materials
• To reflect on the celebration • To explore the meaning of the Mass as a memorial • To explain the meaning of the Eucharistic Prayer	• Poster board, chart paper, or overhead projector • Markers • *Songs of Celebration* CD • Bible

Reflection (20 minutes)

Invite the adults to gather in groups of five or six.

Begin by recalling the ritual moments of the celebration. Lead a guided meditation using the following prompts. Pause after each prompt.
• Play a few verses of the opening song, "Te alabaré, Señor," *Songs of Celebration* CD, track 12.
• Read some verses of the Gospel.
• Ask participants to recall their discussion of the Gospel.
• Call to mind the Memorial Acclamation and the gesture of kneeling.

Small Group Sharing

Pause for a few minutes of silence. Then invite the participants to share their feelings about the celebration in their small group. Encourage them to stay with their feelings. After 10 to 15 minutes, invite sharing with the large group.

Large Group Sharing

Gather the responses of the small groups on poster board, chart paper, or an overhead projector. Ask for feelings and thoughts about the celebration as a whole, and also for specific parts of the celebration that were meaningful to members of the group.

Naming (30 minutes)

Ask the participants to name what they learned from the celebration about God, Jesus, the bodily gesture at prayer, or their own Christian life.

Take each category separately and list responses on poster board, chart paper, or an overhead projector. When the lists are completed, use them to summarize the theology and meaning of the Mass as a memorial and the Eucharistic Prayer.

Affirm, add, or enlarge upon the following points:
• The Eucharist is the memorial of Christ's Passover, the making present of his sacrifice in the Church's liturgy.
• The Memorial Acclamation is always proclaimed after the consecration.
• The mystery of our faith is the dying and Rising of Jesus.
• The Eucharistic Prayer is the Church's great prayer of praise and thanksgiving.
• The Eucharistic Prayer begins by giving thanks and praise for the gifts of creation and goes on to give thanks and remember the gifts of Jesus and the Church.

Reflection and Small Group Sharing (20 minutes)

Ask "What is one thing you will do this week to give praise and thanks to God for the gift of your life?"

Direct participants to reflect in silence for a few minutes and then share their responses with their group.

Closing Blessing (5 minutes)

Gather and begin with the Sign of the Cross.

Leader: God, our Father, we remember and give thanks for all your good gifts.
All: Amen.

Leader: Jesus, our Savior, we remember and give thanks for your death and Resurrection.
All: Amen.

Leader: Holy Spirit, we remember and give thanks that you are with us.
All: Amen.

We Remember and Give Thanks

Goals	Environment	Materials
• To welcome participants in a hospitable environment • To communicate the concept of Eucharist as "thanksgiving" • To help participants come to a deeper understanding of Catholic liturgy, especially the Eucharistic Prayer	• Be sure to clearly identify the meeting place, posting clear directions if necessary. • Tables and chairs arranged for small groups • A prayer setting with large candle, Bible on a stand or table, clear bowl filled with water, and a branch or other instrument for sprinkling	• Beverages and light refreshments • Nametags • Copies of *Call to Celebrate: Eucharist* Family Guide • *Songs of Celebration* CD, track 12 • Copies of **Eucharist Parent/Adult Catechesis Handouts 6:1** and **6:2** (*Sacraments Source Book* CD) • Board or chart paper

Welcome and Opening Prayer (15 minutes)

Welcome parents and other adults and distribute nametags.

Introduce yourself and briefly review the goals and agenda for the gathering.

✳ **If this session was preceded by a large group ritual and reflection, go to We Remember and Give Thanks. If not, continue with the prayer.**

Gather the group around the prayer setting if possible, or have the group pause for a reflective moment.

Introduce the prayer with the Sign of the Cross.

Sing "Te albaré, Señor," *Songs of Celebration* CD, track 12.

Pray these or similar words:

Loving God, we come before you to remember and give thanks for your presence in our lives. We pray especially for... Have participants name their joys and concerns. We offer all of these to you knowing that you are the source of all that is good and life-giving. Amen.

Read *Luke 22:14–20*, then pause for silent reflection.

We Remember and Give Thanks (30 minutes)

Begin by focusing participants' attention on the theme of thanksgiving.

Write the word *Eucharist* on the board or on chart paper, and tell them that the word comes from a Greek word that means "to give thanks."

Review the two main parts of the Mass, the Liturgy of the Word and the Liturgy of the Eucharist (thanksgiving).

Distribute Eucharist Parent/Adult Catechesis Handout 6:1, and invite all to read the directions and complete their lists.

Ask participants to gather in groups of 2 to 3 and share their lists.

Offer input on the Eucharistic Prayer, using this outline as a basis for your remarks:

• **All that we have is a gift from God.**
  • We human beings like to take pride in our accomplishments, but the reality is that all that we accomplish is a gift from God, because God gave us our talents and resources, as well as the opportunities to use them.
  • Our gifts and resources are intended to be used for God's glory and for the service of our brothers and sisters in need. The only thing that we should take any pride in is how we use the talents and materials that God has given us in stewardship.

- **In the Eucharist, we give back to God what God has given to us.**
  - The word *Eucharist* means "thanksgiving." In the Eucharistic celebration, we offer thanks to God for all he has given us.
  - We use simple gifts made from the elements of the earth and formed into something worthy by the work of our hands. Thus, the bread and wine symbolize the integrity of our labor and the dignity of our lives.
  - Through God's grace, those same gifts are transformed into the Body and Blood of Christ, which we will take in as a source of nourishment, an act of intimacy with God, and a gesture of solidarity with one another.

Break for refreshments and conversation.

What Is a Memorial? (30 minutes)

Recall the words that have been used for the Eucharist so far (thanksgiving, sacrifice).

Write the word *memorial* on the board or chart paper, and state that the Eucharist is also a memorial.

Distribute Eucharist Parent/Adult Catechesis Handout 6:2.

Offer input on the Memorial Acclamation, using the handout and this outline as a basis for your remarks:

- To remember is to "re-member," to make the past present again. It is not just recalling. The biblical concept of remembering is that we honor those who have gone before in our remembrance of them.
- In Eucharist, we recall Jesus' Last Supper and his death and Resurrection, which we proclaim as the central mystery of the Christian faith.
- We also pray for, and enter into solidarity with, our brothers and sisters the world over, as well as all believers who ever lived. We do this by participating in the timeless celebration of the Eucharist.

- The Memorial Acclamation is often called the *anamnesis*.
- Note the similarities as well as the subtle differences in the four options for the Memorial Acclamation.

Invite all to participate in the following discussion in small groups of 2 to 3:

- Ask participants to think about the different parts of the Eucharistic Prayer, and to identify what section or phrase stands out for them.
- Ask: What is it about their chosen phrase that makes it memorable?
- Invite volunteers to share their responses.

Parent Moment (10 minutes)

Highlight the three Faith at Home features in the *Child's Book* and show how they will help the parents and family members to participate in the children's preparation.

Emphasize the importance of doing the activities on the Faith at Home page, especially the ritual action.

Closing Prayer (5 minutes)

Gather the participants in a circle around the prayer space and pray these or similar words:

Lord of our longing, you give us every good gift. Your Spirit sustains us in every breath we take and in every beat of our hearts. May we never take you for granted, but rather may we be a people marked by profound gratitude. Amen.

As always, we close by reminding ourselves of our Baptism and our common kinship in God's family. In all that we do, may we reflect the glory of the Father, the Son, and the Holy Spirit. (Sprinkle with water.) Amen.

Thank everyone for their time and participation.

We Remember and Give Thanks

Objectives

- To guide families to experience a celebration of the word, including the gesture of kneeling and the Memorial Acclamation
- To explore the meaning of the ritual action in family groups
- To explain the significance of the Last Supper
- To describe the Consecration, Memorial Acclamation, and Great Amen
- To help families remember and give thanks for gifts from God

Materials

- Copies of the celebration for the assembly (*Sacraments Source Book* CD)
- *Songs of Celebration* CD
- Prayer table
- Bible
- Candle and matches
- Bowl filled with water
- Copies of Scripture Drama 6 pp. CE14–15
- Copies of Activity Master 6 p. CE13
- Props for dramatizing the Gospel story
- Chart or poster paper
- Markers
- Pencils
- *Child's Book*

Welcome and Celebration (10–15 minutes)

Welcome the families in the gathering space.

Distribute copies of the celebration.

Select a family to be in the procession. Have them choose a family member to carry the Bible in procession.

- When families are assembled, walk forward slowly. Follow the child carrying the Bible.
- During the procession, lead families in singing "Te alabaré, Señor," from the *Songs of Celebration* CD, track 12.
- Place the Bible on the prayer table and have the family members return to their seats.
- Light the prayer candle.
- Begin the prayer with the Sign of the Cross and invite the group to follow the order of the prayer. Be sure there is appropriate space to kneel.
- For the proclamation of the Gospel, you may use a Bible or the adapted reading in the *Child's Book* on pp. 56–57.
- Conclude with the opening song from the *Songs of Celebration* CD, track 12.

We Remember individual family unit experience (10 minutes)

Guide family members to reflect on the celebration by asking the following questions:
- What did you see? What did you hear? What did you do?

Ask volunteers to share their responses.

Guide families to think about the meaning of the ritual action of kneeling and the words of the Memorial Acclamation using the activity on p. 54 of the *Child's Book*.

Allow time for family members to read the section together and discuss responses.

Read aloud and discuss the text Signs of Faith: Kneeling.

The Eucharistic Prayer whole-group learning experience (10 minutes)

Select three different family members to each read aloud a paragraph from p. 55 of the *Child's Book*.
- Emphasize that the Eucharistic Prayer tells the story of God's love for humans and that it is a prayer of thanksgiving.

- Encourage families to listen carefully to the words of the Eucharistic Prayer as the priest prays it during the Mass next Sunday.
- Explain that through the power of the Holy Spirit and the words and actions of the priest, the bread and wine become the Body and Blood of Jesus.

Summarize the Signs of Faith: The Priest text.

Jesus Gives Thanks family cluster sharing experience (10 minutes)

Organize the large group into small clusters and invite them to reflect on the following question:
- What happens when families share a meal together?
- Invite volunteers to share their groups' responses with the large group.
- Call attention to the illustration on p. 56 of the *Child's Book*. Explain that Jesus is sharing a meal with his friends.
- Have each family cluster select a leader to read aloud p. 56 of the *Child's Book*.

Scripture whole-group learning experience (15 minutes)

Arrange the space for the Scripture dramatization from pp. CE14–15 of the *Catechist Edition*. Select members of several families to role-play the Scripture reading.

Dramatize the reading. Following the presentation, invite the large group to reflect on the following questions:
- What did Jesus and his disciple remember at the Passover?
- How does your family remember Jesus?

Ask for volunteers to share their responses.

We Remember and Give Thanks family cluster sharing experience (15 minutes)

Guide each group to discuss the following question:
- What do we remember and give thanks for during the Eucharistic Prayer?
- Ask volunteers to share responses and list them on a sheet of chart paper.
- Invite a volunteer to read aloud the first paragraph from p. 58 in the *Child's Book*.

- Recall that when Catholics come together as a community to worship, we want to praise and thank God.
- Summarize the second paragraph, and emphasize the role of the priest as the leader of the Eucharistic prayer, and of all the things we thank God for.
- Brainstorm with families what they are thankful for. Write down their responses on poster paper.
- You may wish to distribute copies of Activity Master 6 on p. CE13 of the *Catechist Edition* for use here or at home.

Ask a family member to read aloud the Signs of Faith Blessed Sacrament text.

Check to be sure families know where the tabernacle is in your parish church.

The Consecration and the Great Amen whole-group learning experience (10 minutes)

Read the section aloud and discuss the significance of the Consecration and the Great Amen.

Discuss how the Eucharist is like the Last Supper.

Say Yes individual family unit experience (10 minutes)

Invite family members to turn to one another and share ways that they can give thanks to God.
- Have family members assist children in completing the activity.
- Select volunteers to come forward and write on the chart paper ways families can give God thanks and praise.

Closing Blessing (5 minutes)

Invite each family to form a family circle.

Begin with the Sign of the Cross.

Pray the prayer on p. 60 of the *Child's Book*.

Conclude by leading families in singing *Songs of Celebration* CD, track 12, "Te albaré, Señor."

Faith at Home individual family unit experience (5 minutes)

Direct families' attention to the Faith at Home page and encourage them to do the activities at home.

We Share a Meal

Before the Celebration		Materials
• This celebration involves sharing food. Choose a gathering space that will be conducive to both a meal and a celebration; the church hall or a gathering place in the parish hall would each be appropriate. You will want the group to be able to see, hear, and move easily during the ritual. • You will need to decide ahead of time what kind of food or meal you want to use in this celebration. It could be something as simple as bread and grape juice or as complex as a "potluck" dinner. • Prepare the group for the ritual action of Sharing a Meal and for the reflection on the sacred Scriptures.	• Select a good reader to proclaim the reading. • Select four people to carry: the Bible, the candle, the bowl of water, and the chrism. Show them where and how to place them in the scantuary or on the prayer table. • Set up a large table of refreshments in center of meeting space. • If not in a church or chapel, place chairs around the table. If there is not enough room for all to sit at one table, arrange room so that food and conversation can be shared in smaller groups. If possible, have tables and chairs set up in another space for adult discussion after the celebration.	• A large, clear bowl with water, a large candle or the Paschal Candle. • A prayer table for the candle, oil of chrism, a baptismal candle, a Bible, and a stand • *Songs of Celebration* CD • Copies of the celebration for the assembly (*Sacraments Source Book* CD)

Gathering Rite

Welcome the gathered assembly.

Rehearse the opening song and go over the ritual action of Sharing the Meal.

Invite the assembly to stand for the procession.

Opening Song

"We Come to the Table," *Songs of Celebration* CD, track 13.

Procession

The presider and persons carrying the bowl with water, candle, and Bible process in while the assembly sings.

Leader: Let us pray.
Make the Sign of the Cross together.

Opening Prayer

Leader: *Loving God, you provide us with everything we need. We are your children. Through your Son, Jesus, we are united with you and one another as one family. Through the power of the Holy Spirit, strengthen us to bring life to others. We ask this through Jesus Christ our Lord.*

All: *Amen.*

Celebration of the Word

Leader: *A reading from the holy Gospel according to John.*
All: *Glory to you, Lord.*
Read John 30:35–58.
Leader: *The Gospel of the Lord.*
All: *Praise to you, Lord Jesus Christ.*
Sit silently.

Reflection

Invite the assembly to reflect on the Gospel. Use the following question:

• What does the image of the Bread of Life suggest to you about your relationship with Jesus?

Ask the assembly to share their responses with one or two people. Be sure to include children in the sharing.

Sharing a Meal

Be seated around the table.

Leader: *Blessed are you, almighty Father,*
who give us our daily bread.
Blessed is your only begotten Son,
who continually feeds us with the word
of life.
Blessed is the Holy Spirit,
who brings us together at this table
of love.
Blessed be God now and forever.

All: *Amen.*

Book of Blessings, 1069

Share the food and conversation at the table.

Leader: *We give you thanks for all your gifts,*
almighty God, living and reigning now
and forever.

All: *Amen.*

Book of Blessings, 1070

Leader: *Let us offer each other the Sign of Peace.*

Closing Prayer

Leader: *Loving God, we thank you for all the*
gifts of life that you have given us—for
food, for families, for friends, and for the
gift of your Son, Jesus. Help us to share
these gifts of life with others. We ask this
in the name of your Son, Jesus.

All: *Amen.*

Children go to their group session and adults go to the appointed space for reflection.

• There is a liturgical catechetical session for adults on p. 134.
• There is a parent/adult catechetical session on pp. 135–136.
• There is an intergenerational catechetical session on pp. 137–138.

We Share a Meal

Goals	Materials
• To reflect on the celebration • To explore the meaning of the Mass as a meal • To explore the Communion Rite	• Poster board, chart paper, or overhead projector • *Songs of Celebration* CD • Markers • Bible

Reflection (20 minutes)

Invite the adults to gather in groups of five or six.

Begin by recalling the ritual moments of the celebration. Lead a guided meditation using the following prompts. Pause after each prompt.
• Play a few verses of the opening song, "We Come to the Table," *Songs of Celebration* CD, track 13.
• Read some verses of the Gospel.
• Ask participants to recall their discussion of the Gospel.
• Call to mind the ritual of Sharing a Meal.

Small Group Sharing

Pause for a few minutes of silence. Then invite the participants to share their feelings about the celebration in their small group. Encourage them to stay with their feelings. After 10 to 15 minutes, invite sharing with the large group.

Large Group Sharing

Gather the responses of the small groups on poster board, chart paper, or an overhead projector. Ask for feelings and thoughts about the celebration as a whole, and also for specific parts of the celebration that were meaningful to members of the group.

Naming (30 minutes)

Ask the participants to name what they learned from the celebration about God, Jesus, the Church, Scripture, or their own Christian life.

Take each category separately and list responses on poster board, chart paper, or an overhead projector. When the lists are completed, use them to summarize the theology and meaning of the Mass as a meal and the Eucharistic Prayer.

Affirm, add, or enlarge upon the following points:
• The Eucharist is the Church's special meal.
• Jesus is the Bread of Life.
• Jesus is truly present in consecrated Bread and Wine.
• Communion gives us an intimate union with Christ. It nourishes us.
• Communion also strengthens our charity, makes us Church, and commits us to the poor.
• We must fast from solid and liquid food, with the exception of water and medicine, for one hour before receiving Communion.

Reflection and Small Group Sharing (20 minutes)

Ask "What is one thing you will do this week to prepare to participate in the Eucharistic banquet?"

Direct participants to reflect in silence for a few minutes and then share their responses with their group.

Closing Blessing (5 minutes)

Gather and begin with the Sign of the Cross.
Leader: God, our Father, we praise and thank you for the gift of life.
All: Amen.
Leader: Jesus, our Savior, we praise and thank you for giving yourself to us in Holy Communion.
All: Amen.
Leader: Holy Spirit, giver of God's gifts, we praise and thank you for helping us live as members of the Body of Christ.
All: Amen.

We Share a Meal

Note: Due to the different nature of this session, which includes eating together, you will need to plan ahead. You may wish to have potluck or other type of meal. The sharing of a meal during the opening prayer or the large group ritual will take more time than the opening prayer in the previous sessions.

Goals	Environment	Materials
• To welcome participants in a hospitable environment • To communicate the concept of Eucharist as a common meal and an experience of deeper investment in the Body of Christ • To help participants come to a deeper understanding of Catholic liturgy, especially the meaning of the reception of Holy Communion	• Be sure to clearly identify the meeting place, posting clear directions if necessary. • Tables and chairs arranged for small groups • A prayer setting with large candle, Bible on a stand or table, clear bowl filled with water, and a branch or other instrument for sprinkling	• A large table of refreshments in the center of the meeting space • Nametags • Copies of *Call to Celebrate: Eucharist* Family Guide • *Eucharist Stories of Celebration* video and guide • *Songs of Celebration* CD • Copies of **Eucharist Parent/Adult Catechesis Handouts 7:1** and **7:2** (*Sacraments Source Book* CD) • Board or chart paper

Welcome and Opening Prayer (15 minutes)

Welcome parents and other adults and distribute nametags.

Introduce yourself and briefly review the goals and agenda for the gathering.

✳ **If this session was preceded by a large group ritual and reflection, go to We Share a Meal. If not, continue with the prayer.**

Gather the group around the prayer setting, if possible, or have the group pause for a reflective moment.

Introduce the prayer with the Sign of the Cross.

Sing "Come to the Table," *Songs of Celebration,* track 13.

Distribute Eucharist Parent/Adult Catechesis Handout 7:1, and follow the order of prayer. At the conclusion of the prayer, have participants move to a place where they can comfortably view the video.

We Share a Meal (30 minutes)

Show Part 3 of the *Eucharist Stories of Celebration* video.

Use the outline and questions in the video guide for this segment of the session.

Pause for a short break.

What Is Holy Communion? (30 minutes)

Introduce the story on p. 8 of the *Family Guide* by saying these or similar words:
• In most times and places throughout the history of the world, sharing a meal has been considered an act of hospitality, friendship, and peace.

Invite a participant to read the story aloud.

Have participants share their responses to the question on p. 8 in pairs.

Distribute Eucharist Parent/Adult Catechesis Handout 7:2, and invite the participants to review it during the week.

Parent Moment (10 minutes)

Highlight the three Faith at Home features in the *Child's Book* and show how they will help the parents and family members to participate in the children's preparation.

Emphasize the importance of doing the activities on the Faith at Home page, especially the ritual action.

Closing Prayer (5 minutes)

Gather the participants in a circle around the prayer space and pray these or similar words:

Jesus, our Lord, you love us so much that you become our nourishment in the Sacrament of Eucharist. Help us to become nourishment for one another through acts of service and lives of virtue, as we strive to be worthy of the graces we receive in our reception of your Body and Blood. Amen.

As always, we close by reminding ourselves of our Baptism and our common kinship in God's family. In all that we do, may we reflect the glory of the Father, the Son, and the Holy Spirit. (Sprinkle with water.) Amen.

Thank everyone for their time and participation.

We Share a Meal

Objectives

- To guide families to experience a celebration of the word, including the Sharing of a Meal and the Sign of Peace

- To explore the meaning of the ritual action in family groups

- To explain the connection between the Eucharist and eternal life

- To describe what happens at the Communion Rite

- To help families reflect on the meaning of Holy Communion

Materials

- Copies of the celebration for the assembly (*Sacraments Source Book* CD)
- *Songs of Celebration* CD
- Prayer table
- Bible
- Candle and matches
- Bowl filled with water
- A large table for refreshments in center of meeting space
- Simple, healthy refreshments (bread, grape juice, fruit)

- Copies of Scripture Narration, pp. CE18–19
- Copies of Activity Master 7, p. CE17
- Blank sheets of white paper
- Pencils
- Chart or poster paper
- Markers
- *Child's Book*

Welcome and Celebration (10–15 minutes)

Welcome the families in the gathering space.

Distribute copies of the celebration.

Select a family to be in the procession. Have them choose a family member to carry the Bible in procession.
- When families are assembled, walk forward slowly. Follow the child carrying the Bible.
- During the procession, lead families in singing "We Come to the Table," *Songs of Celebration* CD track 13.
- Place the Bible on the prayer table and have family members return to their seats.
- Light the prayer candle.
- Begin prayer with the Sign of the Cross and invite the group to follow the order of the prayer.
- Direct families to gather around the large table for the ritual of Sharing a Meal.
- Pray the Blessing Prayer.
- Share the meal.
- At the end of the meal, invite families to exchange the Sign of Peace.

- If the group is too large to gather around the prayer table for the ritual action, have the families stand in place and then invite them to come to the water, one family at a time to make the Sign of the Cross with the water.
- For the proclamation of the Gospel, you may use a Bible or the adapted reading in the *Child's Book* on pp. 66–67.
- Conclude with the opening song from *Songs of Celebration* CD, track 13.

Special Meals individual family unit experience (5 minutes)

Guide families to reflect on the celebration by asking the following question:
- What did you see? What did you hear? What did you do?

Ask volunteers to share their responses.

Guide families to think about sharing a meal by using the activity on p. 64 of the *Child's Book*.

Direct families to read the text Signs of Faith: Sign of Peace.

The Eucharist as a Meal *whole-group learning experience* (10 minutes)

Read aloud the first paragraph on p. 65 of the *Child's Book*.
- Ask families to think about what special meals they share.
- Invite volunteers to tell why the meal they chose is special.

Invite families to reflect on the following question:
- Why is the Eucharist a special meal?

Ask for volunteers to share their responses.
- Select a family member to read aloud the next two paragraphs.

Discuss the picture for the Signs of Faith: Paten, Ciborium, and Chalice. If possible have these vessels available for participants to see.

We Share the Bread of Life *family cluster sharing experience* (10 minutes)

Organize the large group into small clusters. Have each family cluster select a leader. Provide a sheet of blank paper for each group.
- Direct each family cluster to think about the different meals Jesus shared with others and to summarize one story on the paper provided.
- Invite group leaders to share stories with the large group.
- Point out that Jesus will feed us, just as he fed others.

Scripture *whole-group learning experience* (15 minutes)

Select members of several families to narrate the Gospel story. Use the text on pp. CE18–19 of the *Catechist Edition*.

Invite the large group to reflect on the following questions:
- What is Jesus telling the people about himself?
- What do you think Jesus means when he says he is the Bread of Life?
- How can your family share in Jesus' life?

Have family members assist children with the activity.

Ask for volunteers to share their responses and pictures.

The Communion Rite *family cluster sharing experience* (15 minutes)

Invite family clusters to reflect on what happens during the Communion Rite.
- You may wish to use Activity Master 7 on p. CE17 of the *Catechist Edition* to guide the reflection.
- Direct group leaders to read p. 68 of the *Child's Book* aloud to their group. Give each family cluster the task of listing on a sheet of paper what happens when we receive Holy Communion.
- Invite group leaders to share their groups' responses with the large group.

Summarize the text Signs of Faith: Lamb of God.

Holy Communion *whole-group learning experience* (10 minutes)

Write the terms *Host, deacon,* and *extraordinary minister* on poster paper. Define these terms as you discuss the information on p. 69 of the *Child's Book*.
- Invite group leaders to share their groups' responses with the large group.

Read aloud from the text.

Ask for volunteers to come forward and demonstrate the correct way to receive Holy Communion.

Discuss the question:
- Why are we happy to share in the Lord's Supper?

Receive Jesus *individual family unit experience* (10 minutes)

Invite children preparing to receive Jesus for the first time in Holy Communion to share their thoughts and feelings with family members.
- Allow time for children to complete the activity on p. 70 of the *Child's Book*.

Closing Blessing (5 minutes)

Invite each family to form a family circle.

Begin with the Sign of the Cross.

Pray the prayer on p. 70 of the *Child's Book*.

Conclude by leading families in singing, *Songs of Celebration* CD, track 13, "We Come to the Table."

Faith at Home *individual family unit experience* (10 minutes)

Direct families' attention to the Faith at Home page and encourage them to do the activities at home.

We Go Forth

Eucharist Session 8–Whole Community Ritual

Before the Celebration

- Choose a gathering space that will be conducive to prayer and that will accommodate the size of the group; the church, a chapel, or a gathering place in the parish hall would each be appropriate. You will want the group to be able to see, hear, and move easily during the ritual.

- Prepare the group for the ritual action of Blessing for Mission and for the reflection on the sacred Scriptures.

- Select a good reader to proclaim the reading.

- Select four people for the entrance procession: to carry the Bible, the candle, the bowl of water, and the chrism. Show them where and how to place them in the sanctuary or on the prayer table.

- If not in a church or chapel, place chairs in semicircular rows around the prayer space. Leave enough space for people to move in and out of the rows. If possible, have tables and chairs set up in another space for adult discussion after the celebration.

Materials

- A large, clear bowl with water, or if the celebration is in the church, use the baptismal font or pool
- A large candle or the Paschal candle
- A prayer table for the candle, oil of chrism, a baptismal candle, a Bible, and a stand
- *Songs of Celebration* CD
- Copies of the celebration for the assembly (*Sacraments Source Book* CD)

Gathering Rite

Welcome the gathered assembly.

Rehearse the opening song, and go over the ritual action of Blessing for Mission.

Opening Song

"Lead Us to the Water," *Songs of Celebration* CD, track 14.

Procession

The presider and persons carrying the bowl with water, candle, and Bible process in while the assembly sings.

Leader: Let us pray.
> Make the Sign of the Cross together.

Opening Prayer

Leader: Loving God, open our hearts to the Holy Spirit as we listen to your word. We ask this through Jesus Christ our Lord.
All: Amen.

Celebration of the Word

Leader: A reading from the Acts of the Apostles. Read Acts 2:1–13.
The Gospel of the Lord.
All: Thanks be to God.
Sit silently.

Reflection

Invite the assembly to reflect on the reading. Use the following question:
- What is the most surprising part of the Pentecost story for you?

Ask the assembly to share their responses with one or two people. Be sure to include children in the sharing.

Closing Prayer

Blessing for Mission

Ask the children who have been part of the preparation process to come forward with their families and gather around the baptismal font or the bowl with water. Ask the rest of the assembly to gather behind them. Invite everyone to extend their hands in blessing with you over the First Communicants.

Leader: *Just as the disciples were filled with the Holy Spirit and went out to tell the good news in word and action, so are you. Bow your heads and ask for God's blessing. Jesus went about the earth doing good. He left us his example to follow. May his love be the guide for all you do.*

All: *Amen.*

Leader: *Jesus came to serve others. May he lead you to serve your brothers and sisters in their need.*

All: *Amen.*

Leader: *Through his death and Resurrection, Jesus brought new life to the world. May he strengthen you to spread the Good News to all those you meet.*

All: *Amen.*

Adapted from the *Book of Blessings*, 585

Direct everyone to come forward and make the Sign of the Cross with the water.

Leader: *Go forth now to love and serve the Lord.*
All: *Thanks be to God.*

Children go to their group session and adults go to the appointed space for reflection.

- There is a liturgical catechetical session for adults on p. 141.
- There is a parent/adult catechetical session on pp. 142–143.
- There is an intergenerational catechetical session on pp. 144–145.

We Go Forth

Goals	Materials
• To reflect on the celebration • To explore the meaning of blessing and mission • To present the meaning of the Closing Rites of the Eucharist	• Poster board, chart paper, or overhead projector • Markers • *Songs of Celebration* CD • Bible

Reflection (20 minutes)

Invite the adults to gather in groups of five or six.

Begin by recalling the ritual moments of the celebration. Lead a guided meditation using the following prompts. Pause after each prompt.
• Play a few verses of the opening song, "Lead Us to the Water," *Songs of Celebration* CD, track 14.
• Read some verses of the Gospel.
• Ask participants to recall their discussion of the Gospel.
• Recall the assembly extending their hands in blessing and then coming to the water.

Small Group Sharing

Pause for a few minutes of silence. Then invite the participants to share their feelings about the celebration in their small group. Encourage them to stay with their feelings. After 10 to 15 minutes, invite sharing with the large group.

Large Group Sharing

Gather the responses of the small groups on poster board, chart paper, or an overhead projector. Ask for feelings and thoughts about the celebration as a whole, and also for specific parts of the celebration that were meaningful to members of the group.

Naming (30 minutes)

Ask the participants to name what they learned from the celebration about God, Jesus, the Church, or their own Christian life.

Take each category separately and list responses on poster board, chart paper, or an overhead projector. When the lists are completed, use them to summarize the theology and meaning of the blessing and mission.

Affirm, add, or enlarge upon the following points:
• Blessings are actions that use words and actions to ask God to show kindness to us.
• There are many kinds of blessings.
• We can bless one another.
• The word *Mass* comes from a Latin word that means "to be sent."
• Participating in the Eucharist changes us.
• We are sent forth from the Eucharist with a mission to do God's work.
• The Holy Spirit helps us live out our mission.
• Our mission includes witnessing to Jesus' presence in word and action.

Reflection and Small Group Sharing (20 minutes)

Ask "What is one thing you will do this week to give praise and thanks to God ?"

Direct participants to reflect in silence for a few minutes and then share their responses with their group.

Closing Blessing (5 minutes)

Gather and begin with the Sign of the Cross.

> *Leader: God, our Father, sends us forth to tell the world about your love.*
> *All:* Amen.
>
> *Leader: Jesus, our Savior, send us forth to serve others.*
> *All:* Amen.
>
> *Leader: Holy Spirit, guide us to see opportunities where we can witness and be of service.*
> *All:* Amen.

Eucharist Session 8–Parent/Adult Catechesis

We Go Forth

Goals	Environment	Materials
• To welcome participants in a hospitable environment • To communicate the concept of being sent on a mission • To help participants come to a deeper understanding of the Eucharist as a transforming power for mission	• Be sure to clearly identify the meeting place, posting clear directions if necessary. • Tables and chairs arranged for small groups • A prayer setting with large candle, Bible on a stand or table, clear bowl filled with water, and a branch or other instrument for sprinkling	• Beverages and light refreshments • Nametags • *Songs of Celebration* CD • Copies of **Eucharist Parent/Adult Catechesis Handouts 8:1** and **8:2** (*Sacraments Source Book* CD) • Board or chart paper

Welcome and Opening Prayer (15 minutes)

Welcome parents and other adults and distribute nametags.

Introduce yourself and briefly review the goals and agenda for the gathering.

✳ **If this session was preceded by a large group ritual and reflection, go to We Go Forth. If not, continue with the prayer.**

Gather the group around the prayer setting if possible, or have the group pause for a reflective moment.

Introduce the prayer with the Sign of the Cross.

Sing "Lead Us to the Water," *Songs of Celebration* CD, track 14.

Read *Acts 2:1–41*, then pause for silent reflection.

Lord God, continue to shower your Holy Spirit on us that we may proclaim your greatness and goodness to the whole world. We ask this in Jesus' name. Amen.

Distribute Eucharist Parent/Adult Catechesis Handout 8:1, and invite all to read the directions and complete their lists.

We Go Forth (30 minutes)

Begin the session in the large group. Review the Pentecost story, and make a comparison to the story of the Apostles in the Upper Room after Easter (*John 20*).

Ask: What were some of the changes for the Apostles?

Invite participants to think about an event in their lives that changed them and moved them from inaction to action. Allow time for them to reflect silently about what happened and how their behavior was different after the event. Then have them gather in groups of 3 to 4 and share their stories. Ask them to listen without comment to each person's story.

Ask volunteers to share what they heard as causes for people to change. Jot the causes down on the board or on chart paper.

Ask participants to gather in groups of 2 to 3 people to share their lists.

Summarize the sharing, and note there are many different reasons that move people to change.

Write the phrase, *Eucharist is a Sacrament of Conversion*, on the board or on chart paper, and make the following points:

- We are changed by participating in the Eucharist.
- What food does for the life of our body, Communion accomplishes in our spiritual life.
- It unites us more closely with Christ.
- It strengthens our charity.
- It commits us to the poor.
- The words *source* and *summit*, when used in reference to the Eucharist, give a sense of moving out.
- The Eucharist is not so much a "Jesus and me" experience as it is an experience of "Jesus in me and us for the sake of the life of the world."
- We are sent forth to bring life to the world; to move from inaction to action.

Break for refreshments and conversation.

What Is Mission? (30 minutes)

Gather the large group.

- Distribute **Eucharist Parent/Adult Catechesis Handout 8:2.**
- Allow time for participants to read the quote from the *Constitution on the Sacred Liturgy*.
- Organize the large group into smaller groups of 5 to 6, and instruct each group to choose one of the points and discuss the question.
- At the end the discussion, ask volunteers to share responses to each point.

Parent Moment (10 minutes)

Highlight the three Faith at Home features in the *Child's Book* and show how they will help the parents and family members to participate in the children's preparation.

Emphasize the importance of doing the activities on the Faith at Home page, especially the ritual action.

Closing Prayer (5 minutes)

Gather the participants in a circle around the prayer space and pray these or similar words:

Jesus, our Lord, you send us forth to be your hands and feet. Give us a double portion of your Spirit so that we may ignite faith in others and that through our witness others may come to know you. Amen.

As always, we close by reminding ourselves of our Baptism and our common kinship in God's family. In all that we do, may we reflect the glory of the Father, the Son, and the Holy Spirit. (Sprinkle with water.) Amen.

Thank everyone for their time and participation.

We Go Forth

Objectives

- To guide families to experience a celebration of the word, including a Blessing for Mission
- To explore the meaning of the ritual action in family groups
- To help families understand that we are sent forth from Mass to carry God's love to others
- To explain that the Holy Spirit is active in our lives today
- To explain why we are sent forth from Mass
- To reinforce the concept of service

Materials

- Copies of the celebration for the assembly (*Sacraments Source Book* CD)
- *Songs of Celebration* CD
- Prayer table
- Bible
- Candle and matches
- Bowl filled with water
- Copies of Scripture Drama 8, pp. CE21–22
- Copies of Activity Master 8, p. CE20
- Chart or poster paper
- Markers
- Blank sheets of white paper
- Pencils
- *Child's Book*

Welcome and Celebration (10–15 minutes)

Welcome the families in the gathering space.

Distribute copies of the celebration.

Select a family to be in the procession. Have them choose a family member to carry the Bible in procession.

- When families are assembled, walk forward slowly. Follow the child carrying the Bible in procession.
- During the procession, lead families in singing "Lead Us to the Water," *Songs of Celebration* CD, track 14.
- Place the Bible on the prayer table and have family members return to their seats.
- Light the prayer candle.
- Begin prayer with the Sign of the Cross and invite the group to follow the order of the prayer.
- Have the group come forward for the Blessing for a Mission.
- Raise your right hand as you pray the blessing.
- Invite families to come forward and make the Sign of the Cross with the water.
- When all have made the Sign of the Cross, lead the closing prayer.

- For the proclamation of the Gospel, you may use a Bible or the adapted reading in the *Child's Book* on pp. 76–77.
- Conclude with the opening song from the *Songs of Celebration* CD, track 14.

Being Blessed individual family unit experience (10 minutes)

Guide family members to reflect on the celebration by asking the following questions:
- What did you see? What did you hear? What did you do?

Ask volunteers to share their responses.

Guide families to reflect further on the Blessing for a Mission, using the activity on p. 74 of the *Child's Book*. Allow time for family members to share their responses to the activity.

Invite a family member to read aloud the text Signs of Faith: Blessing. Remind the family members that there are Blessings that they can use at home in the *Family Guide* pp. 12–13.

Sent on a Mission family cluster sharing experience (15 minutes)

Arrange the large group into small clusters and invite them to explore being sent from Mass to carry God's love to others, using p. 75 of the *Child's Book*.
- Be sure each group selects a leader for this section.
- Provide a sheet of poster paper and a marker for each group.

- Direct the group leader to read aloud to his or her group from p. 75 of the *Child's Book.*
- Invite groups to write ideas about how they can carry God's love to others on the poster paper provided.
- Ask volunteers to share their group's responses.

Summarize the Signs of Faith: Witness.

The Holy Spirit whole-group learning experience (10 minutes)

Invite families to reflect on the following question:
- What happens when we receive the Holy Spirit?
- List the responses on poster paper in front of the large group.
- Remind families that they pray to the Holy Spirit whenever they pray the Sign of the Cross.
- Recall that the Holy Spirit comes to us in a special way in the Sacraments of Initiation.
- Summarize the first paragraph on p. 76 of the *Child's Book.* Emphasize that the Holy Spirit guides us in our mission to teach about God.

Scripture whole-group learning experience (15 minutes)

Select members of several families to narrate the Scripture story, using the text on pp. CE21–22 of the *Catechist Edition.*

Invite the large group to reflect on the following questions:
- What did the Holy Spirit do for the disciples?
- How does the Holy Spirit help you?

Allow time for volunteers to share their responses to the questions.

We Are Sent family cluster learning experience (15 minutes)

Organize the large group into the same small family clusters as earlier. Direct each group to reflect on the following question:
- What are some ways that we can love and serve Jesus?
- Have the group leader write all responses on the reverse side of the same poster paper used earlier.
- Following the activity, select a group leader to read aloud the bulleted text on p. 78 of the *Child's Book.*
- Recall that Jesus sent his followers out on a mission. Tell families that we are also sent on a mission.

Summarize the text Signs of Faith: Deacon. You may want to distribute copies of Activity Master 8 on p. CE20 of the *Catechist Edition* for reinforcement.

Go Forth individual family unit experience (10 minutes)

Remind families that during the Mass we hear God's message in the Liturgy of the Word and receive Holy Communion during the Liturgy of the Eucharist.

Summarize the first paragraph on p. 79 of the *Child's Book.*

Direct each family to:
- Read the next two paragraphs together.
- Discuss responses to the question on the bottom of the page.
- Decide on one way your family helps others.

Invite each family to stand and share with the large group one way they help others.

Sent to Serve individual family unit experience (5 minutes)

Provide each family with a blank sheet of white paper and pencils. Direct them to:
- Divide the paper into two columns.
- In the first column, list ways that members of your family show love and care for each other.
- In the second column, write down ways the family might continue to show love and care.
- Encourage families to display the activity in their homes as a reminder.

Thank families for their participation, and remind them that when Mass ends, we are sent out to serve God and others.

Closing Blessing (5 minutes)

Invite each family to form a family circle.

Begin with the Sign of the Cross.

Pray the prayer on p. 80 of the *Child's Book.*

Conclude by leading families in singing *Songs of Celebration* CD, track 14, "Lead Us to the Water."

Faith at Home individual family unit experience (5 minutes)

Direct families' attention to the Faith at Home page and encourage them to do the activities at home.

The Bread of Life

Gathering and Opening Prayer (60 minutes)

Materials Needed

- Various types of breads or rolls representing various regions and countries of the world (such as: rye roll, Eastern Europe; pita, Middle East; soda bread, Ireland; croissant, France; pizza, Italy; bagel, Israel; tortilla, Mexico; scone, England; wonton, China; lefse, Scandinavia; fry bread, Native Americans; chapati, India; sourdough roll, United States)
- Colorful napkins
- Scripted index cards
- Large table or altar
- Copies of the **Family Eucharist Retreat Handout 1**
- Pencils

Welcome the participants. Have facilitators distribute nametags and invite families to enjoy the light refreshments as they find a place to sit.

Before the celebration, prepare 7–10 children for the processional. Demonstrate how they are to process into the worship space each holding one of the breads in a colorful napkin. Walk them through the placing of the bread on the table/altar and give them their scripts. The scripts can be written on index cards upon which are printed the words: "This pita bread represents the people of the Middle East."

Invite families to sit in a circle around the large altar or table. Or, you may also choose to pray in the church, with the altar as the focus.

Opening Celebration

Sing "We Come to the Table," *Songs of Celebration* CD, track 13.

Have children process into the worship space carrying the various breads representing different countries.

People around the world rely upon grain made into bread to live. We all share the common need for bread to sustain us. As each type of bread is placed upon the center table, let us give thanks for the nation it represents.

Have each child come forth naming the bread and the country, people, or region it represents. After the bread is placed upon the table, the children may be seated with their families.

Read *John 6:5–13*. (The Gospel may be read or acted out.)

Invite the families to move to their assigned tables to reflect on the Gospel. If you are in the church, have families cluster in pews or seats.

Distribute Family Eucharist Retreat Handout 1 and have families discuss the questions and complete the handouts.

Encourage family members to explain their responses to one another.

Ask the families to talk about why Jesus asked the disciples to gather up the leftovers, then have each family write an ending to the story that illustrates what Jesus might have done with the twelve baskets of leftovers.

Invite the participants to share some of these story endings in the large group.

Conclude the activity with these or similar words:

In the Eucharist, we gather to break the bread and share the cup of wine, which is Jesus' own Body and Blood. We become what we eat—the Body of Christ and the bread of life for others. Jesus instructed the disciples to gather the leftovers so that nothing would be lost. This is important to remember, because in Jesus' eyes, everyone is important and loved. In Holy Communion, we become one with Jesus so that we can go into the world and give Jesus to others. When we receive Jesus in the Eucharist, we are given the courage to help people in need.

Close this celebraton with a verse from the opening song.

Rotation and Break (5 minutes)

Activity Centers

Direct the participants to note the color code on their nametag and ask them to move to the appropriate center.

Tell the group that the lunch break will occur after the families have visited two centers. The remaining two centers can be visited after lunch.

Activity 1: Mobile (20 minutes)

Materials Needed
- *Look at the Moon* by May Garelick* or a similar book
- Vine-type plant
- Model Magic or other self-hardening clay
- Colored paper plates cut in half with four holes punched into the straight edge and one hole punched into the top edge
- Wooden skewer or similar object
- 5 lengths of narrow ribbon for each participant
- Permanent markers

Assemble the group.

Read aloud *Look at the Moon* by May Garelick.

Ask "What was it that connected the little girl to all the various animals and places?"

Invite one of the parents to read *John 15:1–5, 7–8.*

Show the participants the plant and explain how it is an example of what Jesus was talking about in the Gospel story.

Invite families to make a clay mobile showing how we are all connected to Jesus: Direct them to illustrate the half plate with a symbol that represents Jesus and to write the family name on the back of the plate.

Have them use the clay to mold four objects symbolizing people, pets, sports, or other important connections in their lives. When the objects are completed, pierce a hole into the top of each with the skewer and connect them to the bottom of the plate with the strands of ribbon. String one ribbon through the top of the plate to hang the mobile. These can be hung in a central place in the home to remind family members that we are all one in the Body of Christ. Rotation and Break (5 minutes)

Activity 2: Reflection on Being the Body of Christ (20 minutes)

Materials Needed
- Bible
- Copies of **Family Eucharist Retreat Handout 2**
- Pencils

When the group is assembled:

Read *1 Corinthians 12:12–22, 25–27.*

Explain that Paul was speaking to the early followers of Jesus about how each person is important to the Church.

Discuss the reading using the following questions:
- What do you think Paul was trying to teach the early Christians?
- When did you become a member of Christ's Body?

Look at the Moon, May Garelick. Mondo Publishing, New York, NY, 1996.

- When you think about the people who are part of the Body of Christ, who are the weakest? Who are the ones most hurting? Who are the members of the body who are thought of as not important?
- What can we do to help the Body of Christ thrive?

Direct the families to work together on **Family Eucharist Retreat Handout 2**. This sheet can be placed on the refrigerator at home as a reminder to do something together to help the hurting and weak members of the Body of Christ each week as a preparation for First Eucharist.

Lunch (30–45 minutes)

Meal Prayer

Blessed are you, O God, for the food we are about to share. We are thankful for Jesus, who is our living bread. This bread calls us to share ourselves unselfishly as food for one another. This bread is a sign of our unity with people all over the world. Let us remember the many nations that live on the planet earth as we are nourished by the food before us. We remember those who have prepared this meal and pray for those who have no food to eat this day. And so we pray together "Bless us, O Lord."

Activity 3: Tour of the Church (20 minutes)

Pastor (deacon or catechist) takes the families into the sacristy to let the children and their parent(s) see and touch the vessels used for Eucharist, the altar cloths, the sink where the vessels are washed, the tabernacle, and the altar. Each can be explained as to the significance and use. These or similar words may be used:

- The chalice is a large cup used at Mass to hold the wine that becomes the Blood of Christ.
- The paten is a dish that holds the bread that becomes the Body of Christ.
- The ciborium is a larger vessel that may be used to distribute Communion. It is also used to hold the Blessed Sacrament in the tabernacle.
- The decanter or flagon is the bottle-like pitcher used to hold the wine that will be consecrated at Mass. It is carried to the altar during the procession of gifts.

- Bread and wine are used at Mass, carried to the altar during the procession of gifts, and consecrated to become the Body and Blood of Christ.
- Communion cups are used at communion when the people receive from the cup. They are kept on the credence table and brought to the altar when the gifts are brought forth.
- The credence table is the small table by the side of the altar on which the bread and wine are placed before being brought to the altar for consecration.
- The purificator is a white cloth used to cleanse the chalice and communion cups after each person drinks and when the Mass is completed.
- The corporal is a white linen cloth upon which are placed the vessels containing the bread and wine used during the Mass.
- The pall is the stiff, square, white cover that is placed over the chalice.
- The altar is the table upon which the Eucharist is celebrated. It contains an altar stone consecrated or blessed by the bishop.
- An altar cloth covers the table.
- The tabernacle is the place where the consecrated hosts are kept.
- The monstrance is a vessel designed to expose the consecrated Host to the assembly either for adoration in a church or for carrying in a solemn procession.
- The sanctuary lamp is an oil lamp or wax candle that is near the tabernacle. It is always lit when the Blessed Sacrament is reserved in the tabernacle as a sign of honor to the Lord.
- The pyx is a vessel used to carry Holy Communion to the sick.

Rotation and Break (5 minutes)

Activity 4: Making Gratitude Lists (20 minutes)

Materials Needed
- Various colors of construction paper (red, pink, and green scraps need to be included)
- Scissors
- Glue sticks
- Markers
- A large poster board for each family

Explain that in the Eucharist, we give thanks to God for the gift of Jesus, people, and all creation.

Direct the families to make lists of reasons they are thankful to God. Each family should then select the six most important ones. Have families work together to list these reasons on a large poster board, and decorate the board.

Invite families to share their lists and display them in the meeting room.

Closing Prayer (20 minutes)

Materials Needed
- Large table or altar with the bread upon it
- Paper and pencils for each family
- Clown or mime artist
- Water-soluble paint
- *Songs of Celebration* CD
- Bible

Gather the families seated in a circle back at the prayer table.

Assign beforehand a catechist or facilitator in the audience to loudly say, "Everyone needs." Then the clown or mime artist acts out one of the following: food, water, a home, clean air, medicine, to play, school, peace, work, love, safety, God, and anything you might want to add.

Encourage the children to guess what the mime artist or clown is acting out.

Continue by having different voices proclaim the phrase "Everyone needs" before each action.

Invite the families to be mindful of the families of the world who do not have these things and to prepare a petition for families in various countries naming their need. During this time, the clown or mime artist will go around the room marking the cheek of each child with a cross to symbolize Jesus.

Invite everyone to gather around the table and have a member of each family pray their petition aloud.

Have the facilitators and other adults break the breads into enough pieces for each person to have a piece. Distribute the bread.

Read *John 6:48, 51–57* (Bread of Life).

Sing the closing song, "We Come to the Table," track 13, *Songs of Celebration* CD.

Thank the families for participating in the retreat.

Children's Eucharist Retreat
Sharing Bread

This is a day retreat for children. You should conduct it close to the time of the celebration of the Sacrament. If you have fewer than 15 children, you may want to conduct the activities in consecutive order.

Outline	Environment	Materials
1. Gathering and Opening Prayer 2. Activity Centers • Activity 1: Making Bread • Activity 2: Making Mobiles • Activity 3: Learning to Receive the Eucharist 3. Snack 4. Closing Prayer	• At least 4 group facilitators (2 per group) • 1 volunteer to bake bread • Prayer table	• Nametags (color coded for activity centers) • *Songs of Celebration* CD • Napkins, cups, drinks • Additional materials needed are listed within each activity

Gathering and Opening Prayer (10 minutes)

Gather children and facilitators in a circle around the prayer table.

Play selections from *Songs of Celebration* CD as background music.

Lead the opening prayer with these or similar words: *God, our Father, we give you thanks for the gift of your Son Jesus. Help us to become ready to receive him as the Bread of Life in Holy Communion. We ask this in Jesus' name, who lives with you and the Holy Spirit forever and ever. Amen.*

Explain that the Eucharist is made of bread, and that they will be making bread and talking about why it is important.

Organize the large group into two smaller groups. Both groups will bake bread simultaneously. They will separate to do the two remaining activities.

Activity Centers

Direct the participants to note the color code on their nametag and ask them to move to the appropriate center with their facilitators.

Activity 1: Making Bread (40 minutes)

Materials Needed
• Samples of different types of bread
• Copies of **Children's/Candidates' Eucharist Retreat Handouts 1** and **2**
• Pencils

Gather in a cafeteria or classroom. Follow the directions for making bread on the **Children's/Candidates' Eucharist Retreat Handout 1**.

Show the children different kinds of bread. These might be pita bread, muffins, nut bread, and so on. Lead a discussion about how often children eat bread, as toast, in sandwiches, and with butter. Tell the children that bread is an ancient food; even before Jesus was born, it helped people sustain life. Guide the discussion to help the children discover that our Eucharist is special bread, because it gives us eternal life and is a special way that Jesus is always with us.

Distribute the **Children's/Candidates' Eucharist Retreat Handout 2**. Have children work in pairs or small groups to write a prayer of thanks for bread. When children have finished, select one or more prayers to share at snack time.

Rotation and Break (5 minutes)

Activity 2: Making Mobiles (40 minutes)

Materials Needed
• Crayons or markers
• Scissors
• Glue
• Small paper plates with punched holes
• Dowels or wire hangers
• Yarn or string
• Tape
• **Children's/Candidates' Eucharist Retreat Handout 3**

Gather in the classroom with the catechist or a volunteer.

Distribute the Children's/Candidates' Eucharist Retreat Handout 3, and explain each of the symbols and how it relates to the sacrament. Tell the children that they will be making a mobile with the symbols.

Distribute materials, or have them available at tables where 3 to 5 children can comfortably work. Have children color the symbols, then cut them out and glue them to the paper plates. Show children how to tie the yarn or string through the hole and suspend the plate from the hanger or dowel. Have children label their mobiles with their names. Store the mobiles where children can retrieve them when they leave.

Engage children in a discussion about their favorite symbol and why they prefer it.

Rotation and Break (5 minutes)

Activity 3: Learning to Receive the Eucharist
(40 minutes)

Materials Needed
• Unconsecrated hosts and wine

Gather in the parish church or classroom with a priest, deacon, or minister of Holy Communion.

Explain that, just as we have special manners we use when eating, we have special manners for receiving Communion. Tell children that they will learn these manners today. Emphasize that the elements that they are receiving today are not consecrated; because they are practicing today, they are not receiving the real Eucharist.

Demonstrate for small groups of children the correct way to hold their hands, receive the Host, and place the Host in their mouths. Similarly, show children how to take the cup and a sip of the wine. Teach children to say "Amen" in response to the minister's words.

Direct children to line up to receive the unconsecrated elements. Gently correct where necessary, and praise their efforts and behavior.

Answer any questions.

Sing "We Come to the Table," *Songs of Celebration* CD, track 13. Teach the children the words and actions; when necessary, explain their meaning. Sing the song as time permits.

Snack (20 minutes)

Note: The children will be anxious to eat the rolls, especially if they could smell them baking! Have drinks and napkins ready, and invite children to find a place at the tables. Serve the rolls in baskets at tables. Check with parents beforehand to be certain that no child has wheat, gluten, or other allergies that could cause an adverse reaction. Before the children enjoy their efforts, read one of the children's thanksgiving prayers. As the children are eating, walk among the tables, asking how they are enjoying their snack. Point out that they, like the people who make hosts for the Eucharist, took simple natural things to make a special meal. After the snack, read another child's thanksgiving prayer.

Closing Prayer (20 minutes)

Assemble the group again in the large gathering space.

Praise the children for their participation and thank the leaders for their help.

Recap the activities for the day; elicit from the children what they learned.

Emphasize the following major points:
• Jesus chose bread for his special way to be with us.
• Many symbols remind us of the Eucharist.
• We use special, respectful manners when receiving the Eucharist.

Ask everyone to join you in the closing prayer:
Lord Jesus, we thank you for being with us today. Thank you for bringing us together to learn more about the Eucharist. We have learned that bread is a special food that brings us life. The Eucharist is even more special, because it brings us eternal life. We have learned some symbols of the Eucharist and their meanings. We have also learned how to receive you respectfully. Help us to remember all that we have learned. Thank you for this special day. Amen.

Conclude with "We Come to the Table" from the *Songs of Celebration* CD.

Make any announcements and distribute prayers and the mobiles that the children made.

Songs of Celebration CD

Chapter 1—Track 7
Yes Lord, I Believe!
© 2000 John Burland

Chapter 2—Track 8
Glory to God
Marty Haugen. © GIA Publications

Chapter 3—Track 9
Create in Me
© Tom Kendzia. Published by OCP

Chapter 4—Track 10
Open My Eyes
© Jesse Manibusan. Published by OCP

Chapter 5—Track 11
We Praise You
© Damean. Published by OCP

Chapter 6—Track 12
Te alabaré, Señor/I Will Praise You, Lord
Tony Alonso. © GIA Publications

Chapter 7—Track 13
We Come to the Table
© 2004 John Burland

Chapter 8—Track 14
Lead Us to the Water
© Tom Kendzia. Published by OCP

Eucharist
Optional Music Suggestions

Chapter 1

1. "Pan de vida," © Jaime Cortez. Published by OCP
2. "Taste and See," James Moore. © GIA Publications

Chapter 2

1. "Gloria," © Bob Hurd. Published by OCP
2. "Pan de vida," © Jaime Cortez. Published by OCP

Chapter 3

1. "Salmo 50: Oh Dios, crea en mí," © Eleazar Cortes. Published by OCP
2. "Loving and Forgiving," © Scott Soper. Published by OCP

Chapter 4

1. "Abre mis ojos," (Open My Eyes). © Jesse Manibusan. Published by OCP
2. "Jesus, Bread of Life," (refrain). Dvorak/Schaubel. © WLP

Chapter 5

1. "Demos gracias al Señor," © Al Valverde. Published by OCP
2. "Give Thanks and Remember," Jack Miffleton. © WLP

Chapter 6

1. "We Remember," Marty Haugen. © GIA Publications
2. "One Bread, One Body," © New Dawn, John Foley. Published by OCP

Chapter 7

1. "Cancion del cuerpo de Cristo," David Haas/trad. Hawaiian melody/trans. Donna Pena. © GIA Publications
2. "Let Us Break Bread Together," African-American Traditional

Chapter 8

1. "Id y enseñad/Go and Teach," © Gabarain. Published by OCP
2. "Eat This Bread," Les Presses de Taize. © GIA Publications

Mystagogy for Eucharist

Mystagogical Catechesis

Mystagogical catechesis is the name given to the process of gradually uncovering the meaning of the mysteries of sacraments that have already been celebrated. This type of catechesis was first done by the early Church Fathers in sermons preached to the neophytes after their initiation at the Easter Vigil. We still possess some of those sermons. They are instructions rich in images and symbols that help the newly initiated come to a fuller understanding of the sacraments they have celebrated and are now living out. Mystagogical catechesis is based on the principle that as we live out the commitments of sacraments, we experience a fuller, deeper, more personal and communal meaning of them.

The Rite of Christian Initiation

The Rite of Christian Initiation, which was promulgated after the Second Vatican Council, restored the catechumenate and the full initiation process. It designates the Easter Season as the Period of Mystagogy and sets it aside as a period for both the neophytes and the assembly to grow together "in deepening their grasp of the paschal mystery and in making it part of their lives through meditation on the Gospel, sharing in the eucharist, and doing the works of charity." (*RCIA*, 244)

Here are some practical suggestions to involve children and their families in mystagogical catechesis:

- Shortly after the celebration of First Communion, gather children and/or family members to reflect on their experience of the celebration. Use the process outlined in the *Catechist Edition* for reflecting on the celebration.

- Periodically hold gatherings of those who have recently celebrated First Communion to reflect on the Scripture readings that are in the child's Eucharist book or other meal stories from the Gospels. Focus the gatherings on how the children are experiencing themselves as the Body of Christ.

- Over a period of 18 months, select three short-term (2–3 hours) service projects and invite the children and their family members to participate in them. Situate the service project in an initial "Sending Forth" ritual and a reflection process at the end of the project.

- Plan a family gathering during the Easter season with the families of children who have celebrated First Communion and the families of neophytes to share their experiences of coming to the table and entering more fully into the life of the parish.

- Encourage members of the assembly to seek out and welcome the children who have celebrated First Communion.

- Encourage catechists in all levels of your catechetical program to create prayer spaces that include the primary symbols of water, oil, cross, Bible or lectionary, bread and wine. Encourage them to help children reflect on the symbols often.

CALL to CELEBRATE

Sacraments Source Book

Reconciliation

Reconciliation
Scope and Sequence

	Chapter 1 WE ARE CALLED	Chapter 2 WE ARE WELCOMED	Chapter 3 WE REFLECT
Ritual Focus	Signing with the Cross	Renewal of Baptismal Promises	Reverencing the Word
Scripture	God Gives Everyone Life (Acts 17:16–34)	Zacchaeus (Luke 19:1–10)	The Great Commandment (Luke 10:25–28)
Faith Focus	• In Baptism, God calls us to a life of happiness with him. • A sacrament is a holy sign that comes from Jesus and gives us grace. • Jesus is the greatest sign of God the Father's love.	• At Baptism we are called to walk in the light. • Sin is a choice. • The Sacrament of Reconciliation forgives sins committed after Baptism.	• We prepare for the Sacrament of Reconciliation with an examination of conscience, using the word of God. • The Holy Spirit guides us in examining our conscience. • Conscience is the capacity to know right from wrong.
Catechism of the Catholic Church	1420–1421, 1425–1429	1441–1445	1454
Liturgical Focus	Sacraments of Initiation	Reception of the Penitent	The Role of Scripture
Signs of Faith	baptismal name Baptism Holy Trinity	holy water candles Reconciliation room	bowing Bible Precepts of the Church

	Chapter 4 WE ARE SORRY	Chapter 5 WE ARE FORGIVEN	Chapter 6 WE GO FORTH
Ritual Focus	Examination of Conscience and Act of Contrition	Prayer Over the Children	Sprinkling Rite and Sign of Peace
Scripture	A Woman Who Was Sorry (Luke 7:36–38, 45–48, 50)	The Forgiving Father (Luke 15:11–24)	Jesus Appears to the Disciples (John 20:19–23)
Faith Focus	• The Holy Spirit helps us be sorry for our sins. • Sorrow for sin is the most important part of the Sacrament of Reconciliation. • A penance is a prayer or action that shows we are truly sorry for our sins.	• God is always ready to forgive us. • God wants us to be one with him. *Reconciliation* means "bringing together again, or reuniting." • Through the power of the Holy Spirit and the ministry of the priest, we are reconciled with God and one another.	• The Sacrament of Reconciliation is a sacrament of conversion. • The mission of reconciliation is to bring forgiveness and peace to others. • The Holy Spirit remains with us to help us grow and become more like Jesus.
Catechism of the Catholic Church	1450–1453	1455–1460	1468–1470
Liturgical Focus	Confession of Sins and Penance	Prayer of Absolution	Proclamation of Praise and Dismissal
Signs of Faith	kneeling contrition penitent	laying on of hands Advent/Lent purple stole	sprinkling with holy water Sign of Peace bishops and priests

Reconciliation
Sunday Connection
Bulletin Inserts, General Intercessions, and Parish Blessings

Use these as a way to involve the parish assembly in the preparation for sacraments.

Session 1 We Are Called

Bulletin Insert   During the week, our young people who are preparing to celebrate the Sacrament of Reconciliation for the first time will be reflecting on being called to live in friendship with God through participation in the sacraments. Join them by taking time to think about the ways participation in the sacraments has brought you into a closer relationship with God's love.

Intercession   For young people who are preparing to celebrate the Sacrament of Reconciliation for the first time, that they may be encouraged by the active participation and faith of this assembly.

Parish Blessing   God, our loving Father, these young people come before you as your children. They belong to you. Send the Holy Spirit upon them as they begin this time of preparation that they may come to know your presence in all they do. We ask this blessing through Christ our Lord.

Session 2   We Are Welcomed

Bulletin Insert   During the week, our young people who are preparing to celebrate the Sacrament of Reconciliation for the first time will be reflecting on how Jesus welcomes sinners. Join them by reading and reflecting on the story of Zacchaeus (*Luke 19:1–10*).

Intercession   For young people who are preparing to celebrate the Sacrament of Reconciliation for the first time, that they may always be open to the forgiving and transforming love of Jesus.

Parish Blessing   God, our loving Father, these young people gather with us, your people, to give you glory. Send the Holy Spirit upon them to help them recognize you in all the ways you show yourself to them and to continually give you thanks and praise. We ask this blessing through Christ our Lord.

Session 3   We Reflect

Bulletin Insert   During the week, our young people who are preparing to celebrate the Sacrament of Reconciliation for the first time will be reflecting on the importance of the Scriptures as a guide for our lives. Join them by reading and reflecting on The Great Commandment (*Luke 10: 25–28*) and the Beatitudes (*Matthew 5:3–12*).

Intercession   For young people who are preparing to celebrate the Sacrament of Reconciliation for the first time, that they will continue to love God's word and be guided by it in their actions.

Parish Blessing   God, our loving Father, these young people come before you to listen and be fed by your word. Send the Holy Spirit upon them that may hear your word and be empowered to live by it. We ask this blessing through Christ our Lord.

Session 4   We Are Sorry

Bulletin Insert   During the week, our young people who are preparing to celebrate the Sacrament of Reconciliation for the first time will be reflecting on sorrow for sin and confession. Join them by reflecting on the actions and patterns in your life that distance you from a deeper relationship with Jesus and the Church. Pray to the Holy Spirit to awaken sorrow and contrition in you.

Intercession   For young people who are preparing to celebrate the Sacrament of Reconciliation for the first time, that they may be blessed with the ability to say "I am sorry."

Parish Blessing   God, our loving Father, these young people come before you seeking to do your will, but knowing that sometimes they turn away from you. Send the Holy Spirit upon them to help them know you as always kind and merciful. We ask this blessing through Christ our Lord.

Session 5 We Are Forgiven

Bulletin Insert   During the week, our young people who are preparing to celebrate the Sacrament of Reconciliation for the first time will be reflecting on the gift of forgiveness. Join them by reflecting on how you have given and received the gift of forgiveness in your life.

Intercession   For young people who are preparing to celebrate the Sacrament of Reconciliation for the first time, that they may come to know the gift of God's gracious forgiveness in the sacrament and in daily life.

Parish Blessing   God, our loving Father, these young people come before you knowing you are a forgiving God. Send the Holy Spirit upon them that they will be both enlightened and strengthened to ask for and be strengthened by your forgiving love. We ask this blessing through Christ our Lord.

Session 6 We Go Forth

Bulletin Insert   During the week, our young people who are preparing to celebrate the Sacrament of Reconciliation for the first time will be reflecting with their families and catechists about how the sacrament empowers us to live out our mission of being forgivers and reconcilers. Join them by reflecting on your experience of being a forgiver and reconciler.

Intercession   For young people who are preparing to celebrate the Sacrament of Reconciliation for the first time that they may be strengthened to go forth and live as forgiving and reconciling disciples.

Parish Blessing   God, our loving Father, these young people come before you ready to do your will. Send the Holy Spirit upon them that they may be witnesses of peace and reconciliation as they live their lives as your disciples. We ask this blessing through Christ our Lord.

Reconciliation
Catechist Orientation

Goals

- To welcome catechists in a hospitable environment
- To affirm the important role of the catechist
- To reflect on the catechists' experience of First Penance
- To inform the catechists about *Call to Celebrate: Reconciliation:*
  - the philosophy of the program
  - the content
  - the resources available

Materials

- Beverages and light refreshments
- Nametags
- Copies of *Call to Celebrate: Reconciliation* Child's Book
- Copies of *Call to Celebrate: Reconciliation* Catechist Edition
- Copies of *Call to Celebrate: Reconciliation* Family Guide
- *Songs of Celebration* CD
- A prayer table covered in a purple cloth with a candle, a Bible on a stand, a clear glass bowl with holy water, and a branch or another instrument for sprinkling
- Matches or lighter

Welcome and Opening Prayer (30 minutes)

Welcome the catechists and distribute nametags.

Begin the session with welcoming words and introduce yourself.

Have the catechists introduce themselves to one another.

Review the goals and agenda for the gathering.

Gather the group around the prayer setting.

Begin the prayer by singing or listening to "We Are Called," *Songs of Celebration*, track 1.

Light the candle and lead the catechists in the following reflection. Pause after each question.
- Recall your own First Penance day.
- Where was it? Who was there? Did you celebrate individually or with a group?
- Do you remember any sensate experiences smell, sound or touch?
- What were your feelings as you anticipated the celebration? As you celebrated it?
- How were you prepared for the event?
- Was there anything that stood out for you as memorable about your preparation or celebration?

Invite catechists to share any significant memories they may have of their own First Penance.

Read *John 20:19–23.*

Allow time for silent reflection.

Pose and then discuss the question:
- How do you want the children you will be catechizing to hear the message of this Gospel?

Close with a blessing. Ask the catechists to stand, and extend your hands over them as you say:
> *Lord God, in your loving kindness, strengthen and direct these catechists. Let your Spirit uphold them as they prepare to share their time and talent with your children. We ask this through Christ our Lord. Amen.*

Program Overview (15 minutes)

Components

Distribute copies of the *Catechist Guide, Child's Book, Songs of Celebration* CD, and *Family Guide* for **Call to Celebrate: Reconciliation**.

Explain what each is for and have catechists page through them.

Scope and Sequence

Invite catechists to turn to the Table of Contents on p. iii of the *Catechist Edition*. Go through it quickly, pointing out the articles in the front pages and the resources in the back pages.

Note the number of chapters (6) in the *Child's Book.*

Turn to the Scope and Sequence section on pp.vi–vii Explain that scope and sequence section gives the overview of the content for each chapter. Note each of the features in the left column, and go through one chapter column to familiarize catechists with the format. Go through the Ritual Focus row and point out that the flow of the chapters is based on the steps in the Rite of Penance. Review the Rite, if necessary.

Tell catechists that each chapter is structured with a three-step process: Celebrate, Remember, and Live, and point out the family-oriented Faith at Home page.

Lesson Overview (30 minutes)

Child's Book

Use Chapter 2 of the *Child's Book* and show the process of a session:

Celebrate
- celebration and reflection

Remember
- proclamation and breaking open the Bible reading
- understanding the doctrine
- learning about the ritual action of the sacrament

Live
- making connections to their lives and their families

Point out the *Faith at Home* boxes in the *Remember* section and the *Signs of Faith* feature in the *Celebrate and Remember* pages.

Catechist Edition

Use Chapter 2 of the *Catechist Edition* as a guide.

Familiarize catechists with the background and resources in the left-hand column on p. 12A.

Encourage them to read and reflect on the essay in the main column as they are planning their lessons. Note the reflection questions and Catechist Prayer.

Review the planner on p. 12B. Note the materials needed for each lesson, and have catechists turn to the pages noted to find the Activity Masters and Scripture Dramas, Narrations, Pantomimes and more.

Go to pp. 12–21 the catechists that the side wrap gives a step-by-step lesson plan for the *Child's Book* pages, and the bottom boxes gives them additional background, activities, and tips. Instruct them to page through the lesson and then ask for any questions.

Turn to the Catholic Source Book, pp. 62–73. Have catechists page through it and make note of the additional activities provided in the wrap.

Break for refreshments and conversation.

Administrative Details (10 minutes)

Elicit any questions the catechists have about the components and resources.

Allow time for administrative details, such as calendars and class lists.

Remind them of the next session which will be catechist training on liturgical catechesis. This is the method they will be using throughout the program.

Ask them to read pp. iv–xv before the training session.

Closing Prayer (10 minutes)

Gather the catechists in a circle around the prayer space.

Sing "We Are Called," *Songs of Celebration* CD, track 1, or another appropriate song from your parish repertoire.

Make the Sign of the Cross and say:
Let us call to mind the goodness of God who gives us all good things. I bless you with this water to remind you of the gift of your Baptism and your call to hand on the faith. (Sprinkle the group with water.) Let us join in the prayer that Jesus has taught us.

Pray the Lord's Prayer together.

Thank catechists for their attendance.

Reconciliation
Catechist Training

Goals

- To introduce the method of liturgical catechesis
- To present the underlying meaning of the Sacrament of Reconciliation
- To show how to design a prayer space and lead prayer
- To explain sacraments as actions of a faith community

Materials

- A table covered with a white cloth
- A Bible on a stand
- A large candle
- Candles for each participant
- Matches or a lighter
- A large, clear glass bowl with water
- Plants and flowers, if appropriate
- *Songs of Celebration* CD

- Copies of the following articles from the *Sacraments Source Book* CD:
  - "What Is Liturgical Catechesis?"
  - "How to Lead Prayer"
  - "Role of the Prayer Leader"
  - "What Is a Sacrament?"
  - "Reconciliation"
  - "History of Reconciliation"
- Poster board or chart paper
- *Reconciliation Stories of Celebration* video

Advance Preparation

Familiarize yourself with the ritual action in the opening prayer.

Select three persons to carry the holy water, candle, and Bible in procession.

Rehearse the suggested song "We Are Called," *Songs of Celebration* CD, track 1.

Opening Prayer Service and Reflection (20 minutes)

Sing together "We Are Called," *Songs of Celebration* CD, track 1.
As you sing, walk forward slowly. Follow the persons carrying the holy water, candle, and Bible.

Lead the opening prayer.

Leader: *Let us begin. God, our loving Father, we are gathered here in your presence. Send us your Holy Spirit to help us live as disciples of your Son, Jesus. We ask this through Jesus Christ our Lord.*

All: *Amen.*

Leader: *On the day of our Baptism, we were claimed for Christ. By water and the Holy Spirit we received the gifts of faith and new life. Let us once again remember those promises together.*

Come forward and gather around the holy water and candle.

Do you say "no" to sin, so that you can live always as God's children?

All: *We do.*

Leader: *Do you believe in God, the Father almighty?*

All: *We do.*

Leader: *Do you believe in Jesus Christ, his only Son, our Lord?*

All: *We do.*

Leader: *Do you believe in the Holy Spirit?*

All: *We do.*

Leader: *This is our faith. This is the faith of the Church. We are proud to profess it in Christ Jesus.*

All: *Amen.*

Leader: *Come to the water, make the Sign of the Cross, and thank God for the gift of our Baptism.*

When everyone has made the Sign of the Cross, light small candles from the large candle and distribute them to each catechist, saying:

[Name], You are the light of Christ.

Have catechists return to their seats and continue:

Leader: *Loving God, in Baptism we were united to your Son, Jesus. Open our hearts to the Holy Spirit as we remember our Baptism. We ask this through Jesus Christ our Lord.*

All: *Amen.*

Leader: *The Lord be with you.*

All: *And also with you.*

Leader: *A reading from the Acts of the Apostles*

Read Acts 17:16–34.

The word of the Lord.

All: *Thanks be to God.*

Leader: *What image or phrase is important for you in this reading?*

When the discussion is finished, continue the prayer:

Let us stand and pray as Jesus taught us.

Pray the Lord's Prayer together.

Let us offer each other the Sign of Peace.

Reflection on Prayer (20 minutes)

Organize the catechists into smaller groups of five or six.

Invite the catechists to recall the ritual moments of the celebration. Do a guided meditation using the prompts from the celebration. Pause after each prompt.

Pause for a few minutes of silence. Then invite the groups to share their feelings about the celebration in their small group. Encourage them to stay with their feelings. After 5 to 7 minutes, invite sharing with the large group.

Naming (20 minutes)

Ask the participants to name what they learned about God, Jesus, the Church, or their own Christian life from the celebration.

Take each category separately and list their responses on the board or on chart paper. When they have completed their lists, use phrases from their lists to summarize what they have said about Baptism, the Church, and faith. Comment on how much "content" they came up with from their experience of reflecting on the celebration.

Distribute the article, "What Is Liturgical Catechesis?" Summarize the main parts of the article, and explain that this is the model of catechesis upon which **Call to Celebrate** is based. Emphasize that this is what they have just done.

Rotation and Break (5 minutes)

Setting up a Prayer Space and Leading Prayer (20 minutes)

Gather catechists around the prayer space and pass out "How to Lead Prayer." Give catechists ideas on setting up a prayer space in their meeting place. Note where and how they can obtain materials for the space, and emphasize the importance of a prayer environment.

Distribute the article, "Role of the Prayer Leader," and summarize it for the catechists. Practice leading the procession and prayer gestures with them.

Rotation and Break (5 minutes)

A Theology of Sacrament and Eucharist (30 minutes)

Play Part 3 of the *Reconciliation Stories of Celebration* video. After catechists have viewed the video, use the questions in the guide for discussion.

Summarize these important points:
- Sacraments are *actions* of God and a faith community.
- In the Sacrament of Reconciliation, we *experience the forgiveness of God* through the words and actions of the priest.
- There are two different ways the Church celebrates the sacrament. Refer catechists to the outline of the individual and communal rites in the *Child's Book*, pp. 68–69.

Distribute the articles, "What Is a Sacrament?," "Reconciliation," and "History of Reconciliation." Encourage catechists to read the articles later.

Closing Blessing (5 minutes)

Thank the catechists for attending the session.

Extend your hands over the catechists and pray in these or similar words:

God, the Father of mercies, has sent his Son into the world. Through the power of the Holy Spirit, may you continue to be transformed into the Body of Christ and witness his love in the world. Amen.

Reconciliation
Parent Orientation

Goals	Environment	Materials

• To welcome parents and families in a hospitable environment
• To affirm the importance of parent and family participation in the process
• To introduce parents and families to the *Call to Celebrate: Reconciliation* program
• To inform parents and families about the parish policies and procedures relating to celebration of the Sacrament of Reconciliation
	• Be sure to clearly identify the meeting place, posting clear directions if necessary.
	• Tables and chairs arranged for small groups
	• A prayer setting with large candle, Bible on a stand or table, clear bowl filled with water, and a branch or other instrument for sprinkling
		• Beverages and light refreshments
		• Nametags
		• Copies of *Call to Celebrate: Reconciliation* Family Guide and Child's Book
		• *Songs of Celebration* CD
		• *Reconciliation Stories of Celebration* video
		• Copies of the following from the *Sacraments Source Book* CD:
		  • **Reconciliation Parent Orientation Handouts 1** and **2**
		  • "Celebrating Rituals at Home– Letter"
		  • **At Home Ritual Preparation Handouts 1–6**

Welcome and Opening Prayer

Welcome parents and other adults and distribute nametags.

Introduce yourself and briefly review the goals and agenda for the gathering.

Begin the prayer.

Light the candle and lead parents and family members in the following reflection. Pause after each question:
• *Recall the day of your child's Baptism.*
• *Where was it?*
• *Who was there?*
• *Can you recall any significant things that happened that day?*
• *Do you recall any feelings you may have had during the ceremony?*
• *Was there any moment of the ceremony of your child's Baptism that stood out as memorable for you?*

Invite parents and family members to share with one or two other persons any significant memories they may have of that day.

Distribute Reconciliation Parent Orientation Handout 1: Parent's Prayer.

Call the group back together. Ask the parents and family members to stand.

Lead the parents and family members in the Parent's Prayer.

View Video

Show Part 1 of the *Reconciliation Stories of Celebration* video.

Use the questions in the video guide for discussion.

Break for refreshments and conversation.

The *Call to Celebrate: Reconciliation* Program

Distribute the *Child's Book* and walk the parents and family members through the Table of Contents.

Point out that the program:
• introduces the child to an understanding of the Rite of Penance.
• is a preparation for a lifetime of celebrating God's forgiveness and reconciliation.
• introduces children to the sacrament through its rituals and prayers.

Use one chapter of the *Child's Book* to show parents and family members the process of a session.

Celebrate
• celebration and reflection

Remember
• proclamation and breaking open the Scripture reading
• understanding the doctrine
• learning about the ritual action of the sacrament

Live

- making connections to their lives and their families

Highlight the three Faith at Home features in the *Child's Book* and show how they will help the parents and family members to participate in the child's preparation.

Emphasize the importance of doing the activities on the Faith at Home page, especially the ritual.

Describe the *Call to Celebrate: Reconciliation Family Guide* using one of the two implementation models below.

❇ **For programs where the catechesis is done in a group with a catechist and includes family support**

Distribute the *Call to Celebrate: Reconciliation Family Guide*. Point out the difference in the two parts of the guide:

- the first part is for parents and family members to use for their own reflection on forgiveness, conversion, and reconciliation.
- the second part is for those who will be doing the child's preparation at home.

Mention the availability of the *Songs of Celebration* CD, which will enhance their time with the child and support the child's learning.

Emphasize that this time of assisting the child and using the *Family Guide* is an opportunity for parents and family members to grow in their own relationship with God. It will help them understand forgiveness, conversion, and reconciliation in their own lives.

Distribute Reconciliation Parent Orientation Handout 2: Frequently Asked Questions and go through it with parents and family members. Answer any other questions they may have.

Go to Parish Policies and Procedures.

❇ **For programs where the catechesis is done in the home**

Distribute the *Call to Celebrate: Reconciliation Family Guide*. Point out the difference in the two parts of the guide:

- the first part is for parents and family members to use for their own reflection on forgiveness, conversion, and reconciliation.
- the second part is to help these parents and family members to complete the sessions at home.

Go through one session of the *Family Guide* and show parents and family members how to use the outline. Point out:

- the parent background essay, an important piece to understanding what the session is about.
- the easy to follow overview.
- the People of Faith story for each session and the significance of telling these stories to children so they can hear and visualize how others lived out their baptismal call.

Emphasize how essential the ritual prayer is to the session. Go through the prayer as it is written in the session and talk about ways to prepare a prayer space and environment at home. Direct the parents and family members to page 14 of the *Family Guide* for tips on how to lead the ritual prayer.

Distribute Reconciliation Parent Orientation Handout 2, "Celebrating Rituals at Home—Letter," and **At Home Ritual Preparation Handouts 1–6.**

Parish Policies and Procedures

Explain the commitment the parish expects of parents and family members for this preparation.

Distribute appropriate schedules or calendars for parent meetings and other gatherings such as retreats, parish assembly gatherings, dates for the celebration, and other pertinent information.

Closing Prayer

Gather the parents and family members in a circle around the prayer space and pray together:

Let us call to mind the goodness of God who gives us all good things. I bless you with this water to remind you of your Baptism and your call to hand on the faith. (Sprinkle the group with water.)

Let us join in the prayer that Jesus taught us.

Pray the Lord's Prayer together.

 Encourage parents and family members to go to **www.harcourtreligion.com** for more ideas and suggestions.

We Are Called

Before the Celebration

- Choose a gathering space that will be conducive to prayer and that will accommodate the size of the group; the church, a chapel, or a gathering place in the parish hall would each be appropriate. You will want the group to be able to see, hear, and move easily during the ritual.
- Prepare the group for the ritual action of Signing with the Cross and for the reflection on the sacred Scriptures.
- Select a good reader to proclaim the reading.

- Select three people for the entrance procession: to carry the Bible, the candle, and the bowl of water. Show them where and how to place them in the sanctuary or on the prayer table.
- If not in a church or chapel, place chairs in semicircular rows around the prayer space. Leave enough space for people to move in and out of the rows. If possible, have tables and chairs set up in another space for adult discussion after the celebration.

Materials

- A large, clear, bowl with water, or if the celebration is in the church, use the baptismal font or pool
- A large candle or the Paschal candle
- A prayer table for the candle, a Bible, and a stand
- *Songs of Celebration* CD
- Copies of the celebration for the assembly (*Sacraments Source Book* CD)

Gathering Rite

Welcome the gathered assembly.

Rehearse the opening song, and go over the ritual action of Signing with the Cross.

Invite the assembly to stand for the procession.

Opening Song

"We Are Called," *Songs of Celebration* CD, track 1.

Procession

The presider and persons carrying the bowl with water, candle, and Bible process in while the assembly sings.

> *Leader:* Let us pray.
> *Make the Sign of the Cross together.*

Celebration of the Word

> *Leader:* The Lord be with you.
> *All:* And also with you.
> *Leader:* A reading from the Acts of the Apostles.
> Read Acts 17:16–34.
> The word of the Lord.
> *All:* Thanks be to God.
> *Sit silently.*

Reflection

Invite the assembly to reflect on the reading. Use the following question:
- What did the reading tell you about God?

Ask the assembly to share their responses with one or two people. Be sure to include children in the sharing.

Signing with the Cross

Leader: *Let us call to mind the goodness of God, who gives us all good things. God gives us life and breath, and in him we live and move and have our being.*

Invite the children who are preparing for the Sacrament of Reconciliation to come forward to the water with their family members. Have family members place their hands on the children's shoulders as the presider signs each of them individually and says:

Leader: *[Name], God calls you by name to live in love with him always.*

Child: *Amen.*

Have several catechists do the signing if there is a large crowd. When the children have been signed, invite the rest of the assembly to come forward to the water and sign each other with the Sign of the Cross.

Leader: *Let us join in the prayer that Jesus has taught us.*
Pray the Lord's Prayer.

Closing Prayer

Leader: *Creator God, our source of life, bless us, protect us from all evil, and bring us to everlasting life.*

Child: *Amen.*

Children go to their group session and adults go to the appointed space for reflection.

- There is a liturgical catechetical session for adults on p. 166.
- There is a parent/adult catechetical session on pp. 167–168.
- There is an intergenerational catechetical session on pp. 169–170.

We Are Called

Goals
• To reflect on the celebration
• To explore the meaning and symbolism of water and signing
• To review the connection between Baptism and Reconciliation

Materials
• Poster board, chart paper, or overhead   • *Songs of Celebration* CD
• Markers   • Bible

Reflection (20 minutes)

Invite the adults to gather in groups of five or six.

Begin by recalling the ritual moments of the celebration. Lead a guided meditation using the following prompts. Pause after each prompt.
• Play a few verses of the opening song, "We Are Called," *Songs of Celebration* CD, track 1.
• Read some verses of the Gospel.
• Ask participants to recall their discussion of the Gospel.
• Call to mind the ritual of calling the candidates by name and signing them with holy water.
• Ask: "What was it like to come forward and sign and be signed with water?"

Small Group Sharing

Pause for a few minutes of silence. Then invite the participants to share their feelings about the celebration in their small group. After 10 to 15 minutes, invite sharing with the large group.

Large Group Sharing

Gather the responses of the small groups on poster board, chart paper, or an overhead projector. Ask for feelings and thoughts about the celebration as a whole, and also for specific parts of the celebration that were meaningful to members of the group.

Naming (30 minutes)

Ask the participants to name what they learned from the celebration about being called by name, the Sign of the Cross, or their own Christian life.

Take each category separately and list responses on poster board, chart paper, or an overhead projector.

When the lists are complete, use them to summarize the theology and meaning of the sacraments, symbols, and the Sign of the Cross.

Affirm, add, or enlarge upon the following points:
• God's call is a call to share his own life.
• Water symbolizes life and death and cleansing; the waters of Baptism cleanse us from all sin.
• Being signed with the Sign of the Cross is the mark of the Christian—of one who belongs to God.
• Sacraments are visible signs of the invisible reality of God's presence. They use primary symbols of water, oil, bread, and wine, along with words and gestures.
• The Sacrament of Reconciliation celebrates forgiveness for the sins committed after Baptism.

Reflection and Small Group Sharing (20 minutes)

Ask "What will you do this week to deepen your relationship with the God who calls you by name?

Direct participants to reflect in silence for a few a minutes and then share their responses with their group.

Closing Blessing (5 minutes)

Gather and begin with the Sign of the Cross.

Leader: God, our Father, you have given us life and called us by name.
All: We give you thanks and praise.

Leader: Jesus, Son of God and our Savior, you show us how to live.
All: We give you thanks and praise.

Leader: Holy Spirit, you guide and strengthen us to live worthy of the Christian name.
All: We give you thanks and praise.

We Are Called

Goals	Environment	Materials

Goals
- To explore the participants' experience of God
- To help the participants understand the connection between the Sacrament of Reconciliation and the Sacrament of Baptism
- To share childhood experiences of the Sacrament of Reconciliation

Environment
- Be sure to clearly identify the meeting place, posting clear directions if necessary.
- Tables and chairs arranged for small groups
- A prayer setting with large candle and a Bible on a stand or table

Materials
- Beverages and light refreshments
- Nametags
- Copies of *Call to Celebrate: Reconciliation* Family Guides
- *Songs of Celebration* CD, track 1
- Copies of **Reconciliation Parent/Adult Catechesis Handout 1:1** (*Sacraments Source Book* CD)
- Pens or pencils for writing
- *Child's Book*
- Board or chart paper

Welcome and Opening Prayer (15 minutes)

Welcome parents and other adults and distribute nametags.

Introduce yourself and briefly review the goals and agenda for the gathering.

✳ **If this session was preceded by a large group ritual and reflection, go to We Are Called. If not, continue with the prayer.**

Gather the group around the prayer setting, if possible, or have the group pause for a reflective moment.

Sing "We Are Called," *Songs of Celebration* CD, track 1.

Pray these or similar words:

God, you are the source of life. You have made all things. We live with the breath of your life in us. We give you praise and thanks for these gifts. We ask your forgiveness for those times we have disregarded your life-giving presence or turned away from it. Send your Holy Spirit among us that we will share more fully in your life and presence. Amen.

We Are Called (30 minutes)

Select one person to proclaim *Acts 17:16–34*.

Distribute Reconciliation Parent/Adult Catechesis Handout 1:1.

Review the directions with participants and direct them to spend quiet time in reflection and writing.
- After an appropriate amount of time, organize the large group into smaller groups of 4 to 5 people and ask them to share the responses from their reflection.
- Remind them that they may share as little or as much as they want or that they may pass.
- At the conclusion of the discussion, gather feedback from the small groups by asking for their responses to the questions.

Emphasize the following points:
- Many experiences shape our image of God, and people have different images and experiences of God.
- We need a faith community to help us sustain the image of God we believe in, which is a God who created everything in harmony and a God who calls us to act with justice, love tenderly, and serve one another.

- In Baptism, we are called live in harmony with God, other people, ourselves, and creation but we know that we often fail. We sin.
- Through the Church, God offers us a way to come back and to be strengthened to live out our call through the Sacrament of Reconciliation.

Break for refreshments and conversation.

Childhood Memories of the Sacrament of Reconciliation (30 minutes)

Ask participants to open their *Family Guide* to p. 4. Read aloud or have someone else read the story, "Childhood Memories."

Guide a discussion with the group using the questions in the *Guide* on p. 4.

Invite all to participate in the following discussion in their small groups:
- What do you most hope to impart to your child during this preparation time? Make a group list of your hopes.

Parent Moment (10 minutes)

Highlight the three Faith at Home features in the *Child's Book* and show how they will help the parents and family members to participate in children's preparations.

Emphasize the importance of doing the activities on the Faith at Home page, especially the ritual action.

Closing Prayer (5 minutes)

Gather the participants in a circle around the prayer space and pray these or similiar words.

Thank everyone for their attendance, and close with the prayer below.

Loving God, you have made us in your image and likeness. You protect us and guide us through the difficulties and perils of this world. While we have fallen into sin and failed to love, you are steadfast in your love for each of us. We ask for the grace to remain united in your great and forgiving love all the days of our lives. Grant this in the power of your Holy Spirit and through the dying and rising of Jesus. Amen.

 Encourage parents and family members to go to **www.harcourtreligion.com** for more ideas and suggestions.

We Are Called

Objectives

- To guide families to experience a celebration of the word, including being Signed with Holy Water
- To explore the meaning of the ritual action in family groups
- To explain that at Baptism we become children of God
- To reinforce that God gave us life
- To help families increase their understanding of sacraments as signs of God's love
- To encourage families to express how they show they are members of the Church

Materials

- Copies of the celebration for the assembly (*Sacraments Source Book* CD)
- *Songs of Celebration* CD
- Prayer table
- Bible
- Candle and matches
- Bowl filled with water
- Copies of Scripture Drama 1 for participants, pp. CE2–3
- Copies of Activity Master 1, p. CE1
- Poster paper
- Markers
- Pencils
- *Child's Book*

Welcome and Celebration (10–15 minutes)

Welcome the families in the gathering space.

Distribute copies of the celebration.

Select a family to be in the procession. Have them choose a family member to carry the Bible in procession.

- When families are assembled, walk forward slowly. Follow the child carrying the Bible.
- During the procession, lead families in singing "We Are Called," from the *Songs of Celebration* CD, track 1.
- Place the Bible on the prayer table and have family members return to their seats.
- Light the prayer candle.
- Begin prayer with the Sign of the Cross and invite the group to follow the order of the prayer.
- If the group is too large to gather around the prayer table for the ritual action, have the families stand in place and then invite them to come to the water, one family at a time, to make the Sign of the Cross with the water.
- Invite families gathered to follow the order of the prayer on pp. 4–5 of the *Child's Book.*
- Begin with the Sign of the Cross.

- Call each family forward one by one.
- Invite family members to make the Sign of the Cross on each other's foreheads with holy water while saying, "(Name), God calls you by name to live in love with him always."
- When all families have been signed, invite them to raise their hands in prayer and pray the Lord's Prayer together.
- For the proclamation of the Gospel, you may use a Bible or the adapted reading in the *Child's Book* on p. 6.
- Conclude with the opening song from the *Songs of Celebration* CD, track 1.

God Calls individual family unit experience (10 minutes)

Guide family members to reflect on the celebration by asking the following questions:

- What did you see? What did you hear? What did you do?

Invite family members to turn toward one another and share their responses to the questions.

Guide families to reflect further on being called by name, using the activity on p. 8 of the *Child's Book.* Allow time for family members to share their responses to the activity.

God's Children *family cluster sharing experience* (15 minutes)

Organize the large group into small clusters and invite them to share stories about their own Baptism.

Have each family cluster select a leader to read aloud to their group the text Signs of Faith: Baptism on p. 5 of the *Child's Book*.

Provide each group with a sheet of poster paper and a marker.

Ask family members from each group to name one thing that happens when we are baptized.

Invite group leaders to share their group's responses with the large group.

Direct group leaders to read aloud to their group the paragraphs on p. 5, and facilitate a discussion about what it means to be chosen by God.

God Loves Us *whole-group learning experience* (10 minutes)

Brainstorm with families the following question:
• How does God show his love for us?

List all responses on a sheet of poster paper in front of the large group.

Read aloud the first paragraph of p. 6 of the *Child's Book*.

Ask Where is Paul speaking?

Scripture *whole-group learning experience* (15 minutes)

Select members of several families to narrate the Scripture story, using the text on pp. CE2–3 of the *Catechist Edition*.

Invite the large group to reflect on the following questions:
• What does Paul teach about God?
• How do you answer God's call to love him?

Allow time for volunteers to share responses to the questions.

Use the activity on p. 7 of the *Child's Book* to help families reflect on how God shows love for them.

Signs of God's Love *whole-group learning experience* (10 minutes)

Write the words *original sin* on the next sheet of poster paper in front of the group.

Read aloud the text on p. 8 from the *Child's Book*.

Explain that *original* means first, and this was the first sin.

Point out that God loves us even when we sin. Jesus was sent as a gift to us to show us God still loves us.

Select members of one family to read the bulleted items aloud.

The Sacraments of Initiation *family cluster sharing experience* (10 minutes)

Organize the large group into the same small family clusters as earlier. Direct each group to discuss what is happening in the photographs on pp. 8–9 of the *Child's Book*.

Write the names of the Sacraments of Initiation on the poster paper. As you discuss each specific sacrament, have group leaders point out the corresponding photographs.

Direct group leaders to read aloud p. 9 from the *Child's Book* and facilitate a discussion using the following question:
• What are some signs of God's love in family life?

Summarize the Signs of Faith: The Holy Trinity.

Distribute Activity Master 1 from the *Catechist Edition* for the children. Direct them to use them at home for review.

Being a Member *individual family unit experience* (5 minutes)

Explain to families that they are members of the Church at all times, not only when they are worshiping.

Invite family members to talk about how they show they are members of the Church.

Ask volunteers to share their responses with the large group.

Have family members assist children in completing the activity.

Closing Blessing (5 minutes)

Invite each family to form a family circle.

Begin with the Sign of the Cross.

Pray the prayer on p. 10 of the *Child's Book*.

Conclude by leading families in singing *Songs of Celebration* CD, track 1, "We Are Called."

Faith at Home *individual family unit experience* (5 minutes)

Direct families' attention to the Faith at Home page and encourage them to do the activities at home.

We Are Welcomed

Before the Celebration

- Choose a gathering space that will be conducive to prayer and that will accommodate the size of the group; the church, a chapel, or a gathering place in the parish hall would each be appropriate. You will want the group to be able to see, hear, and move easily during the ritual.

- Prepare the group for the ritual action of Renewal of Baptismal Promises and for the reflection on the sacred Scriptures.

- Select a good reader to proclaim the reading.

- Select three people for the entrance procession: to carry the Bible, the candle, and the bowl of water. Show them where and how to place them in the sanctuary or on the prayer table.

- If not in a church or chapel, place chairs in semicircular rows around the prayer space. Leave enough space for people to move in and out of the rows. If possible, have tables and chairs set up in another space for adult discussion after the celebration.

Materials

- A large, clear bowl with water, or if the celebration is in the church, use the baptismal font or pool
- A branch or aspergellum for sprinkling
- A large candle or the Paschal candle
- A prayer table for the candle, a Bible, and a stand
- *Songs of Celebration* CD
- Copies of the celebration for the assembly (*Sacraments Source Book* CD)

Gathering Rite

Welcome the gathered assembly.

Rehearse the opening song, and go over the ritual action of Renewal of Baptismal Promises.

Invite the assembly to stand for the procession.

Opening Song

"We Are Marching," *Songs of Celebration* CD, track 2.

Procession

The presider and persons carrying the bowl with water, candle, and Bible process in while the assembly sings.

> *Leader:* Let us pray.
> Make the Sign of the Cross together.

Opening Prayer

> *Leader:* Good and gracious God, send us the Holy Spirit to open our hearts to the good news of your Son, Jesus, the Light of the World. We ask this in his name.
> *All:* Amen.

Celebration of the Word

> *Leader:* A reading from the holy Gospel according to Luke
> *All:* Glory to you, Lord.
> Read Luke 19:1–10.
> *Leader:* The Gospel of the Lord.
> *All:* Praise to you, Lord Jesus Christ.
> Sit silently.

Reflection

Invite the assembly to reflect on the Gospel. Use the following questions:

- Which part of the story of Zacchaeus do you like the best? Why?

Ask the assembly to share their responses with one or two people. Be sure to include children in the sharing.

Renewal of Baptismal Promises

Invite the assembly to stand. Ask the children who are preparing for Reconciliation to come forward and gather in a circle with family members around the lit candle. Address the words of the ritual to the whole assembly.

Leader: *Jesus is the Light of the World.*
Light the candle.
Let us renew our baptismal promises:
Do you reject sin, so as to live in the freedom of God's children?

All: *I do.*

Leader: *Do you reject the glamour of evil and refuse to be mastered by sin?*

All: *I do.*

Leader: *Do you reject Satan, father of sin and prince of darkness?*

All: *I do.*

Leader: *Do you believe in God, the Father almighty, creator of heaven and earth?*

All: *I do.*

Leader: *Do you believe in Jesus Christ, his only Son, our Lord?*

All: *I do.*

Leader: *Do you believe in the Holy Spirit, the holy catholic Church, the communion of saints, the forgiveness of sin, the resurrection of the body, and life everlasting?*

All: *I do.*

Based on *Rite of Christian Initiation of Adults*, 581

Sprinkle the children and then the assembly with holy water.

Closing Prayer

Leader: *Loving God, thank you for the Light of Christ. Send us the Holy Spirit to help us live as children of light.*

All: *Amen.*

Children go to their group session and adults go to the appointed space for reflection.

- There is a liturgical catechetical session for adults on p. 173.
- There is a parent/adult catechetical session on pp. 174–175.
- There is an intergenerational catechetical session on pp. 176–177.

We Are Welcomed

Goals

- To reflect on the celebration
- To explore the meaning of the Sprinkling Rite
- To present the meaning of the Welcoming Rite in the Sacrament of Reconciliation

Materials

- Poster board, chart paper, or overhead projector
- Markers
- *Songs of Celebration* CD
- Bible

Reflection (20 minutes)

Invite the adults to gather in groups of five or six.

Begin by recalling the ritual moments of the celebration. Lead a guided meditation using the following prompts. Pause after each prompt.
- Play a few verses of the opening song, "We Are Marching," *Songs of Celebration* CD, track 2.
- Ask: "How did you experience the Rite of Sprinkling?"
- Read a few verses of the Gospel.
- Ask participants to recall their discussion of the Gospel.

Small Group Sharing

Pause for a few minutes of silence. Then invite the participants to share their feelings about the celebration in their small group. After 10 to 15 minutes, invite sharing with the large group.

Large Group Sharing

Gather the responses of the small groups on poster board, chart paper, or an overhead projector. Ask for feelings and thoughts about the celebration as a whole, and also for specific parts of the celebration that were meaningful to members of the group.

Naming (30 minutes)

Ask the participants to name what they learned from the celebration about God, Jesus, the Church, or their own Christian life.

Take each category separately and list responses on poster board, chart paper, or an overhead projector. When the lists are completed, use them to summarize the theology of baptismal promises and the welcome Jesus extends to us in the Sacrament of Reconciliation.

Affirm, add, or enlarge upon the following points:
- Baptism takes away original sin and all personal sin. It welcomes us to the Christian community and makes us members of the Church.
- The ritual of the renewal of baptismal promises helps us recall the power of our Baptism and the power of faith.
- Just as we are welcomed in the baptismal ritual, we are also welcomed in the Sacrament of Reconciliation.
- The **Rite of Penance** states: *The priest should welcome penitents with fraternal charity, and if need be, address them with friendly words* (16).

Reflection and Small Group Sharing (20 minutes)

Ask "What is one thing you will do this week to open yourself to prayer and reflection on the Scriptures?"

Direct participants to reflect in silence for a few a minutes and then share their responses with their group.

Closing Blessing (5 minutes)

Gather and begin with the Sign of the Cross.

> **Leader:** *God, our Father, we praise and thank you for continuing to welcome us back into your love.*
>
> **All:** *We praise you, O Lord, for all your works are wonderful.*
>
> **Leader:** *Jesus, our Savior, we praise and thank you for showing us how to live as welcoming and inclusive people.*
>
> **All:** *We praise you, O Lord, for all your works are wonderful.*
>
> **Leader:** *Holy Spirit, giver of God's gifts, we praise and thank you for forming and shaping us into a welcoming community.*
>
> **All:** *We praise you, O Lord, for all your works are wonderful.*

We Are Welcomed

Goals	Environment	Materials
• To continue to affirm the importance of parent/family participation in this process • To help the participants understand the nature of sin • To encourage participants to understand that when we sin, Jesus always welcomes us back	• Be sure to identify the meeting place, posting clear directions if necessary. • Tables and chairs arranged for small groups • A prayer setting with large candle and a Bible on a stand or table • Quiet music for closing meditiation	• Beverages and light refreshments • Nametags • Copies of *Call to Celebrate: Reconciliation* Family Guide • *Songs of Celebration* CD • Copies of **Reconciliation Parent/ Adult Catechesis Handouts 2:1** and **2:2** (*Sacraments Source Book* CD) • Pens or pencils for writing • Copies of *Growing Faith* pamphlet, #33* • *Child's Book* • Board or chart paper

Welcome and Opening Prayer (10 minutes)

Welcome parents and other adults and distribute nametags.

Introduce yourself and briefly review the goals and agenda for the gathering.

✳ **If this session was preceded by a large group ritual and reflection, go to We Are Welcomed. If not, continue with the prayer.**

Gather the group around the prayer setting, if possible, or have the group pause for a reflective moment and begin the session.

Sing "We Are Marching," *Songs of Celebration* CD, track 2.

Pray these or similar words:

God, you always welcome us into life with you. You have welcomed us into your creation and you welcome us into your love and forgiveness. Send your Holy Spirit to guide us to be welcomers of one another. Amen.

We Are Welcomed (20 minutes)

Select two people to do the scripture readings.

Invite the selected readers to proclaim the readings from Romans.

Direct participants to share with one or two other persons:
• Which of the readings they most identified with.
• What the phrase "If God is on our side, can anyone be against us?" means to them.

Give pairs 3 to 5 minutes to share their responses with each other.

Point out that while we are all capable of sin, and many of us do sin, we must remember that God is always "for us." Our God is a welcoming God.

Distribute Reconciliation Parent/Adult Catechesis Handout 2:1.

Review the directions with participants and invite them to spend quiet time in reflection and writing.

Organize the large group into small groups of 4 to 5 people and ask them to share their responses.

> ***Growing Faith*** project pamphlets can be purchased online by going to **www.harcourtreligion.com.** **GO** ONLINE

What Is Sin? (Part 1) (20 minutes)

Distribute copies of *"What Is Sin?"* *Growing Faith* pamphlet #33. Quickly page through the pamphlet with participants and point out the variety of topics. Indicate that you will not be covering the entire pamphlet at this meeting, but that it is a valuable resource for them.

Summarize the material on the first spread of the pamphlet.

Guide the groups to use the reflection section on p. 1 for their small group discussion, and allow 10 minutes for it. At the conclusion of the discussion, gather feedback from the small groups by asking for their responses to the questions. Ask what questions this discussion raised for participants. Jot the questions down so you can refer to them in the second half of the session.

Break for refreshments and conversation.

What Is Sin? (Part 2) (30 minutes)

Distribute Reconciliation Parent/Adult Catechesis Handout 2:2.

Use the handout as an outline to present the doctrine of sin.

Discuss the scriptural images of sin in a conversational style with the participants. Point out that the images give rise to seeing sin as a deviation from an already established relationship or way of life.

Review the distinction between mortal and venial sin. Point out the importance for parents to help children see that sin is not a mistake or an accident, but a choice.

Refer to the questions raised before the break and respond to them.

Parent Moment (10 minutes)

Invite all to participate in the following discussion in their small groups:

- Knowing what you do now, how would you define sin to your child?

Ask for volunteers to share ideas that surfaced in their groups.

Highlight the three Faith at Home features in the *Child's Book*, and show how they will help parents and family members to participate in children's preparation.

Emphasize the importance of doing the activities on the Faith at Home page, especially the ritual action.

Closing Prayer (5 minutes)

Gather the participants in a circle around the prayer space and pray these or similar words.

Loving God, we give you praise and thanks for all the ways you have welcomed and invited us into your life. We ask for the grace to be open to your invitation and the generosity to be open and welcoming to others. Amen.

Thank everyone for their time and participation.

 Encourage parents and family members to go to **www.harcourtreligion.com** for more ideas and suggestions.

We Are Welcomed

Objectives

- To guide families to experience a celebration of the word, including the Renewal of Baptismal Promises
- To explore the meaning of the ritual action in family groups
- To present the concept of forgiveness
- To show that Jesus welcomes sinners
- To explain how we are welcomed in the Sacrament of Reconciliation

Materials

- Copies of the Celebration for the assembly (*Sacraments Source Book* CD)
- *Songs of Celebration* CD
- Prayer table
- Bible
- Candle and matches
- Bowl filled with water
- Small tree branch
- Copies of Scripture Drama 2 for participants, pp. CE5–6
- Poster paper
- Markers
- Pencils
- *Child's Book*

Welcome and Celebration (10–15 minutes)

Welcome the families in the gathering space.

Distribute copies of the celebration.

Select a family to be in the procession. Have them choose a family member to carry the Bible in procession.
- When families are assembled, walk forward slowly. Follow the child carrying the Bible.
- During the procession, lead families in singing "We Are Marching," from the *Songs of Celebration* CD, track 2.
- Place the Bible on the table and have family members return to their seats.
- Light the prayer candle.
- Begin prayer with the Sign of the Cross and invite the group to follow the order of the prayer.
- Lead the Renewal of Baptismal Promises.
- Dip the small branch in the water, and sprinkle families with water.
- For the proclamation of the Gospel, you may use a Bible or the adapted reading in the *Child's Book* on pp. 16–17.
- Conclude with the opening song from the *Songs of Celebration* CD, track 2.

The Light of Christ individual family unit experience (10 minutes)

Guide family members to reflect on the celebration by asking the following questions:
- What did you see? What did you hear? What did you do?

Ask volunteers to share their responses.

Have family members work with the children to complete the activity on p. 14 of the *Child's Book*.

Ask volunteers to share their drawings.

Read aloud Signs of Faith: Holy Water on p. 14.

Describe where holy water fonts or baptismal pools are located in your parish.

Encourage families to fill a small bottle with holy water next time they go to church and keep it at home.

Explain that family members can make the Sign of the Cross with the holy water and bless themselves, or each other, before leaving the house each day.

Children of Light whole-group learning experience (10 minutes)

Select a family member to read aloud the first paragraph from p. 15 of the *Child's Book*.

Summarize the second paragraph and remind families that sins are deliberate wrong and hurtful actions. Mistakes and accidents are not done on purpose and are not sins.

Select members of several families to give examples of sins, mistakes, and accidents.

Read aloud the third paragraph. Remind families that Jesus is always ready to give us a second chance.

Read aloud the text Signs of Faith: Candles. Remind the group that we are called to be a light to others.

Jesus Brings Good News family cluster sharing experience
(10 minutes)

Organize the large groups into small clusters and have each group select a leader. Provide a sheet of poster paper and a marker for each group.

Invite family cluster groups to reflect on the following question:
• What happens when Jesus welcomes us?

Ask group leaders to list their group's responses on the poster paper.

Invite volunteers to share responses.

Have leaders read the first paragraph on p. 16 of the *Child's Book* aloud to their group members.

Scripture whole-group learning experience (15 minutes)

Arrange the space for the Scripture Drama 2 from pp. CE5–6 of the *Catechist Edition*. Select members of several families to role-play the Scripture reading.

Invite the large group to reflect on the following questions:
• Why do you think Jesus decided to stop at Zacchaeus' house?
• What would you do if Jesus came to your home?

Allow time for volunteers to share responses to the questions and for children to complete the activity.

Second Chance whole-group learning experience (10 minutes)

Point out the picture and text for Signs of Faith: Reconciliation Room. Read aloud the text and make sure everyone is familiar with where the parish Reconciliation room is.

Discuss the question, "How are we welcomed in the Sacrament of Reconciliation?"

Recall that Jesus gave Zacchaeus a second chance to live a good life.

Explain that Reconciliation gives us a second chance, too.

Write the following terms on the next sheet of poster paper: *free will, mortal sin, venial sin*.

Summarize the information on p. 18 of the *Child's Book*. Stop to point out each term on the poster paper as you work through the page.

Ask families to describe the difference between mortal sin and venial sin.

Preparation and Welcome whole-group learning experience
(10 minutes)

Explain the activity on p. 20 of the *Child's Book*.

Tell children preparing to celebrate Reconciliation for the first time to complete the activity with the help of family members.

Encourage children to use words to express their feelings about getting ready for their first celebration of the Sacrament of Reconciliation.

Invite volunteers to share their letters.

Closing Blessing (5 minutes)

Invite each family to form a family circle.

Begin with the Sign of the Cross.

Pray the prayer on p. 20 of the *Child's Book*.

Conclude by leading families in singing *Songs of Celebration* CD, track 2, "We Are Marching."

Faith at Home individual family unit experience (5 minutes)

Direct families' attention to the Faith at Home page and encourage them to do the activities at home.

We Reflect

Before the Celebration

- Choose a gathering space that will be conducive to prayer and that will accommodate the size of the group; the church, a chapel, or a gathering place in the parish hall would each be appropriate. You will want the group to be able to see, hear, and move easily during the ritual.

- Prepare the group for the ritual action of Reverencing the Word and for the reflection on the sacred Scriptures.

- Select a good reader to proclaim the reading.

- Select three people for the entrance procession: to carry the Bible, the candle, and the bowl of water. Show them where and how to place them in the sanctuary or on the prayer table.

- If not in a church or chapel, place chairs in semicircular rows around the prayer space. Leave enough space for people to move in and out of the rows. If possible, have tables and chairs set up in another space for adult discussion after the celebration.

Materials

- A large clear, bowl with water, or if the celebration is in the church, use the baptismal font or pool

- A large candle or the Paschal candle

- A prayer table for the candle, a Bible, and a stand

- *Songs of Celebration* CD

- Copies of the celebration for the assembly (*Sacraments Source Book* CD)

Gathering Rite

Welcome the gathered assembly.

Rehearse the opening song, and go over the ritual action of the Reverencing the Word.

Invite the assembly to stand for the procession.

Opening Song

"Del Señor viene la misericordia," *Songs of Celebration* CD, track 3.

Procession

The presider and persons carrying the bowl with water, candle, and Bible process in while the assembly sings.

> *Leader: Let us pray.*
> *Make the Sign of the Cross together.*

Opening Prayer

Leader: God, our loving Father, you call us to holiness. You want us to be united in you. Send us the Holy Spirit so that our minds and hearts will be open to your word. We ask this through Jesus Christ our Lord.

All: Amen.

Celebration of the Word

Leader: A reading from the holy Gospel according to Luke.

All: Glory to you, Lord.
Read Luke 10:25–28.

Leader: The Gospel of the Lord.

All: Praise to you, Lord Jesus Christ.
Silence.

Reflection

Invite the assembly to reflect on the Gospel. Use the following question:

- How are you like the man who studied the commandments?

Ask the assembly to share their responses with one or two people. Be sure to include children in the sharing.

Reverencing the Word

Invite the children preparing for Reconciliation to come forward one at a time with one family member and bow or place their right hands on the Bible. If the number of children is large, have catechists assist. Say the words below to each of them individually.

> *Leader:* [Name], may God's word always enlighten you.
>
> *Child:* Amen.

Invite the assembly to come forward when the children are finished.

> *Leader:* Let us join in the prayer Jesus has taught us.
> *Pray the Lord's Prayer.*

Closing Prayer

> *Leader:* May the Lord bless us, protect us from all evil, and bring us to everlasting life.
>
> *All:* Amen.

Children go to their group session and adults go to the appointed space for reflection.

- There is a liturgical catechetical session for adults on p. 180.
- There is a parent/adult catechetical session on pp. 181–182.
- There is an intergenerational catechetical session on pp. 183–184.

We Reflect

Goals	Materials
• To reflect on the celebration • To explore the meaning of reverencing the Bible • To present the ways sacred Scripture is used in the Church and in the Sacrament of Reconciliation	• Poster board, chart paper, or overhead • Markers • *Songs of Celebration* CD • Bible

Reflection (30 minutes)

Invite the adults to gather in groups of five or six.

Begin by recalling the ritual moments of the celebration. Lead a guided meditation using the following prompts:
• Play a few verses of the opening song, "Del Señor viene la misericordia," *Songs of Celebration* CD, track 3.
• Ask: "What did you see or hear as the children and families went forward to reverence the Bible?"
• Read a few verses of the Gospel.
• Ask participants to recall their discussion of the Gospel.

Small Group Sharing

Pause for a few minutes of silence. Then invite the participants to share their feelings about the celebration in their small group. After 10 to 15 minutes, invite sharing with the large group.

Large Group Sharing

Gather the responses of the small groups on poster board, chart paper, or an overhead projector. Ask for feelings and thoughts about the celebration as a whole, and also for specific parts of the celebration that were meaningful to members of the group.

Naming (20 minutes)

Ask the participants to name what they learned from the celebration about God, Jesus, the Church, sacred Scripture, or their own Christian life.

Take each category separately and list responses on poster board, chart paper, or an overhead projector. When the lists are completed, use them to summarize the role of sacred Scripture in the Church and the celebration of the Sacrament of Reconciliation.

Affirm, add, or enlarge upon the following points:
• We reverence the Bible because God is present in the sacred Scriptures.
• The word is meant to guide us in the Christian life.
• We listen to the word of God during the Liturgy of the Word at Eucharist and during the Celebration of the Word at a communal celebration of Reconciliation.
• We show our reverence for God's word during the liturgy by our gestures.
• The Bible nourishes our spiritual lives when we study it or pray and reflect on it.
• The *Rite of Penance* states: *For through the word of God Christians receive light to recognize their sins and are called to conversion and to confidence in God's mercy* (17).

Reflection and Small Group Sharing (20 minutes)

Ask "What is one thing you will do this week to open yourself to prayer and reflection on the sacred Scriptures?"

Direct participants to reflect in silence for a few a minutes and then share in their group.

Closing Blessing (5 minutes)

Extend your hands over the group and pray in these or similar words:

Leader: *God of power, look upon your sons and daughters as they seek to deepen their understanding of the word.*

Open their minds and hearts that they may come to know you more fully, and recognize your will for them. We ask this through Christ our Lord.

All: *Amen.*

We Reflect

Goals

- To help participants discover the power of God's word
- To develop the concept of the meaning of conscience more fully
- To help participants come to a deeper understanding of the benefit of an Examination of Conscience
- To teach the participants how to use the Scriptures for an Examination of Conscience

Environment

- Be sure to clearly identify the meeting place, posting clear directions if necessary.
- Tables and chairs arranged for small groups
- A prayer setting with large candle and a Bible on a stand or table

Materials

- Beverages and light refreshments
- Nametags
- Copies of **Call to Celebrate: Reconciliation** Family Guide
- *Songs of Celebration* CD
- Copies of **Reconciliation Parent/ Adult Catechesis Handouts 3:1** and **3:2** (*Sacraments Source Book* CD)
- Pens or pencils for writing
- *Child's Book*
- Board or chart paper

Welcome and Opening Prayer (15 minutes)

Welcome parents and other adults and distribute nametags.

Introduce yourself and briefly review the goals and agenda for the gathering.

Select one of the participants to be a candle bearer for the prayer if you are celebrating the prayer in this session.

✴ **If this session was preceded by a large group ritual and reflection, go to We Reflect. If not, begin with the prayer.**

Gather the group around the prayer setting, if possible, or have the group pause for a reflective moment.

Introduce the prayer with the Sign of the Cross.

Sing "Del Señor viene la misericordia," *Songs of Celebration* CD, track 3.

Pray these or similar words:

Your word, O God, is spirit and light. You speak to us in your word, so that we might know the truth, the path of our lives, and the light of your wisdom. Open our ears to hear your word today. Open our minds to understand your word today. Open our hearts to accept your word today. We ask this in Jesus' name. Amen.

Read Luke 10:25–28.

We Reflect (30 minutes)

Explain that the celebration of the Sacrament of Reconciliation involves listening to God's word in the Scriptures because:

- We seek understanding of how we are to be disciples and followers of Jesus by reading, listening, reflecting, and sharing the word of God in sacred Scripture. That is why an Examination of Conscience begins with reading the sacred Scriptures, and both the communal and individual rites have a place for Scripture readings.
- We believe that in sacred Scripture we hear God's voice, and that this can help us discern God's will. It inspires us and forms our conscience and often leads us to a conversion of heart. These stories in the sacred Scriptures are our stories, too. The power of the word is active and transformative for all who receive it in faith.

Invite all to pause and listen once again to the Gospel of *Luke 10:25–28*. Encourage them to hear the word as if they were one of the people in the story.

Allow a period of silence.

Gather participants into groups of 5 to 6.

Invite them to discuss their responses to the following questions:

- What was the man looking for?
- How is his question relevant for your life today?
- What meaning do the words of Jesus have for you today?

- How does this passage change or cause you to rethink anything about your life?

Conclude the discussion by inviting volunteers to share any insights they had during the small group discussion.

Break for refreshments and conversation.

What Is a Conscience? (15 minutes)

Gather the participants back in the large group.

Write the word *conscience* in large letters on the board or on chart paper.

Ask participants to name what words or images they connect with the word *conscience*.

Point out that a conscience is not able to be seen or located in our bodies, but we know it is there.

Show that our conscience plays at least three different roles. It is active:
- when we have a vision of how things should be.
- when we sense that something is right or wrong.
- after the fact when we look back and know that a choice we made was good or not good.

Summarize by explaining that in preparing for the Sacrament of Reconciliation, we examine our conscience. Conscience is that inner voice that helps us to know right from wrong. The Ten Commandments, the Beatitudes, the life of Jesus, and the teachings of the Church are all guides to help us form our conscience and examine our life and our motives.

An Examination of Conscience (15 minutes)

Distribute Reconciliation Parent/Adult Catechesis Handout 3:1 and explain that there are many ways to use sacred Scripture to examine our conscience.

Explain the directions and have individuals work alone for several minutes to develop questions for an examination of conscience.

Ask them to gather into small groups of 3 to 4 to share their questions and develop more. Move around in the groups to assist where needed.

Gather them back into one large group. Ask them to share something from their work.

Parent Moment (10 minutes)

Highlight the three Faith at Home features in the *Child's Book* and show how they will help the parents and family members to participate in children's preparation.

Distribute copies of **Reconciliation Parent/Adult Catechesis Handout 3:2.** Explain that it lists of some of the scripture passages they or their children might choose for the celebration of Reconciliation.

Emphasize the importance of doing the activities on the Faith at Home page, especially the ritual actions.

Closing Prayer (5 minutes)

Gather the participants in a circle around the prayer space and pray these or similar words:

Your word, O God is power and truth. We have seen it with our own eyes and stand before you with wonder. Cleanse our hearts and make us your holy people. Amen.

Raise the sacred Scriptures and invite all to bow and reverence the word of God.

Read *Galatians 5:22–26.*

Extend your hands and pray this blessing, inviting all to join you in saying the "Amens":

May we truly hear and heed God's living word. Amen.
May the light of God's word shine forth in our lives. Amen.
May we walk in God's way. Amen.
May the almighty and merciful God bless us, the Father, the Son, and the Holy Spirit. Amen.

Thank everyone for their time and participation.

Encourage parents and family members to go to **www.harcourtreligion.com** for more ideas and suggestions.

We Reflect

Objectives

- To guide families to experience a celebration of the word, including Reverencing the Word
- To explore the meaning of the ritual action in family groups
- To present how the Bible is used in liturgy
- To explain the Examination of Conscience and the place of Scriptures in Reconciliation celebrations

Materials

- Copies of the celebration for the assembly (*Sacraments Source Book* CD)
- *Songs of Celebration* CD
- Prayer table
- Bible
- Candle and matches
- Bowl filled with water
- Copies of Scripture Drama 3, pp. CE8–9
- Activity Master 3, p. CE7
- Chart or poster paper
- Bibles for family groups
- Markers
- Pencils
- *Child's Book*

Welcome and Celebration (10–15 minutes)

Welcome the families in the gathering space.

Distribute copies of the celebration.

Select a family to be in the procession. Have them choose a family member to carry the Bible in procession.

- When families are assembled, walk forward slowly. Follow the child carrying the Bible.
- During the procession, lead families in singing "Del Señor viene la misericordia," from the *Songs of Celebration* CD, track 3.
- Place the Bible on the prayer table and have family members return to their seats.
- Light the prayer candle.
- Begin prayer with the Sign of the Cross and invite the group to follow the order of the prayer.
- Invite families to form a line.
- Have them come forward one by one and reverence the Bible.
- For the proclamation of the Gospel, you may use a Bible or the adapted reading in the *Child's Book* on pages 26–27.
- Conclude with the opening song from the *Songs of Celebration* CD, track 3.

God's Word individual family unit experience (10 minutes)

Guide family members to reflect on the celebration by asking the following questions:

- What did you see? What did you hear? What did you do?

Invite family members to turn toward one another and share their responses to the questions.

Guide families to reflect further on reverencing the Word, using the activity on p. 24 of the *Child's Book*.

Allow time for family members to share their responses to the activity.

Summarize the text for Signs of Faith: Bowing.

God Speaks to Us family cluster sharing experience (15 minutes)

Organize the large group into small clusters and have each group select a leader.

Provide each group with a sheet of poster paper, markers, and a Bible.

Direct the group leaders to select members of their group to read aloud the text from p. 25 of the *Child's Book*.

Explain that each group will discuss their favorite Bible stories and choose one story to illustrate on the poster paper. Keep the illustrations simple, perhaps drawing one symbol or depicting one key element of the story.

Invite each leader to stand and share his or her group's Bible story illustration with the large group. After all groups have shared, point out the Bibles to the group leaders. Have leaders pass the Bible around to their members so they can look through it while leaders read aloud the text Signs of Faith: The Bible.

Loving God and Neighbor whole-group learning experience (10 minutes)

Invite families to think about how family rules help show everyone how to behave.

Ask for volunteers to share some of their family rules with the large group.

Invite families to reflect on the following question:

- What is the greatest commandment?

List all responses on a sheet of poster paper in front of the large group.

Recall that the Ten Commandments are in the Old Testament. They are laws from God.

Read aloud the first paragraph on p. 26 of the *Child's Book*.

Scripture whole-group learning experience (15 minutes)

Select members of several families to dramatize the Scripture story, using pp. CE8–9 of the *Catechist Edition*.

Write the term *Great Commandment* on the poster paper in front of the large group. Point out that the Great Commandment includes the Ten Commandments in one short sentence.

Draw two tablets on the next sheet of poster paper. Write the numbers 1–3 on one tablet and 4–10 on the other. As you read the second paragraph on p. 27 of the *Child's Book*, use this graphic to reinforce the division of the commandments.

Invite the large group to reflect on the following questions:

- What was Jesus trying to tell the man in the Scripture story?
- When does following a commandment make you happy?

Allow time for volunteers to share responses.

Distribute Activity Master 3 from the *Catechist Edition* for use at home.

The Examination of Conscience whole-group learning experience (10 minutes)

Write the terms *Examination of Conscience, precepts,* and *holy* on a sheet of poster paper in front of the

large group. As you discuss p. 28 from the *Child's Book*, point to the terms you have written.

Recall with families that God gave us free will.

Point out that your conscience helps you know right from wrong and if you have used your free will to make loving choices. As you read and discuss the *Child's Book*, call attention to the bulleted questions.

Tell families that these types of questions help them think about the choices that they make.

We Listen to God's Word family cluster sharing experience (10 minutes)

Organize the large group into the same small family clusters as earlier.

Ask leaders to facilitate their group's discussion about: how studying Scripture helps us to know how we are called to live. Have them read aloud to their group from p. 29 of the *Child's Book*.

Point out to families that conscience helps us know what is right and wrong. In the Sacrament of Reconciliation, we examine our conscience.

Explain that we hear Scripture readings and a homily during a communal Reconciliation celebration.

Showing Love individual family unit experience (5 minutes)

Invite family members to talk about ways they show love for one another.

Have families work together to complete the activity on p. 30 of the *Child's Book*.

Closing Blessing (5 minutes)

Invite each family to form a family circle.

Begin with the Sign of the Cross.

Pray the prayer on p. 30 of the *Child's Book*.

Conclude by leading families in singing *Songs of Celebration* CD, track 3, "Del Señor viene la misericordia."

Faith at Home individual family unit experience (5 minutes)

Direct families' attention to the Faith at Home page and encourage them to do the activities at home.

Reconciliation Session 4—Whole Community Ritual

We Are Sorry

Before the Celebration

- Choose a gathering space that will be conducive to prayer and that will accommodate the size of the group; the church, a chapel, or a gathering place in the parish hall would each be appropriate. You will want the group to be able to see, hear, and move easily during the ritual.

- Prepare the group for the ritual action of Examination of Conscience and Act of Contrition, and for the reflection on the sacred Scriptures.

- Select a good reader to proclaim the reading.

- Select three people to carry: the Bible, the candle, and the bowl of water in procession. Show them where and how to place them in the sanctuary or on the prayer table.

- If not in a church or chapel, place chairs in semicircular rows around the prayer space. Leave enough space for people to move in and out of the rows. If possible, have tables and chairs set up in another space for adult discussion after the celebration.

Materials

- A large, clear bowl with water, or if the celebration is in the church, use the baptismal font or pool
- A branch or aspergellum for sprinkling
- A large candle or the Paschal candle
- A prayer table for the candle, a Bible, and a stand
- *Songs of Celebration* CD
- Copies of the celebration for the assembly (*Sacraments Source Book* CD)

Gathering Rite

Welcome the gathered assembly.

Rehearse the opening song, and go over the ritual action of Examination of Conscience and Act of Contrition.

Invite the assembly to stand for the procession.

Opening Song

"Remember Your Love," *Songs of Celebration* CD, track 4.

Procession

The presider and persons carrying the bowl with water, candle, and Bible process in while the assembly sings.

> *Leader: Let us pray.*
> *Make the Sign of the Cross together.*

Opening Prayer

> *Leader: Loving God, send us the Holy Spirit to open our ears and hearts that we may hear your word and be filled with the courage to live it. We ask this through Jesus Christ our Lord.*
> *All: Amen.*

Celebration of the Word

> *Leader: A reading from the holy Gospel according to Luke.*
> *All: Glory to you, Lord.*
> *Read Luke 7:36–38, 44–48, 50.*
> *Leader: The Gospel of the Lord.*
> *All: Praise to you, Lord Jesus Christ.*
> *Sit silently.*

Reflection

Invite the assembly to reflect on the Gospel. Use the following question:

• What did the Gospel reading say to you about being sorry?

Ask the assembly to share their responses with one or two people. Be sure to include children in the sharing.

Examination of Conscience and Act of Contrition

The sinful woman showed Jesus she was sorry for her sins. Let us think about what we want to tell Jesus we are sorry for.

Ask the assembly to be seated and use the quiet time for an examination of conscience. Invite them to use these questions as starting points:

• Have I loved and honor God's name?
• Have I prayed to God often during the day?
• Have I kept Sunday as a holy day?
• Have I cared for and respected my parents?
• Have I shared what I have with others?
• Have I acted with kindness to family and friends?
• Have I told the truth?

> **Leader:** *Christ our Lord came to call sinners into his Father's Kingdom. Let us now kneel and pray an Act of Contrition.*
> *Kneel.*

> **All:** *My God, I am sorry for my sins with all my heart. In choosing to do wrong and failing to do good, I have sinned against you whom I should love above all things. I firmly intend, with your help, to do penance, to sin no more, and to avoid whatever leads me to sin. Our Savior, Jesus Christ, suffered and died for us. In his name, my God, have mercy. Amen.*
> *Stand.*

Closing Prayer

> **Leader:** *Lord, our God, you know all things. You know that we want to be more generous in serving you and our neighbor. Look on us with love and hear our prayer.*
> **All:** *Amen.*

Children go to their group session and adults go to the appointed space for reflection.

• There is a liturgical catechetical session for adults on p. 187.
• There is a parent/adult catechetical session on pp. 188–189.
• There is an intergenerational catechetical session on pp. 190–191.

We Are Sorry

Goals
• To reflect on the celebration
• To explore the meaning of sorrow for sins
• To discuss the examination of conscience and the Act of Contrition

Materials
• Poster board, chart paper, or overhead projector   • *Songs of Celebration* CD
• Markers   • Bible

Reflection (20 minutes)

Invite the adults to gather in groups of five or six.

Begin by recalling the ritual moments of the celebration. Lead a guided meditation using the following prompts. Pause after each prompt.
- Play a few verses of the opening song, "Remember Your Love," *Songs of Celebration* CD, track 4.
- Ask: "What was the overall environment of the celebration? What did you hear? See? Feel?"
- Read a few verses of the Gospel.
- Ask participants to recall their discussion of the Gospel.
- Repeat some of the words of the examination of conscience.
- Repeat some of the words of the Act of Contrition.

Small Group Sharing

Pause for a few minutes of silence. Then invite the participants to share their feelings about the celebration in their small group. After 10 to 15 minutes, invite sharing with the large group.

Large Group Sharing

Gather the responses of the small groups on poster board, chart paper, or an overhead projector. Ask for feelings and thoughts about the celebration as a whole, and also for specific parts of the celebration that were meaningful to members of the group.

Naming (30 minutes)

Ask the participants to name what they learned from the celebration about, Jesus, the Church, or examination of conscience and sorrow for sin.

Take each category separately and list responses on poster board, chart paper, or an overhead projector. When the lists are completed, use them to summarize the significance of the examination of conscience, sorrow for sin, and the Act of Contrition.

Affirm, add, or enlarge upon the following points:
- Conscience is that capacity in us that helps us discern: what is good or how things ought to be, the rightness and wrongness of present or past actions.
- Conscience is informed by sacred Scripture and the teachings of the Church.
- When we examine our conscience, we consult the Scriptures and the teachings of the Church.
- The Rite of Penance presents several different models for an examination of conscience.
- Sorrow for sin involves naming the sin, asking for forgiveness, and resolving not to sin again.

Reflection and Small Group Sharing (20 minutes)

Ask: "What is one thing you will do this week to open yourself to reflecting on the habits, actions, and patterns of your life as they relate to sin and forgiveness?"

Direct participants to reflect in silence for a few a minutes and then share in their group.

Closing Blessing (5 minutes)

Gather and begin with the Sign of the Cross.

> **Leader:** *God calls us to conversion; let us ask him for the grace to see our lives as he does, and let us ask for the gift of true sorrow for our sins.*

Extend your hands over the group and pray these or similar words.

> **Leader:** *Lord, hear the prayers of those who call on you, forgive those who confess to you, and grant us your pardon and peace. We ask this through Christ our Lord.*
>
> **All:** *Amen.*

We Are Sorry

Goals	Environment	Materials
• To examine the experience of conversion • To help the participants come to a deeper understanding of the nature of sorrow for sin	• Be sure to clearly identify the meeting place, posting clear directions if necessary. • Tables and chairs arranged for small groups • A prayer setting with large candle, Bible on a stand or table, and a bowl of ashes	• Beverages and light refreshments • Name tags • Copies of *Call to Celebrate: Reconciliation* Family Guide • *Songs of Celebration* CD, track 4 • Copies of **Reconciliation Parent/Adult Catechesis Handouts 4:1** and **4:2** (*Sacraments Source Book* CD) • Pens or pencils for writing • *Child's Book* • *Reconciliation Stories of Celebration* video and guide, part 3 • Board or chart paper

Welcome and Opening Prayer (15 minutes)

Welcome parents and other adults and distribute nametags.

Introduce yourself and briefly review the goals and agenda for the gathering.

✳ **If this session was preceded by a large group ritual and reflection, go to We Are Sorry. If not, continue with the prayer.**

Gather the group around the prayer setting, if possible, or have the group pause for a reflective moment.

Introduce the prayer with the Sign of the Cross.

Sing "Remember Your Love," *Songs of Celebration* CD, track 4.

Introduce the prayer by telling participants that the Sacrament of Reconciliation is part of the process of conversion. Through the power of the Holy Spirit, we can honestly look at the nature of our imperfections, experience sorrow, and be moved to change. Integral to the Sacrament of Reconciliation is the Act of Contrition. Contrition is that sentiment which indicates our willingness to change.

Distribute Reconciliation Parent/Adult Catechesis Handout 4:1.

Pray together the Act of Contrition.

Allow time for participants to silently reflect upon their experience of sorrow and conversion as expressed in that prayer.

Conclude with the Lord's Prayer.

We Are Sorry (30 minutes)

View the third part of the video, *Reconciliation Stories of Celebration*. Follow the outline and directions in the guide.

Break for refreshments and conversation.

What Is Conversion? (30 minutes)

Ask the group to gather in groups of 5 to 6.

Distribute Reconciliation Parent/Adult Catechesis Handout 4:2. Using the handout as a guide, have the participants quietly describe a moment of conversion in their own lives.

Invite participants to share their stories in their small groups. Remind them they may share as little or as much as they want, or they may pass.

Summarize the nature of conversion in these or similar words:
• It is always a movement away from one thing (person, attitude, behavior) toward another.
• Usually it is triggered by dissatisfaction.

- We are different after a conversion.
- Religious conversion has all the same characteristics, but at its heart, religious conversion is the movement of our being toward God.
- We believe the Holy Spirit is within us to empower our conversion away from persons, attitudes, behaviors, or patterns that keep us from God.
- The process of conversion transforms the way we relate to others, to ourselves, to the world, to God, and to all of creation.
- Conversion is a continuous lifelong process that draws us closer to God and one another.
- As we develop the habit of examining our values, attitudes, and lifestyles, and discover the areas where we "miss the mark," we experience the next step in the conversion process, which is contrition.
- Contrition moves us forward to firmly resolve to break away from habits, actions, and attitudes that blind us to love.

Parent Moment (10 minutes)

Highlight the three Faith at Home features in the *Child's Book* and show how they will help the parents and family members to participate in children's preparation.

Emphasize the importance of doing the activities on the Faith at Home page, especially the ritual action.

Closing Prayer (5 minutes)

Gather around the prayer table, if possible.

Explain that ashes are a symbol of sorrow and contrition for sin.

Invite each person to come forward and sign himself or herself with ashes, saying, "Turn away from sin and believe the good news." During the signing, sing or play "Remember Your Love," *Songs of Celebration* CD, track 4.

Close by praying the Lord's Prayer together.

Thank everyone for their time and participation.

Encourage parents and family members to go to **www.harcourtreligion.com** for more ideas and suggestions.

Reconciliation Session 4—Intergenerational Catechesis

We Are Sorry

Objectives

- To guide families to experience a celebration of the word, including the Examination of Conscience and Act of Contrition
- To explore the meaning of the ritual action in family groups
- To present the importance of asking forgiveness
- To explain the role of confession and penance in Reconciliation
- To reinforce the idea of contrition for sins

Materials

- Copies of the celebration for the assembly (*Sacraments Source Book* CD)
- *Songs of Celebration* CD
- Prayer table
- Bible
- Candle and matches
- Bowl filled with water
- Copies of Scripture Readers' Theater 4, p. CE11
- Copies of Activity Master 4, p. CE10
- Chart or poster paper
- Markers
- Crayons
- Pencils
- *Child's Book*

Welcome and Celebration (10–15 minutes)

Welcome the families in the gathering space.

Distribute copies of the celebration.

Select a family to be in the procession, and choose a child from that family to carry the Bible.
- When families are assembled, walk forward slowly. Follow the child carrying the Bible.
- During the procession, lead families in singing "Remember Your Love," from the *Songs of Celebration* CD, track 4.
- Place the Bible on the prayer table and have the family members return to their seats.
- Light the prayer candle.
- Begin prayer with the Sign of the Cross and invite the group to follow the order of the prayer.
- For the proclamation of the Gospel, you may use a Bible or the adapted reading in the *Child's Book* on pp. 36–37.
- Invite families to be quiet and to reflect on the questions for the Examination of Conscience.
- Have families kneel.
- Invite families to stand for the closing prayer.
- Conclude with the opening song from the *Songs of Celebration* CD, track 4.

Sorrow for Sin individual family unit experience (10 minutes)

Guide family members to reflect on the celebration by asking the following questions:
- What did you see? What did you hear? What did you do?

Ask volunteers to share their responses.

Guide families to reflect further on being called by name, using the activity on p. 34 of the *Child's Book*.

Allow time for family members to share their responses to the activity.

Discuss the experience of kneeling, and have a family member read aloud the text Signs of Faith: Kneeling.

Ask for Forgiveness family cluster sharing experience (15 minutes)

Organize the large group into small clusters and have each group select a leader. Provide each group with a sheet of poster paper and a marker.

Ask leaders to brainstorm with their group what it feels like when family members say they are sorry and ask forgiveness. List all responses.

Invite volunteers to share their groups' responses.

Direct leaders to read aloud to their group, the first two paragraphs on p. 35 of the *Child's Book*.

Emphasize the importance of genuine sorrow in the process of forgiveness and read aloud the text Signs of faith: Contrition.

Sinners Come to Jesus whole-group learning experience
(10 minutes)

Invite families to reflect on the following question:
- How do people tell Jesus they are sorry?

List all responses on poster paper in front of the large group.

Remind families of the prayer of sorrow that they prayed in the opening celebration.

Point out that there are many ways to show sorrow.

Say that the Scripture story shows a way that a woman showed she was sorry.

Scripture whole-group learning experience (15 minutes)

Select members of several families to tell the Scripture story using the Readers' Theater 4, p. CE11 of the *Catechist Edition.*

Invite the large group to reflect on the following questions:
- How did the woman show Jesus she was sorry for her sins?
- How do members of your family say they are sorry when they have done something wrong?

Allow time for volunteers to share responses to the questions and to complete the activity.

Distribute Activity Master 4, p. CE10 from the *Catechist Edition* to be used by children at home to reinforce the Gospel reading.

The Confession of Sin family cluster sharing experience
(10 minutes)

Organize the large group into the same small family clusters as earlier. Direct each group to reflect on the following question:
- Why do we confess our sins?

Have the group leader write all responses on the reverse side of the same poster paper used earlier.

Remind families that like the woman in the Gospel story, we need to show that we are sorry for our sins.

Direct leaders to read the bulleted material aloud to their group from p. 38 of the *Child's Book,* to explain the parts of the Sacrament of Reconciliation. As they come to the terms *confess, contrition,* and *penance,* have group members circle each term in the *Child's Book.*

Invite family cluster groups to share how they can plan their actions so that they will act in a loving fashion.

Sorrow and Penance whole-group learning experience
(10 minutes)

Talk with families about the types of penances that they might receive in the sacrament.

Write the terms *action* and *prayer* on the poster paper in front of the group. Point out that their penances can be either or both of these.

Ask families why we do penances.

Inform families that some prayers are called *acts.* Refer to p. 39 in the *Child's Book,* where several acts of contrition are printed. Discuss what these prayers have in common.

Discuss the following question:
- How does confession help us?

Showing Sorrow individual family unit experience (5 minutes)

Invite family members to share with one another a time when they were sorry.

Explain the activity on p. 40 of the *Child's Book.* Point out that the space is divided into three sections. Each panel can show a separate part of the story.

Allow time for families to complete the activity.

Invite volunteers to share their stories.

Closing Blessing (5 minutes)

Invite each family to form a family circle.

Begin with the Sign of the Cross.

Pray the prayer on p. 40 of the *Child's Book.*

Conclude by leading families in singing *Songs of Celebration* CD, track 4, "Remember Your Love."

Faith at Home individual family unit experience (5 minutes)

Direct families' attention to the Faith at Home page and encourage them to do the activities at home.

We Are Forgiven

Before the Celebration

- Choose a gathering space that will be conducive to prayer and that will accommodate the size of the group; the church, a chapel, or a gathering place in the parish hall would each be appropriate. You will want the group to be able to see, hear, and move easily during the ritual.

- Prepare the group for the ritual action of the Prayer over the Children and for the reflection on the sacred Scriptures.

- Select a good reader to proclaim the reading.

- Select three people for the entrance procession: to carry the Bible, the candle, and the bowl of water. Show them where and how to place them in the sanctuary or on the prayer table.

- If not in a church or chapel, place chairs in semicircular rows around the prayer space. Leave enough space for people to move in and out of the rows. If possible, have tables and chairs set up in another space for adult discussion after the celebration.

Materials

- A large, clear bowl with water, or if the celebration is in the church, use the baptismal font or pool
- A large candle or the Paschal candle
- A prayer table for the candle, a Bible, and a stand
- *Songs of Celebration* CD
- Copies of the celebration for the assembly (*Sacraments Source Book* CD)

Gathering Rite

Welcome the gathered assembly.

Rehearse the opening song, and go over the ritual action of the Prayer over the Children.

Invite the assembly to stand for the procession.

Opening Song

"Children of God," *Songs of Celebration* CD, track 5.

Procession

The presider and persons carrying the bowl with water, candle, and Bible process in while the assembly sings.

Leader: *Let us pray.*
    Make the Sign of the Cross together.

Opening Prayer

Leader: *Good and gracious God, you are always ready to forgive us. Send us the Holy Spirit. Open our hearts and minds to know your forgiving love. We ask this in the name of your Son, Jesus.*

Celebration of the Word

Leader: *A reading from the holy Gospel according to John.*
All: *Glory to you, Lord.*
    Read Luke 15:11–32.
Leader: *The Gospel of the Lord.*
All: *Praise to you, Lord Jesus Christ.*
    Sit silently.

Reflection

Invite the assembly to reflect on the Gospel. Use the following question:
- What does the Gospel story tell you about God?

Ask the assembly to share their responses with one or two people. Be sure to include children in the sharing.

Prayer over the Children

Leader: *In the scripture story, Jesus told us about a father who loved his son very much. He watched and waited for him to come home. God, our Father, loves us, too. Even when we turn away from him, he waits to welcome us home.*

Invite the children who are preparing for Reconciliation to come forward with a family member. Place your open hands on the head of each child and say:

Leader: *[Name], God loves you and will always forgive you.*
Child: *Thanks be to God.*

If the number of children is large, have several catechists assist.

When the all children have been blessed, invite the assembly to place their open hands on the head of the person next to them and remind them of God's love and forgiveness.

Leader: *Let us ask God our Father to forgive us and free us from evil.*
Pray the Lord's Prayer.

Closing Prayer

Leader: *May the God of peace fill your hearts with every blessing. May he strengthen you with the gift of hope. May he grant you all that is good.*
Child: *Amen.*

Children go to their group session and adults go to the appointed space for reflection.

- There is a liturgical catechetical session for adults on p. 194.
- There is a parent/adult catechetical session on pp. 195–196.
- There is an intergenerational catechetical session on pp. 197–198.

We Are Forgiven

Goals
• To reflect on the celebration
• To explain the ritual of absolution
• To explore forgiveness and reconciliation

Materials	
• Poster board, chart paper, or overhead projector	• *Songs of Celebration* CD
• Markers	• Bible

Reflection (20 minutes)

Invite the adults to gather in groups of five or six.

Begin by recalling the ritual moments of the celebration. Lead a guided meditation using the following prompts:
• Play a few verses of the opening song, "Children of God," *Songs of Celebration* CD, track 5.
• Read some verses of the Gospel.
• Ask participants to recall their discussion of the Gospel.
• Recall the ritual with the children and their family members; ask: "What did you see, what did you hear?"

Small Group Sharing

Pause for a few minutes of silence. Then invite the participants to share their feelings about the celebration in their small group. After 10 to 15 minutes, invite sharing with the large group.

Large Group Sharing

Gather the responses of the small groups on poster board, chart paper, or an overhead projector. Ask for feelings and thoughts about the celebration as a whole, and also for specific parts of the celebration that were meaningful to members of the group.

Naming (30 minutes)

Ask the participants to name what they learned from the celebration about God, Jesus, the Church, forgiveness, and the gesture of laying on hands.

Take each category separately and list responses on poster board, chart paper, or an overhead projector. When the lists are completed, use them to summarize the meaning of forgiveness and the ritual of absolution.

Affirm, add, or enlarge upon the following points:
• God's forgiveness is infinite.
• To experience forgiveness and pardon one must admit one's sin.
• The community has a role in forgiveness.
• God forgives sin through the ministry of the priest and the community.
• The absolution of the priest is always accompanied by a gesture of laying on of hands or at least an extension of the right hand. This signifies the power of the Holy Spirit and recalls the gesture of Jesus as he blessed and healed people.
• Reconciliation means bringing together again or reuniting and occurs when two people or communities ask and grant forgiveness and work to restore the relationship.

Reflection and Small Group Sharing (20 minutes)

Ask "What is one thing you will do this week to experience forgiving and asking for forgiveness?"

Direct participants to reflect in silence for a few minutes and then share their responses with their group.

Closing Blessing (5 minutes)

Gather and begin with the Sign of the Cross.

Leader: God, our Father, we praise and thank you for your generous forgiveness.
All: We give you thanks and praise.

Leader: Jesus, our Savior, we praise and thank you for showing us how to forgive.
All: We give you thanks and praise.

Leader: Holy Spirit, giver of God's gifts, we praise and thank you for enlightening us and giving us the courage to seek forgiveness.
All: We give you thanks and praise.

We Are Forgiven

Goals	Environment	Materials
• To help the participants discover the importance of forgiveness • To deepen their appreciation of the extent of God's forgiveness • To discover the graces and benefits of the Sacrament of Reconciliation	• Be sure to clearly identify the meeting place, posting clesr directions if necessary • Tables and chairs arranged for small groups • A prayer setting with large candle, a Bible on a stand or table, clear bowl filled with water, and incense	• Beverages and light refreshments • Nametags • *Songs of Celebration* CD • Copies of **Call to Celebrate: Reconciliation** Family Guide • Copies of **Reconciliation Parent/ Adult Catechesis Handouts 5:1** and **5:2** (*Sacraments Source Book* CD) • Pens or pencils • Overhead projector and transparencies or PowerPoint capability • Board or chart paper

Welcome and Opening Prayer (15 minutes)

Welcome parents and other adults and distribute nametags.

Introduce yourself and briefly review the goals and agenda for the gathering.

✳ **If this session was preceded by a large group ritual and reflection, go to We Are Forgiven. If not, begin with the prayer.**

Gather the group around the prayer setting, if possible, or have the group pause for a reflective moment.

Introduce the prayer with the Sign of the Cross.

Sing "Children of God," *Songs of Celebration* CD, track 5.

Light the incense and pray these or similar words:
God of love, you always envelop us with an embrace of love in spite of our weakness and sin. Fill us with a new sense of peace, knowing that you are pure love and mercy. Lead us in the light of your unconditional love that we might love one another. Let this, our prayer, rise up to you like the fragrance of incense. We ask this in Jesus' name. Amen.

We Are Forgiven (30 minutes)

Invite the participants to get comfortable in their seats.

Suggest that they close their eyes as you recall the story of the prodigal son and lead them in the following reflection.

Pause where appropriate:
- The son is greedy. He wants it all. His major concern, and sometimes ours as well, is his new self-centered lifestyle. (Pause.)
- The self-centeredness and lack of focus catch up with him after a while and he "comes to his senses," saying, "I will break away and return to my father." Before he ever gets out of the pigpen, he admits his sinfulness. He expresses contrition and determines his own penance. "I will say to him, 'Father, I have sinned against God and against you.... Treat me like one of your hired hands.'" He returns to his father and the father runs to meet him. (Pause.)
- Through one loving gesture, the father forgives the son, and the son hasn't even made his confession yet! "Quick!" says the father. "Let us celebrate." And why? Because a sinner has converted, repented, confessed, and returned. (Pause.)
- The older brother is looking on. He is angry. This is unfair! His problem is a universal human one. It's tough for most of us to say, "I'm sorry." It is even tougher to say, "You're forgiven." And it is most difficult of all to say gracefully, "I accept your forgiveness." To be able to do that, we must be able to forgive ourselves.

Ask the participants to gather in groups of 2 to 3 and share their thoughts, feelings, or insights from the reflection on the parable. After a few minutes, invite volunteers to share one thing they learned from the reflection and discussion.

Distribute Reconciliation Parent/Adult Catechesis Handout 5:1 and ask participants to choose the quote that makes the most sense to them.

Invite them to share their choice with at least one other person during the break.

Break for refreshments and conversaton.

What Is Forgiveness? (30 minutes)

Invite participants to share some of their insights from their conversations about the quotes.

Ask participants to open their *Family Guides* to the story "Forgive and Be Forgiven," p. 8.

Read the story aloud, then gather the large group into smaller groups of 5 to 6 people to discuss the two questions at the bottom of p. 9.

Gather the groups back after at least 15 minutes of discussion.

Begin with the last quote on Reconciliation Parent/Adult Catechesis Handout 5:1 from the *Catechism of the Catholic Church*.

Summarize the discussion and make the following points:

- *Forgiveness* means "to absolve, to wipe the slate clean, and to restore."
- Forgiveness is one person's response in the face of injustice or hatred. Reconciliation occurs when two persons can come together in mutual respect. One person can choose to forgive. Two people must change in order to restore mutual respect. Thus, when reconciliation occurs, it is always a sign of God's presence and activity.
- God always wants to forgive us and be reconciled.
- Being sorry and confessing we have done something wrong are essential components in our relationship with God and human beings.
- Forgiveness of sin brings reconciliation with God and the Church.

- Regular celebration of the Sacrament of Reconciliation affords the opportunity for forgiveness and reconciliation.

Read aloud the following statements that describe the effects and graces of the Sacrament of Reconciliation:

- Our union with God and the community of faith is restored.
- We are strengthened as members of the Church community.
- We are at peace and freed from shame and guilt.
- Our relationships are made whole again.
- We are one with all of creation.

Invite the participants to add to these statements. These can be recorded on a transparency or PowerPoint for emphasis.

Parent Moment (10 minutes)

Highlight the three Faith at Home features in the *Child's Book*, and show how they will help the parents and family members to participate in the children's preparation.

Emphasize the importance of doing the activities on the Faith at Home page, especially the ritual action.

Closing Prayer (5 minutes)

Distribute Reconciliation Parent/Adult Catechesis Handout 5:2.

Relight the incense.

Indicate the right and left side of the group for the antiphonal prayer.

Pray together Psalm 139 on the handout.

Ask each person to think about one weakness or sin for which they seek forgiveness, then direct them to pray in the silence of their hearts, seeking God's forgiveness.

Explain that as the incense smoke rises, it is a sign of God's desire to forgive and erase their sins and heal their weaknesses.

Thank everyone for their time and participation.

Encourage parents and family members to go to **www.harcourtreligion.com** for more ideas and suggestions.

We Are Forgiven

Objectives

- To guide families to experience a celebration of the word, including a Prayer over the Children by parents or caregivers
- To explore the meaning of the ritual action in family groups
- To reinforce the concept of God's forgiveness
- To explain the function of absolution in Reconciliation

Materials

- Copies of the celebration for the assembly (*Sacraments Source Book* CD)
- *Songs of Celebration* CD
- Prayer table
- Bible
- Candle and matches
- Bowl filled with water
- Copies of Scripture Echo Pantomime 5, p. CE13
- Copies of Activity Master 5, p. CE12
- Chart or poster paper
- Markers
- Blank sheets of white paper
- Pencils
- *Child's Book*

Welcome and Celebration (10–15 minutes)

Welcome the families in the gathering space.

Distribute copies of the celebration.

Select a family to be in the procession. Have them choose a family member to carry the Bible in procession.

- When families are assembled, walk forward slowly. Follow the child carrying the Bible.
- During the procession, lead families in singing "Children of God," from the *Songs of Celebration* CD, track 5.
- Place the Bible on the prayer table and have family members return to their seats.
- Light the prayer candle.
- Begin prayer with the Sign of the Cross and invite the group to follow the order of the prayer.
- For the proclamation of the Gospel, you may use a Bible or the adapted reading in the *Child's Book* on pages 46–47.
- Invite parents or caregivers to place their hands on the head of their child or on the heads of their children, saying: "(Name), God loves you and will always forgive you."
- Pray the Lord's Prayer.
- Conclude with the opening song from the *Songs of Celebration* CD, track 5.

Reconciliation individual family unit experience (10 minutes)

Guide family members to reflect on the celebration by asking the following questions:

- What did you see? What did you hear? What did you do?

Ask volunteers to share their group's responses.

Guide families to reflect further on being called by name, using the activity on p. 44 of the *Child's Book*.

Allow time for family members to share their responses to the activity.

Refer family members to the text Signs of Faith: Laying on of Hands for more information on the gesture.

Brought Together Again family cluster sharing experience (15 minutes)

Organize the large group into small clusters and have them select a leader. Provide a blank sheet of white paper for each group. Have leaders read aloud to their group the first two paragraphs on p. 45 of the *Child's Book*.

Have family leaders write the title: *Reconciliation*, on top of the sheet of paper provided.

Direct leaders to ask their group members to share any words or actions they have used to make a situation better, and write them down under the title. When groups have completed the activity, ask for a volunteer to read aloud the last paragraph from p. 45 of the *Child's Book*.

God Wants to Forgive whole-group learning experience (10 minutes)

Invite families to reflect on the following question:
- What does Jesus tell us about God's forgiveness?

List all responses on the poster paper in front of the large group.

Recall Scripture stories from earlier sessions about ways Jesus welcomed sinners, ate with them, and forgave them. Tell families that Jesus also told stories about forgiveness.

Scripture whole-group learning experience (15 minutes)

Select members of several families to tell the Gospel story, using the Scripture Echo Pantomime 5 from p. CE13 of the *Catechist Edition*.

Invite the large group to reflect on the following questions:
- When the son returns, what does he want from the father?
- What does this story tell you about God?

Allow time for volunteers to share responses to the questions and complete the activity.

The Sacrament of Forgiveness family cluster sharing experience (10 minutes)

Gather the large group into the same small family clusters as earlier. Direct each group to reflect on the following question:
- How are sins forgiven in the Sacrament of Reconciliation?

Have the group leader write all responses on the reverse side of the white paper used earlier.

Direct leaders to read aloud the first paragraph from p. 48 of the *Child's Book* to their group.

Have leaders compare the bulleted information about how Reconciliation reunites people with their groups' written responses to the question, and add to the page any information not already listed.

Forgiveness and Absolution whole-group learning experience (10 minutes)

Read the first paragraph aloud from p. 49 of the *Child's Book*.

Write the steps outlined in the paragraph on the poster paper in front of the large group. You may wish to distribute Activity Master 5, p. CE12 of the *Catechist Edition*, for this activity.

Read the Prayer of Absolution twice. The first time, pause after each line to have families tell you what it means. The second time, read it through without pausing.

Write *absolution = forgiveness* on the next sheet of poster paper, and have families explain what this means.

Refer to the photographs on p. 49 to familiarize families with the gestures used during absolution.

Discuss the following question:
- What happens in the Sacrament of Reconciliation?

Serving Others individual family unit experience (5 minutes)

Have families work together to complete the activity on p. 50 of the *Child's Book*. Ask volunteers to share ways their family will show forgiveness this week.

Closing Blessing (5 minutes)

Invite each family to form a family circle.

Begin with the Sign of the Cross.

Pray the prayer on p. 50 of the *Child's Book*.

Conclude by leading families in singing *Songs of Celebration* CD, track 5, "Children of God."

Faith at Home individual family unit experience (5 minutes)

Direct families' attention to the Faith at Home page and encourage them to do the activities at home.

We Go Forth

Before the Celebration		Materials

- Choose a gathering space that will be conducive to prayer and that will accommodate the size of the group; the church, a chapel, or a gathering place in the parish hall would each be appropriate. You will want the group to be able to see, hear, and move easily during the ritual.
- Prepare the group for the ritual action of Sprinkling with Water, the Sign of Peace, and for the reflection on the sacred Scriptures.
- Select a good reader to proclaim the reading.

- Select three people to carry: the Bible, the candle, and the bowl of water in procession. Show them where and how to place them in the sanctuary or on the prayer table.
- If not in a church or chapel, place chairs in semicircular rows around the prayer space. Leave enough space for people to move in and out of the rows. If possible, have tables and chairs set up in another space for adult discussion after the celebration.

- A large, clear, bowl with water, or if the celebration is in the church, use the baptismal font or pool
- A branch or aspergellum for sprinkling
- A large candle or the Paschal candle
- A prayer table for the candle, a Bible, and a stand
- *Songs of Celebration* CD
- Copies of the celebration for the assembly (*Sacraments Source Book* CD)

Gathering Rite

Welcome the gathered assembly.

Rehearse the opening song, and go over the ritual actions of Sprinkling with Water and Sign of Peace.

Invite the assembly to stand for the procession.

Opening Song

"Coming Back Together," *Songs of Celebration* CD, track 6.

Procession

The presider and persons carrying the bowl with water, candle, and Bible process in while the assembly sings.

Leader: *Let us pray.*
Make the Sign of the Cross together.

Opening Prayer

Leader: *Loving God, we come together in your presence to remember that we are your children. You call us to be children of light. Open our hearts to the Holy Spirit that we will understand your word. We ask this through Jesus Christ our Lord.*
All: *Amen.*

Celebration of the Word

Leader: *A reading from the holy Gospel according to John.*
All: *Glory to you, Lord.*
Read John 20:19–23.
Leader: *The Gospel of the Lord.*
All: *Praise to you, Lord Jesus Christ.*
Sit silently.

Reflection

Invite the assembly to reflect on the Gospel. Use the following question:

• Which words or phrases in the Gospel reading are important for you?

Ask the assembly to share their responses with one or two people. Be sure to include children in the sharing.

Sprinkling with Water and Sign of Peace

Invite the children who have been preparing for Reconciliation forward and gather them in a circle around the water. Sprinkle them with holy water and say:

Leader: *You have been baptized in Christ and you are called to bring his light and peace to the world.*
All: *Amen. Alleluia!*
Leader: *Go forth to offer the Sign of Peace to others.*

Direct children to go into the assembly and extend the Sign of Peace.

Closing Prayer

Leader: *God, our Father, send us the Holy Spirit, the giver of peace, that we may go forth as a people of peace and forgiveness.*
All: *Amen.*

Children go to their group session and adults go to the appointed space for reflection.

• There is a liturgical catechetical session for adults on p. 201.
• There is a parent/adult catechetical session on pp. 202–203.
• There is an intergenerational catechetical session on pp. 204–205.

We Go Forth

Goals

- To reflect on the celebration
- To explain the Rite of Sprinkling and Sign of Peace
- To explore the meaning of being reconcilers

Materials

- Poster board, chart paper, or overhead projector
- Markers
- *Songs of Celebration*
- Bible

Reflection (20 minutes)

Invite the adults to gather in groups of five or six.

Begin by recalling the ritual moments of the celebration. Do a guided meditation using the following prompts. Pause after each prompt.
- Play a few verses of the opening song, "Coming Back Together," *Songs of Celebration* CD, track 6.
- Read a few verses of the Gospel.
- Ask participants to recall their discussion of the Gospel.
- Recall the ritual with the children and their family members, and ask, "What did you see, what did you hear?"
- Recall the ritual with the assembly, asking, "What was it like to have the children come into the assembly and offer the Sign of Peace?"

Small Group Sharing

Pause for a few minutes of silence. Then invite the participants to share their feelings about the celebration in their small group. Encourage them to stay with their feelings. After 10 to 15 minutes, invite sharing with the large group.

Large Group Sharing

Gather the responses of the small groups on poster board, chart paper, or an overhead projector. Ask for feelings and thoughts about the celebration as a whole, and also for specific parts of the celebration that were meaningful to members of the group.

Naming (30 minutes)

Ask the participants to name what they learned from the celebration about God, Jesus, the Church, and going forth.

Take each category separately and list responses on poster board, chart paper, or an overhead projector. When the lists are completed, use them to summarize the meaning of forgiveness and the ritual of absolution.

Affirm, add, or enlarge upon the following points:
- The Rite of Sprinkling always recalls our Baptism.
- At the Eucharist, the Rite of Sprinkling may replace the Penitential Rite.
- Confession of sins and forgiveness leads us to be reconcilers in the world.
- The Sacrament of Reconciliation is a sacrament of conversion.
- The community of the baptized is called to live as forgiving and reconciling people.

Reflection and Small Group Sharing (20 minutes)

Ask "What is one thing you will do this week to extend forgiveness and reconciliation to someone?"

Direct participants to reflect in silence for a few minutes and then share their responses with their group.

Closing Blessing (5 minutes)

Gather and begin with the Sign of the Cross.

Leader: May the Father bless us, for he has adopted us as his children.
All: Amen.

Leader: May the Son come to help us for he has received us as brothers and sisters.
All: Amen.

Leader: May the Spirit be with us for he has made us his dwelling place.
All: Amen.

We Go Forth

Goals	Environment	Materials
• To help the participants come to a deeper understanding of the meaning of Jesus' gift of peace in them • To draw from the participants some of the qualities that we bring to the world when we are reconciled to Christ and one another • To inspire the participants to be ambassadors of reconciliation to the world	• Be sure to clearly identify the meeting place, posting clear directions if necessary. • Tables and chairs arranged for small groups • A prayer setting with large candle, Bible on a stand or table, and tapers	• Beverages and light refreshments • Nametags • Copies of **Call to Celebrate: Reconciliation** Family Guide • *Songs of Celebration* CD • Copies of **Reconciliation Parent/ Adult Catechesis Handouts 6:1** and **6:2** (*Sacraments Source Book* CD) • Pens or pencils for writing • Board or chart paper

Welcome and Opening Prayer (15 minutes)

Welcome parents and other adults and distribute nametags.

Introduce yourself and briefly review the goals and agenda for the gathering.

✳ **If this session was preceded by a large group ritual and reflection, go to We Go Forth. If not, continue with the prayer.**

Gather the group around the prayer setting, if possible, or have the group pause for a reflective moment and begin the session.

Open the prayer by inviting all to stand and sing "Coming Back Together," *Songs of Celebration* CD, track 6.

Peace Be with You (15 minutes)

Read the Gospel of *John 20:19–23.*

Encourage the participants to quietly recall the story of Jesus appearing to the disciples. Lead them in the following reflection.

Pause where appropriate:

• Call to mind some of the fears you experience in your life today. (Pause)
• Listen again as Jesus speaks to you, "Peace be with you." What do you feel as you hear these words? (Pause)

• Think about Jesus sending you forth into the world to be his ambassador of peace and reconciliation. (Pause)
• What emotions rise in you as you hear him say, "As the Father has sent me, so I send you?" (Pause)
• How have you carried out the healing and forgiving work of Jesus in your lifetime? (Pause)

Invite the participants to share one thing from their reflection with another person.

Ask the group to share their ideas on this question:
• How does forgiveness bring inner peace? (You may choose to note their ideas on an overhead transparency or Powerpoint for all to see.)

Then ask:
• In what ways does the celebration of God's forgiveness in the Sacrament of Reconciliation bring about conversion—inner change?

Conclude the prayer by asking participants to stand and share the Sign of Peace with one another.

Break for refreshments and conversation.

We Go Forth (15 minutes)

Distribute copies of **Reconciliation Parent/Adult Catechesis Handout 6:1** and review the directions.

Allow at least 15 minutes for this reflective process.

Gather the participants in groups of 5 to 6 people.

- Pose the following questions to the group and invite them to share one or more responses in their small groups: What does it mean to be light for the world? How can we be messengers of reconciliation in our families or at work? What responsibilities do we have to others in the Body of Christ?
- At the conclusion of the small group sharing, draw together their comments and read *Matthew 25:31–46.*
- With input from the whole group, name the attitudes, actions, and qualities that we all strive for as followers of Jesus challenged to be Christ in the world today.

What Is Mission? (15 minutes)

Gather the group back and make the following points about the mission to be reconcilers:

- When we use the term mission in reference to the Church and the baptized, we are talking about being sent to accomplish God's plan.
- The Church is missionary by its very nature because it exists to continue the work of the Risen Lord through the power of the Holy Spirit. We are called to continue the forgiving work of Jesus.
- The words: "whose sins you shall forgive…" apply also to us as members of the Church because the Church accomplishes its mission through the ministry of the baptized.

- Through the Sacraments of Initiation, Baptism, Confirmation, and Eucharist, each of us is empowered for mission. We are sent forth from the baptismal waters to "walk always as a child of the light" and to keep the flame of faith alive in our hearts.
- Each of us is called to be a witness to the forgiveness of God in our daily lives.

Parent Moment (10 minutes)

Highlight the three Faith at Home features in the *Child's Book* and show how they will help the parents and family members to participate in the children's preparation.

Emphasize the importance of doing the activities on the Faith at Home page, especially the ritual action.

Closing Prayer (5 minutes)

Distribute copies of **Reconciliation Parent/Adult Catechesis Handout 6:2.**

Invite all to come forward and light a taper from the large candle as all sing "Coming Back Together," *Songs of Celebration* CD, track 6.

Read *1 Corinthians 5:16–19.*

Invite all to commit themselves to the mission of reconciliation using the commitment prayer on **Reconciliation Parent/Adult Catechesis Handout 6:2.**

Close by offering one another a Sign of Peace.

Thank everyone for their time and participation.

Encourage parents and family members to go to **www.harcourtreligion.com** for more ideas and suggestions.

We Go Forth

Objectives	Materials

Objectives

- To guide families to experience a celebration of the word, including Sprinkling with Water and Sign of Peace
- To explore the meaning of the ritual action in family groups
- To present the mission of the Church to forgive sins
- To help families increase their understanding of what it means to be a reconciler

Materials

- Copies of the Celebration for the assembly (*Sacraments Source Book* CD)
- *Songs of Celebration* CD
- Prayer table
- Bible
- Candle and matches
- Bowl filled with water
- Copies of Scripture Narrative 6, p. CE16
- Copies of Activity Master 6, p. CE15
- Small branch with leaves
- Chart or poster paper
- Markers
- Pencils
- *Child's Book*

Welcome and Celebration (10–15 minutes)

Welcome the families in the gathering space.

Distribute copies of the celebration.

Select a family to be in the procession. Have them choose a family member to carry the Bible in procession.

- When families are assembled, walk forward slowly. Follow the child carrying the Bible.
- During the procession, lead families in singing "Coming Back Together," from the *Songs of Celebration* CD, track 6.
- Place the Bible on the prayer table and have the family members return to their seats.
- Light the prayer candle.
- Begin prayer with the Sign of the Cross and invite the group to follow the order of the prayer.
- For the proclamation of the Gospel, you may use a Bible or the adapted reading in the *Child's Book* on pp. 56–57.
- Have families stand.
- Dip the branch into the water, and then use it to sprinkle families as you say the prayer.
- Invite families to offer each other the Sign of Peace.
- Conclude with the opening song from the *Songs of Celebration* CD, track 6.

We Share individual family unit experience (10 minutes)

Guide family members to reflect on the celebration by asking the following questions:

- What did you see? What did you hear? What did you do?

Ask volunteers to share their responses.

Use the text in the Signs of Faith features to point out how the Sprinkling with Water and Sign of Peace remind us of our Baptism. Use the activity on p. 54 of the *Child's Book* to guide families to reflect on their Baptismal call to bring Christ's light into the world.

Allow time for family members to share their responses to the activity.

We Are Reconciled family cluster sharing experience (10 minutes)

Organize the large group into small clusters and invite them to share with their group what it means to grow and change.

Write the word *conversion* on a sheet of poster paper. Explain that conversion means to grow and change to become more like Jesus.

Write the word *Holy Spirit* on the same poster paper, and explain that the Holy Spirit helps us grow and change so we become more like Jesus.

Direct each family group to select a leader to read aloud to their group p. 55 of the *Child's Book*.

Invite groups to discuss ways family members can be reconcilers at home.

Jesus Shares Peace and Forgiveness whole-group learning experience (10 minutes)

Invite families to reflect on the following question:
• What did Jesus send the disciples to do?

List all responses on the next sheet of poster paper in front of the group.

Read aloud the first paragraph of p. 56 in the *Child's Book*.

Scripture whole-group learning experience (15 minutes)

Select members of several families to narrate the Scripture story, using the text on p. CE16 of the *Catechist Edition*.

Invite the large group to reflect on the following question:
• What did Jesus send the disciples to do?

Remind families that they are also disciples and Jesus wants them to be forgiving too.

Invite families to reflect on the following question:
• In what ways does forgiveness bring peace to your household?

Have volunteers share responses.

Invite families to show how they bring forgiveness and peace to members of their family, using the activity on p. 57 of *Child's Book*. Have volunteers present their drawings to the large group.

Distribute Activity Master 6, p. CE15 of the *Catechist Edition*, and suggest that families make peace flags during the week.

Proclamation of Praise and Dismissal family cluster sharing experience (10 minutes)

Organize the large group into the same small family clusters as earlier. Direct each group to reflect on the following question:
• How do we share reconciliation with others?

Direct leaders to read aloud the first paragraph from p. 58 of the *Child's Book* to their group. For each bulleted item, have leaders invite a group member to give examples of specific actions that would demonstrate that idea.

Have group leaders read aloud the last paragraph to their group.

Go Forth whole-group learning experience (10 minutes)

Explain that just as at the end of every Mass we are sent out to show that we have learned something. So are we sent forth from the Sacrament of Reconciliation to be signs of God's forgiveness.

Read to families the prayer excerpts on p. 59 of the *Child's Book*.

Summarize the mission of forgiveness by reading the last paragraph aloud.

Talk about how the people in the picture feel.

Discuss the question:
• What can you do to be a living sign of God's forgiveness and mercy?

Remind families that we are meant to be signs of God's forgiveness to others.

Being a Reconciler individual family unit experience (5 minutes)

Explain the activity on p. 60 of the *Child's Book* to families.

Allow time for family members to complete the activity.

Have volunteers share their ideas with the group.

Closing Blessing (5 minutes)

Invite each family to form a family circle.

Begin with the Sign of the Cross.

Pray the prayer on p. 60 of the *Child's Book*.

Conclude by leading families in singing, *Songs of Celebration* CD, track 6, "Coming Back Together."

Faith at Home individual family unit experience (5 minutes)

Direct families' attention to the Faith at Home page and encourage them to do the activities at home.

Family Reconciliation Retreat

Forgiveness and Reconciliation

Outline	Environment	Materials
1. Opening Prayer	• Children's Bible	• Nametags (color coded for activity centers)
2. Activity Centers	• At least 4 group facilitators	
• Activity 1: *The Story of the Cracked Pot*	• An adult and several children to act out the Gospel in the opening prayer	• *Songs of Celebration* CD
		• Light refreshments
• Activity 2: Meditation and Examination of Conscience	• A prayer setting with large, lighted candle, Bible on a stand or table, and a clear bowl filled with water	• Lyrics to "Like a Shepherd"*
• Activity 3: Masks		• Additional materials needed are listed within each activity.
• Activity 4: Visit to the Reconciliation Room	• Tables and chairs for family groups	
3. Peer Group Time	• Chairs set in a circle or circles around the prayer setting	
4. Closing Prayer		

Gathering and Opening Prayer (20 minutes)

Welcome the participants and explain the agenda for the gathering. Have facilitators distribute nametags and invite families to enjoy the light refreshments as they find a place to sit in the circle of chairs.

Sing "Coming Back Together," *Songs of Celebration* CD, track 6.

Pause for a moment of silence.

Make the Sign of the Cross
Let us pray. Loving and merciful God, as we gather together this day, we pray for those who are sick, afraid, lost, abandoned, alone, and unhappy. Your love is so wide and deep that there is room enough for every person on this earth. Help us to remember those who most need our love and give us the courage to offer our love to them in your name. Amen.

Proclaim the Gospel according to *Matthew 18:10–14, Parable of the Lost Sheep* from the children's Bible. You may want to have an adult and some children mime the story during the proclamation. If so, you will have to prepare them ahead of time.

Make the following points:
- In this story, we see that Jesus gives full attention to the lost sheep. This means that Jesus will do anything to bring everyone into the loving light of God's family.
- We are to be like Jesus, concerned for ourselves when we wander away from Jesus, and concerned when the bond of love between ourselves and another is broken; that is, when we wander away from each other.
- Jesus desires that we all be one with him and with one another in love.

Sing "Like a Shepherd" by Bob Dufford, SJ.

Invite all to extend a sign of peace to each other.

Activity Centers

Tell the group that the lunch break will occur after the families have visited two centers. The remaining two centers can be visited after lunch.

Direct the participants to note the color code on their nametag and ask them to move to the appropriate center.

---

* "Like a Shepard," ©1976 Robert J. Dufford, SJ. Published by OCP.

Activity 1: *The Story of the Cracked Pot* (20 minutes)

Materials Needed
- **Family Reconciliation Retreat Handout 1**
- Pencils and paper

Gather in a classroom, meeting space or a quiet place in the large hall.

Read *The Story of the Cracked Pot.*

Ask: Did you ever think a cracked pot would be a good thing? What was your favorite part of this story? Did you ever feel ashamed, like the pot did, because you made a mistake or did something wrong? How did you feel when the bearer of the pot pointed out the flowers? Whom does the bearer resemble?

Distribute Family Reconciliation Retreat Handout 1, paper and pencils, and instruct family members to write their own family stories of how Jesus can use each of their "cracks" to make something beautiful and new.

Distribute copies of the story for use at home.

Rotation and Break (5 minutes)

Activity 2: Meditation and Examination of Conscience (20 minutes)

Materials Needed
- CD of reflective music

Gather in a chapel or room away from the activities of the other centers. Play reflective music, place pillows on the floor or provide sitting mats, and put a sign on the door that asks visitors to enter quietly.

Explain that this quiet time will be used to make an examination of conscience.

Remind everyone that we make an examination of conscience:
- to discover a pattern to our shortcomings.
- to discover how we have sinned.
- to prepare for the Sacrament of Reconciliation.

Begin a centering meditation using these or similar words, pausing frequently when appropriate: *Close your eyes and sit in a comfortable position. Think about each breath you take. As you breathe, relax deeper and deeper into a quiet place in your heart. Think about the Holy Spirit, who lives in you and helps you to know God*

and to make good choices. Pray to the Holy Spirit now. Ask him to help you see where you have sinned and where you can do better. (Pause for a few minutes.)

Imagine God pouring love like water all over you. (pause) Feel God loving you even when you failed to love, forgot be kind, or were naughty. (pause) Now think about how you love God in return. Ask yourself: Do I pray and spend time thinking about God? (pause) Do I treat sacred places and things with respect? (pause) Do I join my community of faith in worship each week? (pause) Do I use God's name with respect not as a curse word? (pause) Am I kind to others? Do I speak kindly about others? (pause) Do I forgive others when they hurt me? (Pause for a few minutes.)

Close the meditation by inviting all to pray the Act of Contrition together.

Lunch (45 minutes)

Activity 3: Masks (20 minutes)

Materials Needed
- Poster paper
- Pencils
- Scissors
- Stapler
- Permanent markers
- Feathers
- Stickers
- Yarn and fabric scraps
- Glitter
- Beads
- Variety of found objects
- Glue
- Elastic
- **Family Reconciliation Retreat Handout 2**

Ask the participants to think about how they think others see them. Have them share one by one in family groups, but tell them no one can comment on what is said until the next step.

Invite family members to tell how they look at the others, and what they see inside themselves or others that others may not see.

Invite the families to discuss the many faces they wear, at home, at school, and at play.

Distribute Family Reconciliation Retreat Handout 2 and read the directions aloud.

Ask parents to help children make a mask expressing their inside and outside faces.

Encourage families to take time to discuss the two representations on the masks and what they mean to the children.

Rotation and Break (5 minutes)

Activity 4: Visit to the Reconciliation Room
(20 minutes)

Take the group to the Reconciliation Room. It is ideal if one of the parish priests or confessors takes a role in this visit to the Reconciliation Room. This will offer a chance for children to become acquainted with the minister of the sacrament.

Point out the various items in the room: a table with a cross and Bible, two chairs, and also the traditional screen or grill if this option is available.

Walk the families through the six steps of individual celebration:

1 The priest greets the penitent and makes the Sign of the Cross.
2 A passage from the Scriptures is read (this can be chosen by the priest or the penitent).
3 The penitent confesses his or her sins and accepts a penance from the priest.
4 A prayer of sorrow, usually the Act of Contrition, is prayed.
5 The priest offers absolution.
6 A thanksgiving to God for the forgiveness of sin is expressed and the penitent is dismissed.

Respond to any questions that arise in the group.

Rotation and Break (5 minutes)

Peer Group Time (20 minutes)

Adult Session:

Materials Needed
- Bibles (1 for each group)
  or copies of Scripture passages listed within text below

Gather the parents into several small groups and give each group one of the passages listed below for reflection. These passages can be printed out or Bibles can be distributed among the groups.

Invite the groups to discuss the following questions:
- What does this passage tell you about Jesus' capacity for forgiveness?
- What application can you make for your own life?

Scripture Passages:
Matthew 8:5–13 "The Centurion's Servant"
Mark 9:31–37 "The Deaf-mute"
Luke 5:17–26 "The Paralyzed Man"

Matthew 12:9–15 "A Man with a Shriveled Hand"
Mark 5:1–20 "Expulsion of the Devils in Gerasa"
Luke 8:43–48 "Woman with the Hemorrhage"
John 5:1–15 "Cure at the Pool of Bethesada"
Mark 10:46–52 "The Blind Bartimaeus"
Luke 7:36–50 "The Penitent Woman"
John 8:1–11 "The Adulteress"
John 21:15–19 "Peter's Declaration"

Gather the small groups together and ask volunteers to share their insights or comments.

Make the following points in explaining the concepts of forgiveness, contrition, and reconciliation:

- The Scriptures advocate a large-hearted attitude of forgiveness and tolerance of others' mistakes. We are challenged to forgive seventy times seven. In biblical math, this is a limitless number.
- Forgiveness is the ability to let go of the hurt, and until we can do so, we remain a slave of the hurt—always brooding over our loss and the injustice done to us.
- Forgiveness is not forgetting or denying we have been hurt, nor is it condoning or excusing what has been done to us. It is a conscious choice to turn to the good in the face of wrongdoing.
- Bringing ourselves to contrition is a process guided by God's grace. It takes time and openness to be led through this process. This process includes a sense of remorse, taking responsibility for one's hurtful actions, making restitution, and finally repentance, that is, a turning away from past actions and focusing on a new direction.
- Forgiveness does not automatically achieve reconciliation between ourselves and those who have hurt us. Forgiveness is one person's response in the face of injustice or hatred. Reconciliation occurs when two persons can come together in mutual respect.
- When reconciliation occurs, it is always a sign of God's presence and activity.

Children's Session:

Materials Needed
- The story of Joseph and his brothers from *Genesis* (video, storybook, or interpretive play or mime)

Tell, read, or have the story of Joseph acted out (*Genesis 50:15–21*).

Discuss:

- How did Joseph and his brothers feel when they met each other after so many years.
- How was Joseph able to forgive them?
- Did the brothers need to forgive Joseph?

Explain that it takes both parties to reconcile. God helps us forgive and reconcile.

Closing Prayer (20 minutes)

Gather the participants in a circle.

Ask the families to share what they most enjoyed about the day.

Tell the following parable:

A man was exploring caves by the seashore. In one of the caves, he found a canvas bag holding a bunch of hardened clay balls. It was as if someone had rolled clay balls and left them out in the sun to bake. They didn't look like much, but they intrigued the man, so he took the bag out of the cave with him. As he strolled along the beach, he would throw the clay balls one at a time out into the ocean as far as he could. He thought little about it until he dropped one of the balls and it cracked open on a rock. Inside was a beautiful, precious stone.

Excited, the man started breaking open the remaining clay balls. Each contained a similar treasure. He found thousands of dollars' worth of jewels in the 20 or so clay balls he had left. Then it struck him. He had been on the beach a long time. He had thrown maybe 50 or 60 of the clay balls with their hidden treasure into the ocean waves. Instead of thousands of dollars in treasure, he could have taken home tens of thousands, but he just threw it away.

Conduct the following reflection in these or similar words:

It's like that with people. We look at someone, maybe even ourselves, and we see the external clay vessel. It doesn't look like much from the outside. It isn't always beautiful or sparkling, so we discount it. We see that person as less important than someone more beautiful or stylish or well-known or wealthy. But we have not taken the time to find the treasure hidden inside that person by God.

There is a treasure in each and every one of us. If we take the time to get to know another person, and if we ask God to show us that person the way he sees them, then the clay begins to peel away and the brilliant gem begins to shine forth.

Proclaim *Matthew 18:21–35.*

Reflect with the families:

- There is no time when we can refuse to forgive another because each person holds a treasure within.
- God always shows mercy and forgives us no matter what we have done.
- We are to forgive and show mercy just as God forgives us.

Sing "Coming Back Together," *Songs of Celebration* CD, track 6.

Thank the families for participating in the retreat.

Children's Reconciliation Retreat
Walking Together Again

This is a half-day retreat for children. You should conduct it close to the time of the celebration of the Sacrament. If you have fewer than 15 children you may want to do the activities in consecutive order.

<table>
<tr><th>Outline</th><th>Environment</th><th>Materials</th></tr>
<tr><td>

1. Gathering and Opening Prayer
2. Activity Centers
   - Activity 1: Ceremony Review and Music for Reconciliation
   - Activity 2: Forgiveness Skits
   - Activity 3: Personal Prayer of Sorrow and Examination of Conscience
3. Snack
4. Closing Prayer

</td><td>

- At least 3 group facilitators
- Prayer table

</td><td>

- *Songs of Celebration* CD
- Snacks (pretzels)
- Nametags (color coded for activity centers)
- Additional materials needed are listed within each activity.

</td></tr>
</table>

Gathering and Opening Prayer (20 minutes)

Welcome children and facilitators in a circle around the table.

Point out that one meaning of *reconciliation* is to "walk together again."

Play selections from *Songs of Celebration* CD as background music.

Lead the opening prayer.

Lord Jesus, be with us today. Help us to learn more about the Sacrament of Reconciliation, which we will celebrate together soon. Help us teach one another about your forgiveness. Help us learn to fix what is broken in our lives. Help us learn to walk with one another in peace. Help us learn to walk with you, and the Father, and the Spirit again.

Distribute the nametags.

Explain that children will be divided into three groups. Each group will travel together through three activities, then the large group will meet together again for a closing ceremony.

Make any other necessary announcements.

Match children with their facilitators and send them to their first activity.

Activity Centers

Direct the particiants to note the color code on their nametag and ask them to move to the appropriate center.

Tell the group that the snack break will occur after the children have visited the three activity centers.

Activity 1: Ceremony Review and Music for Reconciliation (40 minutes)

Materials Needed
- Order of service for the ceremony, diagram of church building, song sheets, missalettes, or hymnals

Gather in the parish church or classroom. A priest or program director explains the order of service. A music minister teaches the hymns or songs.

Review with the children the order of celebration for their First Reconciliation. If you aren't meeting in the church itself, use a diagram of the church to show where the Reconciliation Room is. Also show any other places in the church where the priests will be hearing confessions.

Show them where to line up to afford privacy to others. Answer any questions.

Distribute the song materials. Teach the children the words, and explain their significance.

Sing the songs as time permits.

Rotation and Break (5 minutes)

Activity 2: Forgiveness Skits (40 minutes)

Materials Needed
- **Children's/Candidates' Reconciliation Retreat Handout 1**
  (*Sacraments Source Book* CD)
- Pencils

Gather in a classroom with a facilitator.

Explain that many of our sins involve hurting others.

Invite the children to think about things that would hurt others, or times when others have hurt them. Tell children that hurting someone's feelings with words or actions can be a sin, too.

Distribute the handout and divide the group into smaller groups of 3 to 5 children.

Tell the children that they will have 15 minutes to plan and rehearse a skit about forgiveness. Suggest that they use the handout as a guide.

Walk among the groups to offer assistance.

Call the group back together. Remind the children to be attentive as all groups present their work.

Ask for a volunteer group to begin, or call on each group in turn until all have performed.
Rotation and Break (5 minutes)

Activity 3: Personal Prayer of Sorrow and Examination of Conscience (40 minutes)

Materials Needed
- **Children's/Candidates' Reconciliation Retreat Handout 2**
  (*Sacraments Source Book* CD)
- Pencils
- Copies of Prayers of Sorrow, Ten Commandments, Beatitudes, Works of Mercy (*Catholic Source Book*)

Gather in a classroom with a facilitator.

Remind children that the Examination of Conscience and Prayer of Sorrow are part of the Reconciliation service. Point out that when the children pray their daily prayers, they can use any prayers they like, even prayers that they write.

Have children work individually or in groups of 2 to 3, depending on abilities and learning styles.

Distribute the handout and go over the directions for writing a prayer of sorrow. You could show them other written prayers of sorrow.

Walk among children offering assistance where needed. When the children are finished, ask volunteers to share their prayers. Praise their work.

Select one child to share his or her prayer at the closing gathering.

Introduce the Examination of Conscience section of the handout. Remind children that sins can hurt our relationship with God or with other people.

Have them work in pairs or small groups to write an Examination of Conscience that they can use every day. If possible, have the Ten Commandments, Beatitudes, and Works of Mercy posted in the room.

Walk among the children to offer affirmations and assistance.

Encourage the children to use their personal prayers every night.

Snack (20 minutes)

At some point in the retreat, incorporate a snack. Pretzels are an ideal treat, especially paired with a small drink. Check to be certain that no child will have an allergic reaction. As children are eating, tell them the story of pretzels.

Long ago, people observed Lent very strictly. They could not eat milk, butter, cheese, or meat. They made bread out of water, salt, and flour. They rolled the dough and shaped it to look like a person with his hands folded over his chest, which was the way that they prayed. They called the bread "little arms," or "bracella" in Latin. The word changed over time to be our pretzel. Today, it reminds us to pray and of our special heritage as Catholics.

Closing Prayer (20 minutes)

Assemble the group again in the large gathering space.

Praise children for their participation and thank the facilitators for their help.

Call each group to share its work. Then ask the selected children to share their prayers of sorrow.

Ask everyone to join you in the closing prayer:
Lord Jesus, we thank you for being with us today. We are ready to receive your forgiveness in the Sacrament of Reconciliation. Thank you for teaching us to walk with one another in peace.

Conclude with one of the selections from the *Songs of Celebration* CD that the children learned today.

Songs of Celebration CD

Chapter 1—Track 1
We Are Called
David Haas. © GIA Publications

Chapter 2—Track 2
We Are Marching
South African Traditional

Chapter 3—Track 3
Del Señor viene la misericordia
© Bob Hurd. Published by OCP

Chapter 4—Track 4
Remember Your Love
© Damean Music, Daigle/Balhoff

Chapter 5—Track 5
Children of God
© Christopher Walker. Published by OCP

Chapter 6—Track 6
Coming Back Together
© John Burland

Optional Music Suggestions

Chapter 1
1. "Donde hay amor y caridad," © Pedro Rublacava. Published by OCP
2. "Yes Lord, I Believe," © John Burland
3. "All People That on Earth Do Dwell," Traditional/Old 100th

Chapter 2
1. "Salmo 99: Nosotros somo su pueblo," © Jaime Cortez. Published by OCP
2. "All Are Welcome," Marty Haugen © GIA Publications

Chapter 3
1. "We Will Journey in Faith," © Dan Schutte. Published by OCP
2. "Grant to Us, O Lord," © Lucien Deiss, WLP

Chapter 4
1. "Un pueblo camina," © Juan Espinosa. Published by OCP
2. "Give Me Jesus," African-American traditional

Chapter 5
1. "Mi alma está sedienta de ti," © Donna Pena. Published by OCP
2. "Amazing Grace," traditional

Chapter 6
1. "Del Señor viene la misericordia," © Bob Hurd. Published by OCP
2. "Without You," © Tom Kendzia and NALK, OCP

Mystagogy for Reconciliation

Mystagogical Catechesis

Mystagogical catechesis is the name given to the process of gradually uncovering the meaning of the mysteries of sacraments that have already been celebrated. This type of catechesis was first done by the early Church Fathers in sermons preached to the neophytes after their initiation at the Easter Vigil. We still possess some of those sermons. They are instructions rich in images and symbols that help the newly initiated come to a fuller understanding of the sacraments they have celebrated and are now living out. Mystagogical catechesis is based on the principle that as we live out the commitments of sacraments, we experience a fuller, deeper, more personal and communal meaning of them.

Although the process of mystagogy is usually connected with the sacraments of Baptism, Confirmation, and Eucharist, it certainly can be used for the other sacraments, since each of them is rich with meaning that is uncovered as we live out our lives.

Here are some practical suggestions to involve children and their families in mystagogical catechesis for Reconciliation:

- Shortly after the celebration of Reconciliation, gather children and/or family members to reflect on their experience of the celebration. Use the process outlined in the *Catechist Edition* for reflection.
- Send out special invitations for scheduled Parish Reconciliation celebrations to children and families who have recently celebrated the sacrament for the first time.
- During Advent and Lent, which are seasons of penitence and conversion, plan gatherings of those who have celebrated Reconciliation for the first time within the past two years to reflect on the Scripture readings that are in the child's Reconciliation book or other healing and forgiveness stories from the Gospels. Focus the gatherings on how the children are experiencing themselves as messengers of peace and reconciliation.
- Arrange with the Director of the catechumenate to invite those who have recently celebrated Reconciliation to be involved in the Scrutiny preparation for children who are in the RCIA.
- Encourage catechists in all levels of your catechetical program to invite children and their families to celebrate the sacrament of Reconciliation frequently and to attend any parish communal celebrations.

A
absolution, 41
assembly, 13, 34, 35, 40, 41

B
Baptism, 7, 9, 11, 14, 18, 31, 41, 241
baptismal promises, 9, 11
baptizein, 8
bishop(s), 10, 11, 16, 18, 30, 40, 41
Blessed Sacrament, 13
Body and Blood of Jesus, 13
Body of Christ, 6, 7, 15, 34, 41, 80, 154
bread and wine, 13

C
catechesis, 32, 36
catechumenate, 9
celebration of the sacraments, 28
chrism, 9, 11
chrismation, 11
Christ, 8, 11, 13
    light of, 8
    sacrifice of, 12
Church, the, 7, 9, 30, 34, 36
communal celebration, 15
communion, 18, 41
community of faith, 31
confession, 14
Confirmation, 7, 11, 18, 33, 35, 41, 80, 214
consecration, 40
conversion, 13, 41

D
deacon(s), 9, 17, 18

E
Eucharist 5, 7, 11, 12, 13, 14, 33, 35, 40, 41, 214
eucharistein, 12
Eucharistic Prayer, 12, 40

F
First Communion, 80, 154

G
Good News, 10, 28
grace, 7, 31

H
Holy Orders, 7, 18
Holy Spirit, 6, 8, 11, 18
Host, 13

I
Invocation of the Trinity, 9

J
Jesus/Jesus Christ, 11, 14, 28, 29, 36

L
laying on of hands, 10, 11
liturgical catechesis, 5, 26, 35,38

Liturgy, 5
Liturgy of the Eucharist, 13
Liturgy of the Hours, 26, 27
Liturgy of the Word, 13

M
Mass, 5, 40
mission, 8, 11, 30
myron, 11
Mystagogical catechesis, 80, 154, 214
mystagogy, 27
mysteries of faith, 5
mysterion, 6

O
original sin, 14

P
Paschal candle, 8
Paschal mystery, 12, 16, 80
Penance, 7, 14, 27, 41
Penitentials, 41
penitents, 41
prayer, 34, 39
priest(s), 9, 11, 14, 15, 16, 17 18, 40
procession, 38

R
Reconciliation, 14, 15, 27, 33, 35, 214
Resurrection, 8, 12
Rite of Christian Initiation, 80, 154
Rite of Penance, 41

S
Sacrament of Baptism, 8
Sacrament of Confirmation, 9, 10
Sacrament of Eucharist, 9
Sacrament of Marriage, 31
Sacrament of Matrimony, 17, 18
Sacrament of Penance, 15, 27
Sacrament of the Anointing of the Sick, 7, 16
Sacrament(s), 5, 6, 7, 31, 32, 34
Sacrament of Reconciliation, 7, 14, 15, 27, 41
Sacraments in Service to Communion, 7
Sacraments of Healing, 7, 14
Sacraments of Initiation, 7, 11
sacramentum, 6
Scriptures, 30
song, 38

T
tabernacle, 13

V
viaticum, 16

W
water, 8
witness, 10, 30, 36

Sacraments Source Book CD Contents

GENERAL CALL TO CELEBRATE RESOURCES

The following resources are available as pdfs in English and Spanish.

What Is Liturgical Catechesis?
How to Lead Prayer
Role of the Prayer Leader
The Role of Music
What Is a Sacrament? (Overview)
Confirmation
Eucharist
Reconciliation
Restored Order
History of Eucharist (the Mass)
History of Reconciliation
Illustrations/Clip Art
Program Components

SESSION HANDOUTS

The following handouts are available as pdfs in English and Spanish. For updated Children's Retreat handouts, go online at **www.harcourtreligion.com**.

Confirmation/Eucharist (Restored Order)

Parent Orientation Handouts
Parent/Adult Catechesis Handouts
Family Retreat Handouts
Candidates' Retreat Handouts

Eucharist

Parent Orientation Handouts
Parent/Adult Catechesis Handouts
Family Retreat Handouts
Children's/Candidates' Retreat Handouts

Reconciliation

Parent Orientation Handouts
Parent/Adult Catechesis Handouts
Family Retreat Handouts
Children's/Candidates' Retreat Handouts

WHOLE COMMUNITY/ INTERGENERATIONAL CATECHESIS CELEBRATIONS

The following handouts are guides of the celebration for the participants. They are available as customizable Word documents in English and Spanish as well as pdf files in English and Spanish.

Confirmation/Eucharist (Restored Order)

Sunday Connection
Whole Community Ritual/Intergenerational Catechesis Participant Pages

Eucharist

Sunday Connection
Whole Community Ritual/Intergenerational Catechesis Participant Pages

Reconciliation

Sunday Connection
Whole Community Ritual/Intergenerational Catechesis Participant Pages

Pacing Plan Chart

Use the updated versions of the Pacing Plan Chart available in English and Spanish online at **www.harcourtreligion.com**.

AT HOME RITUAL PREPARATION

The following resources are available as pdfs in English and Spanish.

Celebrating Rituals at Home–Letter
At Home Ritual Preparation Handouts
Confirmation/Eucharist (Restored Order)
Eucharist
Reconciliation